The History of Here

The History of Here

*A House, the Pine Hills Neighborhood,
and the City of Albany*

Akum Norder

excelsior editions

AN IMPRINT OF STATE UNIVERSITY OF NEW YORK PRESS

Cover photo courtesy of Olivia Raffe.

Published by State University of New York Press, Albany

Excelsior Editions is an imprint of State University of New York Press

For information, contact State University of New York Press, Albany, NY
www.sunypress.edu

Production, Diane Ganeles
Marketing, Kate R. Seburyamo

Library of Congress Cataloging-in-Publication Data

Names: Norder, Akum, author.
Title: The history of here : a house, the Pine Hills neighborhood, and the
  city of Albany / Akum Norder.
Description: Albany : State University of New York Press, Albany, 2018. |
  Includes bibliographical references and index.
Identifiers: LCCN 2017004239 (print) | LCCN 2017020479 (ebook) | ISBN
  9781438467924 (ebook) | ISBN 9781438467900 (pbk. : alk. paper)
Subjects: LCSH: Pine Hills (Albany, N.Y.)—History. | Pine Hills (Albany, N.Y.)—
  Biography. | Pine Hills (Albany, N.Y.)—Social life and customs. | Norder, Akum. |
  Albany (N.Y.)—History. | Albany (N.Y.)—Biography. | Albany (N.Y.)—Social life
  and customs.
Classification: LCC F129.A36 (ebook) | LCC F129.A36 P566 2018 (print) | DDC
  974.7/43—dc23
LC record available at https://lccn.loc.gov/2017004239

To Gary, because I never could have done it without you

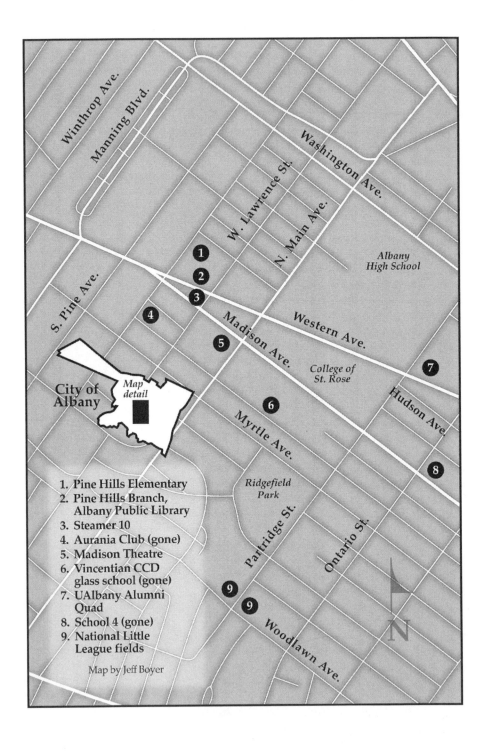

1. Pine Hills Elementary
2. Pine Hills Branch, Albany Public Library
3. Steamer 10
4. Aurania Club (gone)
5. Madison Theatre
6. Vincentian CCD glass school (gone)
7. UAlbany Alumni Quad
8. School 4 (gone)
9. National Little League fields

Map by Jeff Boyer

Contents

Acknowledgments

Thank you, first, to my parents, for showing me that writing can change minds, communities, and lives: to my dad, Steve Norder, for teaching me that the route to understanding the present leads through the past; and to my mom, Lois Norder, for giving me the best writing advice I ever got: that there are no boring topics, only boring writers.

Thank you to my daughters, Cleis and Tavik, who so many times had to hear, "Not now, sweetheart, I'm writing." I love you.

Thank you to the families whose lives were interwoven with my house's story. This book would have been impossible without you. Thank you to Beryl Scott Glover and Catherine Scott for sharing their time and their stories with me. Thanks to Susan Galbraith, another of John Scott's granddaughters, for her thoughtful correspondence and for the loan of a family scrapbook. Thank you to other members of the Scott family for taking the time to help connect me to the relatives with the longest memories.

Thank you to Olivia Raffe, to Bill Willig, to Michael Graham, and to Carl and Anna Patka. I appreciate your willingness to respond to a stranger's queries.

Special thanks to the members of the Stickles and Spencer family, and in particular to Greg Spencer and Lynn Devane: I am humbled by your strength and grace, and can never find words to express my thanks for your trust in me. I'm deeply grateful for the chance to get to know your family, whose stories continue to inspire me.

A heartfelt thank you to everyone who took the time to speak with me.

Thank you to Crystal Wortsman for sharing family photographs, to Carolyn Keefe for helping track down a photo of the School 16 demolition, and to the *Times Union* for its generous access to its photo archives. Further thanks are due to the *Times Union* for hosting the blog on which I hammered out early drafts of some of this material.

Thank you to the Historic Albany Foundation, whose notes on my house's history, delivered as part of their plaque program, sparked my interest to learn more. Thanks to the staff at the Albany County Hall of Records and Albany Public Library who helped me locate documents during my research. Thank you to Tom Tryniski: he has scanned millions of pages from New York state newspapers and made them available to the public on his website, Fultonhistory.com, at his own expense.

Thank you to SUNY Press, and to acquisitions editor Amanda Lanne-Camilli, for seeing potential in this story. Thank you to Ann Pfau and David Hochfelder for their feedback and encouragement, and to Sue Petrie for her insights and advice about the publishing process. Thanks to Jeff Boyer for his excellent map.

Thank you to my neighbors for making the Pine Hills a place I love to live.

And finally, thank you to Gary Hahn, the best editor, and best husband, anyone could ever hope for; who read every draft of every chapter and didn't hesitate to tell me when it wasn't done yet; who created space in our family life for me to write; and who believed in me far, far more than I ever believed in myself. My love and gratitude are yours forever.

I

The View from My Porch

An item from the *Albany Evening Journal* on Thursday, April 3, 1879:

A son of Louis Marx, gardener on Madison avenue, having his mind full of dime novels, took $30 a few days since and left for the Black Hills to dig gold. He was heard from at Chicago this morning, and Marx has sought the aid of Chief Maloy to secure his return home.

I know a thing or two about Louis Marx's family, for reasons I'll explain shortly, and I wonder which of his sons it was who leapt at the chance to leave Albany for the open West.

There were four boys in the Marx household in 1879. One was two years old, and though toddlers do enjoy adventure stories, when they escape the house they never remember to bring money along. So it's probably safe to rule him out. Neither, I suspect, was it the gardener's oldest son, Luie. Luie would have been twenty years old, and had he run off to seek his fortune, he'd probably earned the right to seek it and then find his own way home again.

William, age fifteen, was in the prime of his restless years. No one can do daring and half-formed plans as well as a teenage boy can, and in all likelihood it was William who hopped the train, stopping to check in with the folks once he was eight hundred miles away.

1

But I like to think it was George. Eleven years old in 1879, he had grown up watching the wagons pass through the tollgate on the Great Western Turnpike, not far from his father's house and farm. George could have seen how past the gate, the road stretches arrow-straight to the horizon, offering him a running start into the west. Maybe the pull of that road just became too strong. If at age fifteen a journey to Chicago is a dime-novel adventure, at age eleven it's an epic. Maybe I vote for George because I have a daughter who's on the brink of eleven, and I see so clearly how life swells up inside her like the opening notes of a musical. All it would take is a downbeat and a lungful of air for her to break into song.

Whichever it was, William or George, the son of the Albany market gardener was restless for change. He didn't find it in the Black Hills, but change was coming anyway. All the Marxes would have to do was stand still, and it would sweep over them. Within the boys' lifetimes the fields and woods of Albany's western reaches would be graded, tamed, and covered with houses. Their family was the last to farm this side of our street, West Lawrence Street.

Fast forward one hundred thirty years or so, and we're having a party.

Here on our slice of the old Marx farm, we're celebrating our house's hundredth birthday with a gathering of neighbors, friends, and others who have a connection to the house and neighborhood. There's Greg, who grew up in my house in the 1940s. From his third-floor bedroom window he'd shoot matchsticks at the neighbors' slate roof with his Red Ryder BB gun. Once, when he and his Red Ryder were deep in a war story, Greg took a position on the upstairs porch, drew a bead on his enemy, and fired. His enemy, unfortunately, was a cleaning lady leaving a Morris Street apartment. "Within three minutes the cops were at the door," he remembered sheepishly, and that was the end of his sniper days.

And over here: This lady, at the party with her nephew, is the granddaughter of the house's first owner, the man whose name is on the Historic Albany Foundation plaque near the front door. Her family gave me the photograph that sits on the hall vanity: the little boy on the sidewalk looking at—is that a monkey? Yes it is, a monkey in a braid-trimmed coat. To the side, at the foot of the stairs, an organ grinder holds its leash. Those are our stairs, our sidewalk. In the background, our neighbor's house is being built. The year's about 1913.

It's a curious gathering of friends and strangers. Our younger daughter is getting chocolate frosting on my 1930 census map. The neighbors are talking to the guy who sold us the house nine years before. A woman who grew up down the street has brought a stack of postcards to show me; they were sent to her aunt a century ago by a lady who lived in our house. We offer everyone a tour, show them old photographs, feed them cake: it's a birthday party, after all.

Let's call Louis Marx and sons point A and call our 2012 party point B. This book is the story of how my house got from point A to point B.

When you buy an old house, you get more than a house. In its quirks, its alterations, in fragments of memory and traces left behind, you get a bundle of small mysteries. Who used to live here? Why did they come here, and where did they go? Whose name is that written on the attic wall? When did that odd little bathroom get shoehorned in there, and what did the room look like before?

If you're lucky, one or two of your house's mysteries might unfold into stories. I was very lucky. Using public records, newspaper accounts, and interviews, I traced my property forward from the last man who farmed it. I located and spoke with the families of everyone who's ever owned my house, as well as its builder. I was able to learn the answers to my questions, or parts of the answers, and much more.

As I followed these threads, I came to see the development of my house, my street, and my neighborhood as part of Albany's story. And in the lives of its residents, their struggles and triumphs, I saw a reflection of twentieth-century America.

It's not exactly a linear narrative. Sure, it leads forward—time is stubborn like that—but it's not above stopping to look around now and then. That's the kind of walk I like to take: one with plenty of pauses to see where I am and how I got there.

This book follows another path, too: my own. I grew up in one of those families who weren't from here—wherever "here" happened to be.

I guess you'd say we moved around a fair bit. Before I came to Albany at age twenty-one we had lived in nine houses in six towns in four states, my parents following the journalism/teaching job markets. We rented all but one of the houses we lived in. Renting was light: no roots, just passing through. There was something comfortable about being the outsiders. "Comfortable"—is that the right word? Maybe "safe." When you're standing on the margins, away from the action, you're less likely to get hurt.

After I moved to Albany, several things changed. The first was that I fell in love with the city: its history, its distinct neighborhoods, its marvelous architecture. Then came children, then buying a house, and somewhere in there I realized that there might be something to this notion of "community" after all.

Albany's history is much larger, longer, and grander than the lifespan of one little house. And our house is not especially old or particularly grand. Nobody famous ever lived here. But I'm a believer in thinking small. I'm taken by the beauty of how a thousand everyday moments can add up to something extraordinary. And as I looked at the century of change that brought Albany's Pine Hills from farmland to streetcar suburb to modern urban neighborhood, I learned that the legacies of these ordinary people reached far beyond West Lawrence Street.

This is the story of my house, the people it sheltered and the neighborhood it stands in. And it's the story of how Albany became home to this wandering girl.

2

The Junction at the End of Town

He was called Ludwig Marx, or Louis Marx, or sometimes Lewis Marx, or Louis Marks, or Ludwig Marks, in the fluid manner of nineteenth-century immigrant names. Arriving from Hesse-Darmstadt, Germany, he set himself up in the 1860s growing produce to sell downtown at the open-air market. His wasn't a big operation, just seven acres. According to the grid that city planners imposed on top of it, Marx's land extended from Madison Avenue south to Myrtle Avenue, about three blocks long and half a block deep. That grid laid down West Lawrence Street over one of Marx's outbuildings—a sign of the changes to come.

Early on, city directories listed no street address for him, just a location: "House Lydius near junction Western turnpike." Those of us who know Albany know this place well, even if we don't recognize it here: Lydius was the old name for Madison Avenue, and the Western Turnpike was modernized to Western Avenue. The Madison-Western point is the heart of today's Pine Hills neighborhood.

Marx's was just one of the many small farms that dotted Albany's outskirts. But even in his day, the area around the junction of Madison and Western Avenues was no pastoral void. It had been shaped by many years of use into a district that looked both east and west, maybe not quite a neighborhood but not empty, either, populated by farmers and vagrants, wealthy landowners, and, in time, speculators who foresaw that with the rattle of streetcars, life in the old city would soon take on a new rhythm. Transportation built this neighborhood, and in more ways than one.

Its first moment of transit glory had come and gone before Marx's time and earned the area its only state historic marker: the first steam-powered

This advertisement for Pine Hills building lots ran in *The New Albany* magazine, September 1891.

passenger train in the country left from the Lydius-Turnpike junction in 1831.

Why start the railroad up here, so far from the bustle of downtown Albany? Because here the land levels out. From the Junction—and that's how you'll see the name in old accounts, a landmark intersection with a capital J—a train could make a relatively flat run to the outskirts of Schenectady, about thirteen miles away. So passengers boarded cars in downtown Albany, and with the aid of a rope and a stationary engine they were pulled uphill to the Junction, where the locomotive was waiting. At the other end of the journey, coaches would bring the passengers downhill into Schenectady. That, at least, was the plan.

The company behind this grand experiment was the Mohawk and Hudson, one of the first railroads in the country. The locomotive was the *DeWitt Clinton*, one of the earliest built in America. The cars were souped-up stagecoaches fitted to run on rails. And the passengers? They didn't know what they were in for.

A sizable crowd gathered at the Junction to watch as civic officials and honored guests boarded the train, sitting both inside and atop the carriages. A blast from a tin horn, and—thump—the cars, connected by lengths of chain, lurched forward with enough force to throw the passengers from their seats and send their hats flying. The dry pitch pine that fueled the engine spit out black smoke. Burning embers showered down on the honored guests, who by this point probably felt less than honored, because it's hard to maintain your dignity when you're being knocked to the floor with your clothes on fire. One of the riders that day, Judge J. L. Gillis, later described the scene:

> Each of the outside passengers who had an umbrella raised it as a protection against the smoke and fire. They were found to be but a momentary protection, for I think in the first mile the last one went overboard, all having their covers burnt off from the frames, when a general melee took place among the deck-passengers, each whipping his neighbor to put out the fire.

But you know what? The train was moving.

On reaching the first water station the passengers took down some fence rails and lashed them between the cars to take the slack out of the chain; that made the ride a little smoother. Farmers and their families lined the route, at least till the engine neared. Then their spooked horses bolted and upset their carts, sending spectators tumbling in every direction. But the train made it to Schenectady and back, reaching a top speed of thirty miles an hour. And as a mode of transportation, the horses' days were numbered from that moment forward.

In 1844 the train was rerouted to leave downtown Albany through Tivoli Hollow. Up at the Junction, life returned to the gentler sounds of horse-drawn wagons and herds of geese being driven to market. For a little while, at least.

The area around the Junction held another significance for Albany: A tollgate on the Great Western Turnpike stood not far away, near the point where Marion Avenue hits Western today.

Turnpikes were the Thruway of their era. True, they were often wheel-sucking mud, sand, and ruts, and all in all it was easier, if you could, to wait until winter and travel by sleigh. But western expansion after the Revolution needed roads, and of the wretched roads available, turnpikes were often the best. Before the Erie Canal was dug, people heading west could come by river as far as Albany and then start walking. Many of Albany's avenues started off as turnpikes: Central, Delaware, New Scotland, Western.

Chartered in 1799, the Great Western Turnpike was the main route for overland travel to Buffalo—and it remained so until they built Interstate 90 in the 1950s. The turnpike evolved over the years to become part of Route 20, the longest road in the United States, rolling 3,365 miles from Boston to Newport, Oregon, where it ends unceremoniously next to a gas station a couple of blocks from the Pacific Ocean—at least, that's what I can see from Google Street View. Sometime, when I have a few months to spare, I'd like to travel the whole thing. It's tempting to think that I could walk to my neighborhood corner, turn left, and be swept into its west-rolling stream.

This turnpike network meant a lot for Albany, a lot of money. In his history of the city, Jack McEneny described it thus:

All roads led to Albany, not just in a geographic sense but in an economic sense as well. The typical Yankee settler moving with his family from Massachusetts to the fertile valley of the Genesee would not only traverse toll roads owned in part by Albany investors but would often purchase land held by Albany speculators and mortgaged to Albany bankers. Once settled, he would clear his land with Albany tools and supply his farm with provisions ordered from Albany merchants and factories.

Some of that money stayed in the neighborhood: the Marx farm rubbed elbows with a few hotels. Among them were Carrick's, Roadside Inn, and the Klondike, which one old-timer noted was popular with farmers bringing their produce east to the Albany markets. This old-timer, writing to *Knickerbocker News* columnist Charley Mooney in the early 1970s, said he'd learned that from a neighborhood old-timer of *his* youth—a man who remembered picking cherries on Louis Marx's farm.

By the time Marx established his truck garden, the Erie Canal and the railway had thinned turnpike traffic. But the page of the 1870 census that lists Marx and his family suggests a district dependent on both city and farm, locals and travelers. The seven households on the page include the tollgate keeper, an innkeeper, and three market gardeners, counting Ludwig; there are also three garden laborers, a hotel clerk, and a domestic servant.

The land near the Junction wasn't all farms and hotels. To Marx's east were rich neighbors, Andrew and Elizabeth Brown. Their estate, which they called Twickenham, covered a good portion of the land from Partridge Street to West Lawrence, on both sides of Madison Avenue. The Browns and their ten children would summer at Twickenham, a country escape from their downtown residence at Clinton Square.

Another prominent Madison Avenue neighbor was Robert Harper, whose mysterious death in 1870 reads like a tease for a William Kennedy novel. The Albany political figure vanished one January night with a thousand dollars in his pocket. Harper had once been, like Marx, a market gardener; he parlayed a successful business into some smart real estate investments and became quite wealthy. He built his family homestead on a tidy parcel along Madison west of Partridge: The 1870 business directory puts his estate at 145 acres. He served in the state assembly one term, in 1852, representing Albany's Fourth District. He also served as county clerk, city school commissioner, and longtime chairman of the Albany County Democratic Committee.

On January 22, 1870, Harper went downtown to see his lawyer and cash a large check. Afterwards, he ran some errands, and at half past nine at night he was seen eating oysters at Watkins House, a hotel and restaurant at 100 State Street. One account, published several days later, noted, "It is said that he was somewhat under the influence of liquor at this time." Shortly after 9:30, Mr. Simmons, auctioneer, saw Robert Harper walking alone on State Street below Pearl. Then Harper walked down to the Hudson River basin and fell in.

The authorities concluded from the start that the missing man must be somewhere under the docks at the foot of State Street, but the public would have none of it. Seeing an opportunity to bash city police and government, newsmen printed dozens of rumors of Harper's grisly demise at the hands of robbers: He had been seen "with three or four strange men" on State Street, or with one short man on Broadway. His body had been found under a State Street bridge. He had been "decoyed into the suburbs" to be robbed and murdered. He'd had his throat slashed in a brickyard. Albany thrilled to each new terror until the spring rains finally dislodged Harper's body and sent it downriver, where it was found by a Coeymans lighthouse keeper. Harper's money was still in his pocket, and his gold watch had stopped ten minutes after he was seen leaving Watkins House.

Not everyone believed that, of course. But they buried him and moved on, and in the coming years Harper's heirs auctioned off his land holdings in lots. Mr. Simmons, the last man to see Harper alive, presided over some of the sales. This is Smallbany, after all.

So it was in this border territory, between Albany gentility to the east and the open west, that Louis Marks worked and lived in 1870 with his wife, Catharine, and their four children: Louis, Rosana, William, and George. But then Catharine died. By 1880 Ludwig's (and he was Ludwig for this census, Ludwig Marx, with an x) new wife, Fredericka, had borne him a son, little Ludwig, age three. Ludwig senior was in his late fifties when his last child was born; Fredericka was twenty years his junior. Rosa, William, and George were still at home in 1880, William already working as a gardener at age sixteen. The oldest son, Louis—known as Luie—was out on his own.

The 1880 census gives us a glimpse of West Lawrence Street as farm: Mr. Marx grew Irish potatoes on two of his seven acres of land, producing 250 bushels' worth in 1879. In total that year he brought $1,100 worth of produce to market. He owned one horse, one milk cow, and four pigs, but no sheep and no poultry. Compared to his neighbors, he paid very little in wages for farm labor—an advantage, I suppose, of having sons at home.

I am impressed that Marx could get anything to grow in this heavy soil. I don't know a lot about farming, but I know our neighborhood is wet brown clay topped by a veneer of wet grey clay. Digging into this mass takes the force of two feet, one on each shoulder of the spade. Is this the soil the Marxes had to work with? Surely there must have been a better place to farm? Well, maybe not. For one, this land is inside the toll gate, which would have saved Marx money over time. What's more, not far west of here start the sand plains of Albany's Pine Bush, once an ancient lake bed and, later, the largest inland pine barrens in North America. Here and there, as you drive along Washington Avenue, you can still see sand peeking through the grass. In the nineteenth century, the Pine Bush was the site of notorious land swindles. People unfamiliar with the area would think they were buying farmland, and finding it was worthless, they'd try to recoup their loss by foisting the plot onto some other rube. Popular opinion held that the sand plains were a "mistake in nature" and that "not even a diseased dog ought to be allowed to die on the premises, out of respect for the dog." Perhaps that explains why Ludwig Marx put his roots down here: Compared to the pine barrens, clay soil doesn't sound so bad.

I wish I knew more about the Marx family. Luie, William, and George all married eventually, but they don't seem to have had any children who survived them. Rosa married a market gardener and started a family of her own. But little Ludwig, the young son from Marx's second marriage: His story I know. From the April 17, 1882, *Albany Times*:

A shocking accident happened yesterday morning at the house of Ludwig Marx, a two-story frame building at the end of Madison Avenue, near the toll gate. At half past seven o'clock, while the family were at breakfast, they heard the report of a pistol coming from the upper room. Rushing upstairs they found Louis Marx, a boy five years of age, sitting up in bed with a smoking revolver in his hand, while the blood was pouring from a ghastly wound on the left side of his neck, near the jugular vein. Blood was also streaming from his nose and mouth.

The child died two hours later.

The gun belonged to his brother William, who had planned to go hunting Sunday morning with his stepbrother, Frederick Miller, Fredricka's son by an earlier marriage. Fred shared a room with little Ludwig on Saturday night, and before going to bed he had stashed the borrowed pistol under his pillow.

The sharp morning light of April, the family seated around the breakfast table, the noise of the shot, and the moment of stunned, terrible silence that would have followed it—I don't know how you survive that.

But spring pushes on anyway, and there would have been potatoes to plant; and the harsh cheer of summer would bring a new crop of cherries, and you'd load the wagon in the early morning hours and head down Madison Avenue to the market, and things would be the same as every year, and never the same again.

Changes were coming fast to the Marx family's neighborhood, because Albany's eye was turned west. In the 1870s and 1880s, the city spent hundreds of thousands of dollars to build Washington Park. Drawing from the work of noted landscape designers Frederick Law Olmsted and Calvert Vaux—who consulted on Albany's project, though it was ultimately planned by others—the park was laid out at the site of an old parade grounds and cemetery.

Olmsted and Vaux had imagined Washington Park as the key piece in a ring of green spaces and boulevards, providing a charming carriage circuit for a summer's afternoon. Albany tried to carry out such a plan:

the parks commission made a deal with the Great Western Turnpike Company, buying Western Avenue from Washington Park all the way up to the tollgate. In 1876 and 1877 the avenue got the works: granite paving, curbs, sewers, sidewalks, and twin rows of Norway maples. Near the tollgate, where the Western Avenue improvements stopped, the first section of boulevard turned north. The Board of Commissioners of Washington Park adopted a plan to use the city's destitute men—those who otherwise would have "been a charge upon the city poor fund, with no labor performed to show for it, destroying their self-respect and manhood"—as construction labor. In order to "distribute employment as generally as possible," the board's reports explained, the crews of needy men were switched out frequently. It was one of those ideas that worked better on paper: the crew changes meant the work advanced in fits and starts, leading the commissioners to reconsider their plan. Ultimately, the ring of boulevards was never completed, but the section between Western and Washington Avenues nevertheless became a city showplace: bridle paths flank the gracefully curving road, and the houses built along the boulevard are set behind deep green lawns. Today, this stretch of Manning Boulevard is still one of Albany's loveliest streets.

Money followed money as well-heeled Albanians built their houses near Washington Park and beyond it. They turned out onto the West End's avenues and boulevards in their carriages and sleighs, and in their 1886 history of Albany, Howell and Tenney stated that Madison "is considered one of the most fashionable and desirable locations for private residences in the city."

In the mid-1880s, a group of local swells was looking for a place to play sports. The Albany Cricket Club, which had been playing in city parks and rented fields, started a fund to purchase its own pitch. The subscribers—young fellows with old names like Pruyn, Van Valkenburgh, and Van Antwerp—bought some land along Partridge Street that had once belonged to Robert Harper. They decided to expand their offerings beyond cricket, putting in ball fields, a bicycle track, and a clubhouse designed by prominent architects Albert Fuller and William Wheeler. The Ridgefield Athletic Association grounds opened on June 16, 1885.

One of the Ridgefield Association's first projects was just what you'd expect from a group of guys with money, spare time, and a thirst for adventure: A fifty-five-foot-high toboggan run. There's an illustration of the Ridgefield chute in the "Official Programme" of Albany's 1886 bicentennial celebrations, and if it's accurate, then the thing was a monster. It's built up on what appear to be wooden trusses to a height that screams "liability waiver" and even dwarfs the ink-sketched clouds. In other words, it looks awesome. Albany's society set thought so, too, and for a few winters Ridgefield tobogganing was hugely popular, even drawing mention in the *New York Times* and a visit from the governor, the impressively mustachioed David Hill.

Along with all of Albany's westward growth came a need for city services. The neighborhood around the Junction already had a primary school, but by the time Albany really started to unfurl its tendrils out this way the old place was more of a headache than an asset. It had been built in the 1830s as a city of Albany school, a one-story brick building that stood right in the Junction formed by Madison, Western, and West Lawrence. My 1876 map places it in the narrowest point of the triangle, near Allen Street. But a redrawing of administrative boundaries put it outside the Albany school district for some years. When it became a city school once again, in 1870, the Board of Education named it School 18 and added a second story, giving the building a capacity of more than two hundred students. That sounds impressive, but reports to the school board suggest not even half that many usually turned up.

There were probably two reasons for that. The first was a lack of nearby children. Rapid growth was coming to the area around the Junction, but it wasn't here yet. In those years the place that really needed a school was Paigeville,[1] a now-forgotten working-class neighborhood that

---

1. References to the "Paigeville" neighborhood in Albany newspapers and directories trace at least as far back as the early 1860s. It seems likely it was named after John Keyes Paige, a prominent citizen who had his "country seat" there in the middle of the nineteenth century, on land along Lydius between Partridge and Ontario. Mr. Paige was a longtime clerk of the Supreme Court, and he served one one-year term as Albany mayor, 1845–46. He also was president of the Canal Bank when it made history in 1848, according to chronicler Joel Munsell, as Albany's first failed bank. Paige left Albany after that, moving to Schenectady, where apparently disgrace is easier to bear, and he died there nine years later.

used to fan out along Madison and Western near Ontario Street, a half-mile or so to the east. Paigeville residents complained for years that School 18 was too far away for their youngest children to walk to in bad weather.

The second reason for School 18's low attendance might have been that the place was a dump. When the Board of Education assumed control of it in 1870, it concluded the foundation couldn't handle the weight of any more bricks, so the second-story addition was built out of wood. Over the years the building got worse, and in 1888 the Committee on Hygiene urged that it be "closed at the first available opportunity." The classrooms were still heated by coal stoves, and ventilation was a big problem: the air in one classroom, the committee reported, "becomes so vitiated at times, that the teacher is compelled to open all the windows and the door, thus creating a draft, and keep the children marching around the room to prevent their taking cold." The schoolyard, encircled by a gapped and broken fence, turned into a lake of mud in wet weather. What's more, "The exposed location of the school, in the extreme western end of the city, renders the yard and outbuilding a very accessible resort for tramps and other worthless characters."

Well. Can't have that. The district already had a land deal in the works for a Paigeville school, so the board decided to close School 18 and move its blackboards and furniture down to the new digs. School No. 4 was erected in 1892 on the northeast corner of Madison and Ontario.

But the city gave two chits to families near the Junction. The school board reassured them that "as this is a growing section of the city, it will not be long before a new school-house will be needed there." And it gave the School 18 property to the Board of Fire Commissioners, which was looking for a place to put a firehouse. Steamer 10, designed by Albert Fuller, became part of the Albany Fire Department in September 1892. That the neighborhood had earned its own fire station by the 1890s reflects its growth—and the growth the city expected in the future.

An aside, from the irony files: the alternate proposal for Steamer 10 was to build it as an addition on the back of the new School 4 building. The school board didn't think much of that plan, and I can't say I blame them—imagine the kids all rushing to the windows every time the bell clanged—but it's worth noting that School 4's original building was lost to fire on a Saturday night in 1922.

By 1890 the Ludwig Marx house had acquired a number, 1072 Madison, an address that today would fall in the intersection where West Lawrence crosses the avenue. Son William, a machinist at Albany's railroad yards, lived in his father's house. Luie, the eldest son, also a gardener, was boarding down the street. I wish I could check on the size of the farm, see how the potato crop was doing, but most records from the 1890 census were lost in a Washington, DC fire in 1921.

It was undeniable that Albany was changing around the family's farm. Albany Railway, which operated the city's horse-drawn streetcars, ran its first electric car from Quail Street to Broadway and back in April 1890, and the next month put two hundred of its horses up for sale. Soon the trolley would extend all the way up to the Junction. And more than the road improvements, the turnpike, and even the carriage circuit, those trolleys were going to change the neighborhood.

A pair of lawyers named Louis Pratt and Gaylord Logan saw it coming. In the late 1880s they bought a couple of farms west of Allen Street. A broker named Charles J. Peabody threw in his lot with them,[2] and not long afterwards they were selling off plots as the Albany Land Improvement and Building Company. They named their development Pine Hills.

"In ancient times Albany was a walled city! The gates were closed every night," read one ad Pratt and Logan ran in the *Albany Evening Journal*. "Perhaps the limited extent of the territory within the stockade accounts for the very compact way in which the city was built up. . . . Come out in the fresh air! There are no Indians or wild beasts at PINE HILLS! You needn't shut yourself up in a flat or a stuffy block house. We have plenty of room for you at the WEST END." A middle-class development of free-standing homes: for Albany this was a new kind of neighborhood. Pratt and Logan played it up. More than mere

---

2. Some ads and other materials list Pratt, Logan, and Peabody as owners; others name just Pratt and Logan—or even call Pine Hills "the Pratt and Logan Pine Hills subdivision." Pratt was the company's president, Peabody was vice president, and Logan was secretary-treasurer, according to newspaper accounts; in 1892 Peabody secured a seat on the New York Stock Exchange and left Albany.

houses, these were "villas" and "summer resorts" bedecked with "verandas" and "piazzas." Compared to most downtown residences, the Pine Hills lots were huge, giving much more space per family. Light and air could enter the house on all sides, and the separate lots eased concerns about the spread of fire. The developers promoted Pine Hills as "the most healthful and desirable residence section of the city."

Quality was another selling point. Albany Land Improvement put a lot of money into infrastructure (paving, drainage, sidewalks, trees) and tried to ensure that individual properties would follow suit. Covenants were written into many Pine Hills deeds that set standards for quality, including minimum amounts to be spent on a home's construction, and restricted land use—what, how, and where you may build on your property. For Albany, this too was something new; in the late nineteenth century, zoning was an idea just coming in to its own. Building restrictions weren't the only covenants in Pine Hills deeds. Booze sales were out as well. The original contracts prevented property owners from selling "intoxicating liquors" west of Allen Street—part of the "healthful" Pine Hills lifestyle.

Spacious lots in an orderly, wholesome neighborhood—not a bad sales pitch. But none of it would have been possible without the trolleys that allowed people to live farther from their workplaces. Pratt and Logan never forgot that.

Another one of their *Albany Evening Journal* ads:

The magnificent improvements at the West End of Albany are largely due to the excellent service provided by the ALBANY RAILWAY. We took a PINE HILLS CAR at the Postoffice Tuesday evening just after 6 o'clock. The car made 30 stops and carried 55 passengers and reached PINE HILLS, a distance of nearly three miles by the Lark street line, in just 23 minutes. . . . Magnificent public buildings, churches, banks and business houses, schools, clubs, elegant residences, beautiful parks are passed, making this the most notable route traversed by any street car line in America. At the end, PINE HILLS!

The developers offered free trolley tickets for "half-holiday excursions" to Pine Hills. A savvy move: showing potential buyers not just a piece of land but a new way of living.

A number of prominent Albany residents—bankers, lawyers, businessmen—took them up on their deal, building their houses along Pine Avenue and Allen Street. Hoping to entice more buyers, the developers ran ads listing these Pine Hills pioneers by name and occupation. Pratt built his own house at the corner of Western and Pine; from a chair on the porch he could see, rolling forth like a carpet, Madison Avenue's grand approach to his door.

Louis Pratt and Gaylord Logan gave the neighborhood not just its name but also a large part of its character. Their vision of Pine Hills endured even as their own plans sputtered: the Albany Land Improvement Company was wiped out in the financial panic of 1893. The bank foreclosed on its loan, and Pratt and Logan's lots were sold off on the cheap. For the Pine Hills neighborhood, it was a temporary stop; other speculative developers were waiting to take the throttle.

The Pine Hills neighborhood association was established in 1900. It pushed for more streetlights, better trolley service, better sidewalks, better paving, and it asked the city to prohibit heavily loaded sand wagons from entering Albany via Madison Avenue. Not only were the wagons tearing up the street, but "they shake out so much sand that it is absolutely impossible to keep our piazzas clean," the head of the Pine Hills Association told the *Albany Evening Journal*. Nimby, nimby, nimby: newcomers with money fighting unsightly industry or smelly agriculture. It echoes contemporary disputes in the Adirondacks or the Hudson Valley: whose town is this, anyway?

In the Pine Hills, at least, it was becoming clear. In 1902 the new neighbors joined forces to block the building of a "hospital for incurables"—the horror!—that would have gone up on Allen where the Elks hall stands today. By pooling resources to buy the land, they averted this disaster and used the site to establish the fashionable Aurania Club. Society had arrived.

In time, the parents of Pine Hills were complaining that School 4 was too far away for their little ones, even by trolley. School 16 went up on North Allen, opening in 1906 with seats for 364 pupils and a staff of seven female teachers, all graduates of Albany High. They added another teacher the next year as enrollment continued to grow. In 1912, the school gained a four-classroom addition, and still the superintendent wrote in 1913: "So rapid has been the growth of the city in this section that at present this school is seriously crowded."

And what of Ludwig Marx? He passed on, of course, but not before the electric trolley rolled past his house, bringing carloads of new neighbors to a place with a new name. The 1894 city directory is the last edition that includes the old truck gardener; the following year, Fredericka is listed as his widow. Son Luie took ownership of his father's farm; younger brother William and his wife stayed on in the Marx family house. The third brother, George, was a trolley motorman who no longer lived in the neighborhood. And more houses were built, and more lots were drained and graded, and the trolley pushed on, past where the tollgate used to be, riding its tether of electricity into the west.

On May 14, 1910, Luie Marx sold his father's farm to an Albany builder named Lorenz Willig. Some of the Marxes stayed on the land, or part of it: Luie moved into a new home on Morris, and William built a house around the corner at 243 West Lawrence, land that's now topped by the Price Chopper parking lot.

Lorenz Willig moved quickly. In a month, he had filed building plans with the city. And for West Lawrence Street, a new type of growth began.

3

Notes on "From"

"WHAT?! Where is Exit 3? There should be an Exit 3!"

Five minutes in the Capital Region, and already the place had thrown me a curve.

It was August 1994. Twenty-one years old, I was moving from Texas to Albany for a doctoral program. After two and a half days of staring out the windshield of a U-Haul, my eyeballs were rattling. It was bucketing rain. And, okay, playing navigator is not exactly one of my strengths. But dammit, there should have been an Exit 3.

My map showed Exits 2 and 4, and between them the interstate clearly passed over a road that would make a natural highway exit. True, I didn't see it on the map. I figured that, I dunno, it must be a printing error—because why would you build an interstate and skip an exit number? Well, they did, and so my dad and I rolled right over Sand Creek Road, both yelling in frustration to find ourselves still heading north.

It was a prophetic moment, this little Northway quirk. Welcome to Albany: in ways large and small, a city that wasn't quite what I expected it to be.

At first I didn't expect much out of Albany at all. Its main attraction for me was that it was within driving distance of my Massachusetts boyfriend. That's all I wanted: a stopover while we figured out our plans. Other than that, the graduate program looked all right, and the living expenses were better than Boston's, which was my second choice. I felt pretty sure I'd find something to like about Albany; I'd moved around all my life, and I'd yet to see a city with *nothing* to offer. When I tired of Albany, I'd move on.

The first time I'd seen the city, a few months earlier, it was safe to say that I was not impressed. I'd come up for a meeting at the state university campus. Since I was in town I thought I'd start hunting for an apartment, or at least get a feel for where I should look. I asked my graduate advisor what neighborhood she'd recommend.

"There's an area of town that some people call 'the student ghetto,'" she said, pronouncing the words as if they tasted funny. She reached into a file and pulled out a list of student apartment vacancies, which the university housing office provided as a service—though whether it was a service to the students or the landlords is open to debate.

The houses I looked at that day in 1994 needed paint, porch railings, structural repairs, or all three. Unbroken lines of parked cars stretched along both sides of the streets. Sidewalks and yards were littered with paper plates and other trash. If this was Albany, it was dirty, crumbling, and tired. I had just committed to moving seventeen hundred miles away from my family, to a state where I knew not a soul, and looming inside of me was the feeling that I had made a big mistake.

After five or six sag-porched houses, I gave up on the university's list and tried some ads from the newspaper classifieds. They led me to glorious streets of brownstones: tidy row houses, their tall windows dappled by sunlight through trees, flowerpots on their stoops—actual stoops, like something out of a movie. And they might as well have been, for all the chance I'd have to live there on my teaching assistantship salary.

At sunset I went downtown to see the place I'd been looking forward to most of all: the Capitol. I collect state capitols, hoping to visit all fifty of them before infirmity overtakes me. New York's is whimsical and strange, and I liked it very much: each level of its facade is a different style, as if they had kept changing plans midconstruction (in fact, as I learned later, that's what had happened). This was the Albany I'd been hoping for: storied, stately, and surprising. Seen from the Capitol steps, city hall and State Street were majestic. I checked on one more "Apartment for Rent" sign about a block from the Capitol: out of my league.

Though I'd always admired old cities and old houses, I'd never before stared down what it would mean to actually live in them. To avoid the student ghetto, it seemed, I was going to need to find a housemate or look outside city limits. I'm too much of an introvert to set up housekeeping with a stranger. All in all, I felt safer and saner up near my hotel in the suburb of Colonie.

So that's where I settled first, just off the Wolf Road commercial strip, on the fifth floor of a modern apartment complex full of elderly women. It was a boring little apartment, but one with easy parking, quiet neighbors, and no defects. The "welcome" basket was stocked with corporate samples: dish soap, sponges, peanut butter puff cereal. It didn't really make me feel welcome, but I ate the cereal anyway.

The people I met in Albany called me a Texan. I let them, casual acquaintances anyway, because people think they need to know these kinds of things. I love Texas. I did go to college in Texas. And after I was already in college, my parents moved there, too—and, as it turns out, they lived there for the next twenty years before moving again. But all that hardly makes me a Texan.

I never felt I was "from" anywhere—or, at least, it was always complicated. Live in a lot of places, and they all become part of you. But people don't like answers like that. "From" is one of the ways we categorize each other, and people feel entitled to a simple answer.

I was born in the city of Ames, Iowa, but it'd be a stretch to say that's where I'm from. Ames is a university town, and my parents were students there. They were Iowa natives, though, as were their parents, and I lived in the Midwest, in Iowa and Illinois, until I was twelve. So I've got pioneer blood in my veins—which gives me a "from" on a macro level, but it never trickled down into a sense of belonging. The four towns we lived in during those years weren't places with any roots for us, places where our families had any history. And in Iowa you could move to a town and live there for thirty years, and people would still call you an outsider. Your folks—were they from around here? In our case, they never were.

Iowa in the 1970s and early '80s exerted a strong pressure to conform, which wasn't really one of our family values, so people in the towns we lived in never welcomed us much. Neighbors in one place brought a signed petition to our door asking us to leave town: my mother, a reporter, was looking a little too closely at the school board's shenanigans. Parents told their kids not to play with me. I was the girl sitting at the edge of the playground, reading a book and waiting desperately for recess to be over. You'll forgive me if I don't feel like embracing Iowa.

When my mom got a job offer in Louisiana, we left the Midwest and never looked back.

The first question my new classmates and their parents would ask— "What's your name?"—was straightforward enough. But the invariable second question took us by surprise: "What church do you go to?" Er . . . We didn't go to church. My mother advised me to tell people, "We haven't chosen one yet." That worked for our first few months in Louisiana; for the next six years it sounded a little thin. Our "outsider" status thrived.

Though we weren't going to assimilate in the Bible Belt, we also discovered that it was less of a sin not to be a local. There was an air force base in our town, so people were used to seeing families come and go. It had no effect on Louisiana's lively—and infectious—sense of itself. I loved our time there: the music, the unique history—the fact that it was so different from anyplace else, even from other states in the Deep South. Comparing Louisiana with the Midwest opened my eyes to the fact that there were a thousand ways to be American: how people greet each other, how they do business, the assumptions they make—to say nothing of the foods they eat and the stories they believe about themselves. Maybe every place, I wondered, is just as deeply and uniquely itself, if you look hard enough. My explorer's torch was lit.

In Louisiana, belonging was also determined by race, of course; race was a strong dividing and defining factor. Until shortly before I moved there, a law was still on the books that required a person to identify himself as black if he was one thirty-second African American. High school peer groups—and entire high schools—were overwhelmingly either white or black. As I learned to drive I couldn't help noticing how a street would change names, or simply dead-end and pick up again a few blocks later, instead of continuing on into a black part of town.

When I was in college in Texas, and dating Mr. Massachusetts long distance, I couldn't understand why he kept telling his friends and family I was Swiss. "Why would you say that?" I asked him over the phone.

"They want to know what you are," he said.

What I "am"? In Louisiana it had stopped at white or black, Catholic or Baptist. But whether your ancestors came from Germany or England or Poland? Who cared? I don't think Iowa ever cared either: I recalled some story about my great-grandmother scolding my aunt, telling her sternly not to bother about what countries the family had come from: "You're American, and that's all there is to it." My last name is Swiss, but the Norders immigrated in the 1840s, and they married people from all over northern Europe: Germany, Denmark, France, England, Netherlands. I'm a mutt.

"I'm an American!" I insisted to my boyfriend, echoing Grandma. "Why do you care where my ancestors came from?"

But in his world, it meant something. My boyfriend's parents had been the first to marry out of their ethnic groups. Their families had arrived more recently; they still drank slivovitz on holidays, and they knew what cities in Europe the old folks had called home. During my early visits to the Eastern United States I met people who defined themselves and each other by ethnicity to an extent I'd never seen before.

That's what I expected, I guess, when I moved to Albany—the sort of clan loyalty you see in movies about New York. I didn't expect to find a sense of belonging here; I was a graduate student wearing a path between the university and my apartment. None of the people I met were *from* Albany or knew it any better than I did. I had no stake in this town, and no plans to stay.

But from the start, the city fascinated me. I made a friend who lived on North Pearl Street in Arbor Hill, in an old row house with iron bars on the windows and doors. The house abutting hers was a crumbling hull that would eventually lose its back wall. My friend's apartment wasn't a jewel of architectural preservation by any stretch. It was freezing in the winter, and it always smelled like a litter box. But it had soaring ceilings and the mantels of old fireplaces, and from its back deck you could see—well, it was mostly warehouses, but it was *here*, as in, it couldn't have been just anywhere.

Rather than take the interstate to her house just north of downtown Albany, I'd drive slowly down Clinton. On a warm night, Clinton Avenue buzzed with energy. People were everywhere, talking on stoops, sitting outside the corner stores, crossing and recrossing the street. At first it felt unsafe, as if this many people in the street at night meant trouble was brewing. But then I realized I was seeing something new to me: the street as living space. People were hanging out on stoops and sidewalks in the same way I might relax in a living room or on a back patio. It was more communal, much louder, and very compelling.

Back at my apartment complex, an elderly neighbor four doors down passed away. Her body lay undiscovered until the odor brought maintenance men to our floor.

The only thing I liked about my Colonie apartment was the view from my balcony. On clear days the Helderbergs traced the horizon like the rim of a cup. After endlessly flat Texas, I could not get over this mirage of a mountain. It made my chest constrict with loneliness.

Over time I came to realize something my graduate advisor apparently did not know: Albany was filled with apartments. Nearly every neighborhood was a mix of single-family homes and multiunit buildings. I'd never really seen that before. Other than a few grotty wrecks near the universities, houses in the cities I'd known had been single dwellings, and to find an apartment you moved to a multistory development named for whatever it had replaced—"Hillside," maybe, or "The Oaks." And I saw that other people I knew in grad school lived where they could walk to things: a market, or a library, or a laundromat. There seemed something real about that. I tried walking from my apartment to the Shop 'n Save, half a mile away. Someone almost mowed me down as I crossed the five lanes of Wolf Road. From my place, there really wasn't anywhere I could go unless I drove. I suppose if I'd wanted to I could have cut across two paved lots and squeezed through a fence and gone to Colonie Center, but a shopping mall is hardly a place that makes one feel grounded in reality.

And that, I guess, is what coalesced by the end of my first couple of years in Albany: Wolf Road's strip malls and chain restaurants could have been anywhere. I wanted to feel *here*—wherever here was, I wasn't really sure yet, but I wanted it to be a definable place. I wanted someplace with sidewalks, trees, maybe a deli on the corner. A neighborhood.

In the spring of 1995 I went to an end-of-semester picnic at Thacher Park, on the top of the Helderberg Escarpment. Still not that good with geography, it wasn't until I was standing at the overlook that I realized I was seeing the reverse view from my apartment balcony. My building was lost in the expanse stretched out before me; even the university campus was little more than a speck. After a hard, cold spring, the earth was warming at last, and the valley was a haze of new green. It was only when I looked closer that I noticed clusters of roofs peeking out from among the trees: there was so much more out there than the road between Colonie and SUNY Albany.

I found an apartment off New Scotland Avenue, in one of the hundreds of upstairs/downstairs duplexes built across the city in the early twentieth century. Mine was only a half-flat, actually; it had been chopped in two to add another rental unit in the back. But hey, there was 1920s tile work in the bathroom.

The neighborhood was a tidy, comfortable mix of older houses, both single-family homes and the ubiquitous two-family flats. The area was built for walking, with a little strip of shops and restaurants up on New Scotland. What I liked best about the neighborhood, though, were the porches. Come summer, people set them up as second living rooms, decorated with flower baskets, chairs and tables, maybe a rug or a swing. It was cheerful, and I loved it. I imagined that neighbor had inspired neighbor, the way some homeowners nudge each other to ever-larger Christmas light displays. Or maybe it had spread like a virus, all starting from one lady with a box of annuals and a striped awning. A veteran of 1970s ranch houses, I'd never lived in a house with a porch. I'd walk the neighborhood at twilight, when the inside lights were on but the curtains not yet closed, the glow spilling out onto the porch like a welcome mat.

At school, I was struggling—not academically, but philosophically. I was quickly losing faith that I had anything to contribute to my field. What's more, my department was a chaotic place, with factions and acrimony and anonymous notes slipped under doors—and that was among the faculty. We had a succession of department chairs. I found it all ludicrous and immensely depressing. Everyone seemed to be posturing for one another, or looking for a place to stick the knife. No one seemed to find any joy in their work. I couldn't live like that.

I married Mr. Massachusetts to see if that would ease my sense of loneliness and disconnection. It didn't. And over the next year or so, stunned by the mess I'd made of my life, what I did most was walking. I walked my neighborhood so often I discovered that without trying to, I had memorized the street names, in order, from Manning Boulevard to Academy Road. When I couldn't walk, I drove. For hours at a stretch I would drive around Albany, usually at night, taking every street in a neighborhood just to see where it went and how it connected to the other places I knew. Ah, the days of cheap gasoline.

After I'd driven this patchwork of neighborhoods, I wanted to know what I'd seen, so I read William Kennedy's *O Albany*, *Ironweed*, and *Billy Phelan's Greatest Game*. I got a cat and named him after my favorite local architect, Marcus T. Reynolds. I came to learn that "from" isn't much of an issue here: Albany has been absorbing outsiders for hundreds of years. You want to be a New Yorker? So become one.

Eventually I realized that movement isn't progress. Though I'd burned through a lot of gas, time, and shoe leather, sooner or later I was going to have to stop and face my problems, or I'd never go anywhere. I knew I had no future in academia. I knew my marriage was a mistake. But Albany—Albany I wanted to keep.

Well, eventually, things got better, as they nearly always do. I met a fellow who also collected state capitols. Gary wasn't a local—he grew up in Syracuse—but he'd lived in Albany since the mid-'80s. He'd come out walking with me; we would read aloud to each other from a copy of *Albany Architecture*. He loved exploring even more than I did. Cities large and small, important and fading; country villages and old mill towns—he'd study maps, read histories, but best of all put on his tromping shoes and go spend a day walking the streets. He loved every place, loved how they differed from each other. He sought out beauty, nature, and good design, but he didn't shy away from clutter, broken windows, and neglect; he just loved sinking his teeth into whatever was real. What he wanted most was to see each place for what it is, for what makes it unique. More than anyone else I'd ever met, he was *here*, in a moment, in a place. I fell head over heels.

I've lived in Albany now for more than twenty years. That's half of my life, and nearly four times as long as I ever lived in any other place. So am I "from" Albany now? No, not really. "From" doesn't work like that. But for the first time I think of myself as a member of a community—and for a born outsider, that feels like a leap of faith. All love is.

I might not ever have a "from." But I found something better: a home.

4

The Carpenter-Poet

Lorenz Willig was seventy-four years old when life offered him one of its rare gifts: a new perspective.

It was 1941, and Mr. Willig went out to the Albany Airport with his nineteen-year-old grandson, William Madigan. William, a Siena College student, had learned to fly through a government civilian pilot training program, and the young man wanted to take the older one up to the sky for a look at his native city. A newspaper photographer took their picture next to the plane, the willowy youth half a head taller than his bespectacled grandfather, who looked slightly nervous. Both men have their shirtsleeves rolled up; both carry their shoulders and arms in the same loose, capable way.

After the flight, Mr. Willig disembarked with an irrepressible smile. He groped for words to tell a *Knickerbocker News* reporter what he had experienced. His first reaction? He was surprised, he said, to see that Albany had so many buildings.

"I'm a carpenter," he said, "and do you know it took me quite a while to figure out what all those buildings were alongside of Buckingham Lake." They were the recently built Stonehenge apartments.

"I thought I knew all about the new buildings in Albany," he laughed.

Even Lorenz Willig, one of the men who built twentieth-century Albany, hadn't fully realized how much the city had grown.

Willig family lore says that Lorenz built most of the homes bounded by Manning, New Scotland, and Western, as far west as Stonehenge Lane. That's an area of about 250 acres. Even accounting for a little fond hyperbole, there's no question that Lorenz Willig is one of the men who transformed Albany. During his years as a builder, the city unfurled from its dense urban center, becoming a modern city of residential neighborhoods that depended on transportation. You'll find Willig's name in deeds and real estate ads for properties all over the city's western reaches. He had his hand in hundreds, maybe thousands, of deals, buying land and building, selling, and renting houses. My house was one of his projects.

Willig was just one of many builders working in Albany during a period of significant growth. He wasn't famous; he wasn't a civic leader or a captain of industry. But when you consider how much of Albany's housing stock was built in his era, you realize that men like Lorenz Willig did as much to shape Albany and give it its character as any city official, maybe more.

Willig's story is the story of Albany's westward expansion. In part, he was a man who made his living through the good fortune of having the right skills at the right time. Beyond that, he was a farsighted businessman who looked for ways to make things happen, rather than waiting for them to happen. He knew well that he was reforging the city of his birth.

Between 1900 and 1930, Albany's population increased by thirty-three thousand, swelled by immigrants and a shifting rural population. What's more, as the ranks of the middle class expanded, demand for new, more modern dwellings grew. In Albany, as in many places, these trends brought a housing crunch.

"We cannot begin to supply the demand for modern flats or cottages," a real estate agent told a local newspaper in 1903. "Albanians are apparently more prosperous and have more money to spend. Their financial condition being improved, they desire to improve the homes— hence their desire to move into more comfortable and cheerful quarters."

It wasn't just the middle class who needed houses. According to the *Albany Evening Journal* in 1907:

The great need of Albany is homes for the laboring class, at a rental which will be no burden on their resources. Houses of this class are decidedly scarce, little or no building of this character going on except in West Albany. . . . Real estate men are at their wits' end, and are daily turning away applicants who are looking for flats at living rates of rent.

Outmoded, inadequate housing stock and rocketing rent—not a bad time to try your hand at the housing market. People were on the move, and builders like Lorenz Willig were working fast to give them places to move to.

Born in Albany in 1869, the oldest son of a carpenter, Lorenz followed his father into the trade. Over the years, his directory listing shifted from "carpenter" to "real estate." My street was typical of his early building projects: in 1910 he bought a stretch of West Lawrence Street, subdivided the land, built on it, and sold the houses. It was a pattern he would follow over and over again. A 1922 newspaper article described his method:

> Mr. Willig, who is a contractor and builder of many years of experience, told how the company was able to save from 15 to 20 per cent on construction costs through wholesale buying and by the use of gangs of men who did certain parts of work on all the houses, moving from one to the other in succession. The houses are usually from four to five designs with slight exterior modifications so that a street of them presents a varied and pleasing appearance. Money is also saved in the purchase of property at acreage prices and brings the lot costs down to a reasonable figure. There is also a large saving in architect's costs, etc.

He'd buy a carload of materials at a time. Call it the Costco model of home construction: buy in bulk, save per piece. It's interesting to note how Willig maximized his labor, too, with a method that echoes Henry Ford's assembly line operations. But what strikes me most is that despite the steps he took to standardize and streamline the homebuilding process, Willig did not build cookie-cutter houses. Nearly every news article that talks about his homebuilding plans—and there are a number of them, for reasons I'll come back to shortly—emphasizes that the homes would each look different from the outside. So a varied streetscape must have been important to the readers, too.

The houses on my block reflect this variety. The building specs and blueprints[1] for my address are on file down at the county archives. They're part of a set of plans that covers three "villa houses," two in my block and one that stood between Morris and Madison, now gone. Each one was different from its neighbors, with Tudor half-timbering here, an odd little window there, a recessed arch there. The houses all rely, though, on a similar interior layout and use similar materials.

Let's tour mine as it was in 1912, the year Willig finished it—not because it's particularly impressive, but because it's typical of Willig's work. It's just one good old house in a city of good old houses.

The house is set on a hill, sixteen steps up from the sidewalk, high enough to put it above the street. It's a Tudor revival, a motif popular in the early years of the century, with stucco walls, diamond pane windows, and inlaid wood timbers in the gable peak forming curves, rays, and diamonds. There is no driveway. In just a few short years that would be standard issue on every new property, but in 1912 it hadn't happened yet. People were already motoring around Albany, sure, but they kept their cars in garages being built in the city's old stable lanes, streets like Yates, a block away.

Go up the stairs, cross the porch, and reach the door. A little vestibule stands between the storm door and the heavy main door, which has a brass bell, the kind with a key in the middle to twist. Twist it, and when the door opens, step in.

You're in the entryway. On your left is a wooden window bench, warmed by a radiator underneath. Ahead is the staircase; beyond that, the kitchen. From this spot you can see a window no matter which way you turn. To your right, through a wood-framed double doorway, is the living room. It has a trio of slightly bayed windows and a brick fireplace flanked by sconces. From the living room, pocket doors lead into the

---

1. The blueprints were drawn by Harry G. Wichmann, a twenty-two-year-old architect who'd learned his craft through a correspondence course. It's thanks to resources like Google Books that details such as these float up through the digital dishwater.

dining room, which has wood-trim insets on the ceiling and walls, a built-in china cabinet, and a plate rail. In the back of the dining room is a windowed alcove just the right size for a hutch or a desk. A door provides access into the pantry, and from there into the kitchen. From the kitchen, other doors lead to the back porch, to the basement, up the kitchen staircase, or back to the entryway.

Return to the front stairs. The heavy rail feels good under your hand. Seven steps take you halfway up, to a landing where you turn, step, step, and turn for the second set of stairs. But first, look to the other side of the landing: The back staircase meets you here. The main stairs bring the mistress up from the parlor, while the back stairs escort the maid from the kitchen. Mistress and maid share the final seven steps to the second floor.

Seven doorways radiate off the upstairs center hall. One leads to a bathroom, four others to bedrooms. The remaining two flank the stairway: The door on the right conceals the stairs up to the maid's bedroom and to the unfinished attic wings on either side of it. The door on the left opens into a closet.

The house has three porches: the front and back verandas, as the building plans called them, plus a sleeping porch off one of the upstairs bedrooms. The basement has a coal furnace, a stone sink, and another toilet. The fixtures reflect a house on the cusp of two eras: two bedrooms had electric lights; two had gas. Downstairs had both, thanks to combination gas-electric chandeliers, with three arms holding lightbulbs and three sporting gas jets. In the kitchen, the oven had a gas range but was unenameled iron.

The interior woodwork is one of the most striking features of the house. It's typical of craftsman architecture, which had caught on in America just as detail-rich Victorian styles were beginning to look dated and fussy and right around the time Lorenz Willig was launching his building career. The trim above the windows and around the dining room walls might not be fancy enough to catch your eye at first. It's just a series of raised surfaces, blocks on blocks, to give the pieces a little dimension. But each one of those surfaces is a separate piece of wood, put in place with tiny nails. There have been careful human hands at work here.

Making your living building houses takes artistry and business sense, and Lorenz Willig had both in spades. He built and sold single-family houses like mine; he also constructed two-family houses and sold building lots to other developers. When his houses didn't sell, he offered them up for rent with incentives to buy. Part of his skill was in predicting where Albany was going to grow next. But he didn't stop there; he did what he could to accelerate the city's growth. Two projects illustrate the scope of his vision, and how he helped change Albany.

Around 1915, a group of New Scotland Avenue homeowners wanted public transportation for their growing neighborhood. They pushed the United Traction Company to lay trolley line out their way, and when that didn't happen, they organized their own bus company instead. The Woodlawn Improvement Association Transportation Corporation (say *that* three times fast) began in 1917 with a few small buses and a route that ran from downtown out New Scotland Avenue to Allen Street, then up to Washington Avenue. Lorenz Willig, whose own house stood where Allen meets New Scotland, was one of the bus company's founders. During the WIAT's brief existence, he served as its president, vice president, and general manager.

He and his cofounders were right: New Scotland Avenue needed a bus line. A January 1918 news article says that in the WIAT's first year nearly five hundred thousand fares were taken on its four buses. By 1922, according to a trade magazine, the WIAT was carrying nearly 2 million passengers a year. That same magazine presented the WIAT buses as an example of "just how a suburban real estate development can be the foundation of a successful bus business." Of course, that goes both ways—something Lorenz Willig no doubt perceived. Having a New Scotland Avenue bus line made it easier for people to buy the houses Willig was building in the neighborhood—and made his houses more valuable.

The WIAT bus line was taken over by the Albany Transit Company in 1925.

Plenty of other cities were experiencing a similar housing shortage. There was work to be done, money to be made. And if financing was holding back the building boom, well, there were solutions to that, too. In the early 1920s Lorenz Willig became one of the founding directors of the Central New York Mortgage and Homebuilding Company. This was a politically connected corporation: its president was William S. Hackett, who was also president of the Albany City Savings Bank—and, incidentally, the mayor of Albany. The city treasurer and a former state senator were among the founders, too.

Another director was a man named John A. Scott, a prominent Albany real estate man with whom Willig had worked in tandem for years. Remember that name, John Scott, because we'll meet him again later: He was also the first resident of my house.

The company brought its homebuilding plan to cities around the region and beyond, trying to sell it to elected officials and chambers of commerce. This story in the *Saratogian* gives the company pitch:

> Secretary [John] O'Brien gave a history of the inception of the movement by Mayor Hackett, who was the author, and a body of men with high ideals of service to the community as a method of giving needed help to worthy home seekers. He went into the difficulty that a workingman was up against in financing a proposition to build a home when he had only a small amount of capital to begin with, showing how the company was prepared through its system of purchasing a large plot of land, building fifteen to twenty houses at one time on one general plan, to provide a medium whereby a workman is able to secure a home at a figure within his means, even under the present high cost of building. He then introduced Lorenz Willig, as the biggest contractor and builder of homes in this part of the state, as the expert of the company, who would show how it could be done.

Willig would take the floor to outline the cost-saving construction methods he had used in Albany. Scott was one of the money men, explaining how the communities were expected to subscribe, through the purchase of company stock, for a third of the building programs' costs. The company would front the rest, buy the land, build the houses, and finance the mortgages where necessary.

In news stories about these meetings that ran in local papers, the tone was positive. Local officials were intrigued; there was a real need for a builder with a magic formula. The Central New York Mortgage directors made the rounds of small- to midsized regional communities: Amsterdam, Stillwater, Mechanicville, Ballston Spa. The company opened offices in Utica, Schenectady, and Troy. Their plans involved hundreds of homes and hundreds of thousands of dollars.

Yes, the world sure looked bright in 1922. It didn't last, of course. But I'll get to that later, when we meet Mr. Scott again.

Lorenz Willig was far from the only man building Albany in the years before the Great Depression. Many contractors and companies were looking to fill the need for affordable housing.

One solution was mail-order homes. How modern the world must have seemed: every piece, lumber to light fixtures, right down to the nails, could come directly to you, shipped in a railroad boxcar and trucked to the homesite. Everything was numbered, and the house could be assembled by local builders, or even, perhaps, the homeowner. The mass production of materials kept the home prices moderate; the precut lumber reduced labor time, lowering costs further.

Sears, Roebuck was perhaps the best-known company offering kit houses, as they were called. "Skyscrapers are ready-cut. Why not your home?" asked ads that Sears ran in Albany papers in the 1920s. "Build your home the Skyscraper way." The company began offering mail-order homes in 1908 and sold as many as seventy-five thousand of them nationwide between then and 1940. Available floor plans ranged from a modest bungalow to an elegant ten-room colonial.

It's not clear exactly how many Sears kit houses were built in the Capital Region, but there are quite a few. Sears opened a "Modern Home Sales Center" in Albany around 1929; and as Rosemary Thornton, author of *The Houses That Sears Built*, wrote: "Sears didn't open a sales center unless sales in that area were strong, and once a sales office was open, sales typically increased quite a bit." Given an infinite amount of time, I would be seen sneaking around Albany comparing early twentieth-century houses to pictures in a Sears catalogue.

Another notable Albany development project was Winchester Gables, an utterly charming neighborhood that might make you think you took a left turn off South Main and ended up in California. Spanish revival bungalows—stuccoed walls, tiled roofs, heavy wooden doors, and a tower or two—plunked in the heart of Albany? Sure, it's a little strange. But really, it's not like *my* home's mock Tudor architecture makes any historical sense here, either.

These 1920s bungalows were the brainchild of a man named Dan Winchester. He was purchasing manager at JB Lyon, the family printing business, but he moonlighted as a real estate developer. His timing was off, though: sixty houses were planned but only twenty-seven got built before the Depression set in. They're beloved still today for their beauty, their quirk, and their solid construction.

By the way, these Spanish revival houses were built by a firm called Willig and Acker ("Homes our Hobby—the Kozey Kind," as their ads used to say). Willig was Anthony J. Willig, Lorenz's son. When you consider the work of the four Willig sons who followed their father into the building trades, the family's influence on Albany's built environment was substantial indeed.

Bill Willig sits across the table from me at a Saratoga County Cracker Barrel. He has photos, documents, and, best of all, memories of the man who built my house.

He shows me a photo of Lorenz, his grandfather, smiling above a stiff collar. The builder's eyes crinkle in the corners like my husband's do. I'd known Lorenz was a short fellow; his passport application lists him at 5 foot 3 ¼. What I hadn't known was that his wife, Anna, was 5 foot 10. "People would notice it," said Bill, a retired Saratoga Springs attorney. "But they were from the old country, where people didn't give a damn about things like that. They had ten children, so I guess they got on all right."

Bill is proud of his grandfather and his legacy as an Albany builder. He tells me stories he's heard of Lorenz's work, the elaborate staircases and furniture he would do for some of the Pine Hills houses he built. "This man was a bundle of energy. Very strong work ethic." That, Bill says, is the strongest point he can make about his grandfather.

And he must have been as adept with people as he was with wood. Among the papers Bill brought along is a testimonial letter: After World

War I, when he was in his late forties, Lorenz Willig volunteered with the YMCA in Europe, where supervisors praised him for the skill and speed with which he took a multinational crew that lacked a common language and organized it into a quick, efficient building team.

The Willig family homestead on New Scotland Avenue was gone by the time Bill came around, but he tells me a story: Lorenz had a chance to buy a sizable parcel of land in southern Albany, down where Hackett Boulevard later went through. But to finance it he would have had to use his house as collateral, and Anna put her foot down. It was her one rule: she never wanted to risk losing the family home. So no go on the Hackett deal. It would have made his fortune, Bill Willig said.

City directories hint at the family's difficulties during the Depression. The 1931 directory notes that Anna died in late 1930; she was just sixty years old. For the next couple of years, Lorenz apparently turned part of his home into retail space: a tailor and a shoe repair shop share the Willig address. Then, having kept his promise during Anna's lifetime, he let the family home go and moved in with his daughter on Kakely.

Lorenz adapted his work life to the changing economy. In the years before the Depression, city directories list his profession as "contractor." By 1933 Willig had changed his listing; no longer advertising himself as a builder or carpenter, he offered his services as a furniture maker, specializing in lawn chairs.

But his restless creativity—and his hustle—wasn't content with garden furniture.

I love those double-take moments when you learn something unexpected about a person, and suddenly you see them in a new light. With Willig, that moment came in a music copyright catalogue. Lorenz Willig of Albany appears there in the early 1930s, where he gets lyrics credits for a handful of tunes with syrupy titles like "My time is your time any time at all," "Some men fall for dark eyes, but I just fell for blue," and "Your eyes send a wireless message to me." *Songs?* It seemed so out of left field that I assumed it must have been another Lorenz Willig, probably his namesake son.

No, it was Grandpa, Bill told me. Lorenz wrote songs and played the concertina. The 1941 *Knick News* article about his flight over the city fleshed out this side of Willig senior, calling him "a carpenter-poet of wide reputation." In a gush of patriotism about the civilian pilot program, it even quotes one of his pieces:

I'm proud of dear America,
Where freedom had its birth;
Adopted land or native land
Most blessed land on earth.

Land of peace and freedom's rights,
May she forever wave
Her flag of stars and glory stripes,
Dear emblem of the brave!

As the 1930s trudged on, Lorenz expanded his offerings, first advertising as a carpenter again and then, in 1940, reestablishing himself as a contractor. He continued to advertise as a contractor into the early 1950s, when he would have been in his eighties.

Bill remembers visiting Lorenz in the home on Kakely, where he lived in rooms upstairs and had a workshop behind the house. Bill would turn the handle of his grandfather's grindstone to sharpen his father's chisels.

"He never talked a lot about his own jobs or his activities. He would always talk about where my Uncle Lorrie was working, or maybe where Gus was, what David was doing, family stuff, stuff like that. When we'd visit my grandpa, he'd always ask [my dad], 'Are you working, Jim?'"

"Lorenz Willig was a strong believer in hard work," Bill added. "And all of his children were hard workers. My nephews and nieces, too, are hard workers. It's almost genetic."

Bill's father, James, was one of the Willig sons who followed their dad into the trade. "I think [Lorenz] felt guilty about the way he treated my father when he was younger. He was an unwanted ninth child," Bill explained. In the seventh grade Lorenz pulled James out of the classroom and put him to work as a laborer, telling him, "You're too big for school."

Bill remembers his father riding the bus with his toolbox on his shoulder. "One of the lucky things about my dad was he always had a job," Bill said. Still, James wouldn't let Bill work construction. He told his son, "You can get hurt too easily, and you won't want to leave the money behind." So Bill rode *his* bus to Vincentian and went on to be the first in his family to graduate from college. Wanting to distinguish himself from the scores of other college grads, he enrolled in law school. Today, retired after a career in law, he says he knows stories about mid-century Albany politics that can never be told.

Bill's hobby is restoring antique mahogany boats. He carries pictures of them in his wallet; one of them was named "antique boat of the year" in 1979. Lorenz's love of craftsmanship must be genetic, too.

Lorenz Willig died in 1962, at ninety-three, and was buried at Our Lady of Angels. The cemetery sits cheek-to-jowl with the Colonie Center shopping mall, a place the builder would probably admire as a savvy land development deal. He was survived by eight of his children, twenty-four grandchildren, and thirty-four great-grandchildren. He left quite a legacy—in flesh and blood, as well as in wood, stucco, and stone.

I went out once to visit him there, to tip my hat to the man who built my house. On the back of his tombstone is inscribed "mother"— Anna, remember, was the first to pass—and words from the Book of John: "I go to prepare a place for you." It's a fitting verse for a man who spent a lifetime preparing places for others.

5

By Any Other Name

My street, West Lawrence Street, is a puzzle. To start with, there's no East Lawrence Street, so why is it called *West* Lawrence? And since it's a north-south running road, what is it "west" of?

Well, turns out it *is* west of something: North Lawrence Street. That's in Albany's warehouse district, where it runs (wait for it) east to west. These two Lawrence streets have no relationship to each other whatsoever. If you extended each one, letting West Lawrence head north and North Lawrence roll west, they'd eventually cross. As amusing as it'd be to watch mailmen spin in circles at that intersection, it's the sort of thing city planners would tend to avoid. And in the old city directories, West Lawrence Street is alphabetized under "W"—"West" is a part of its name, not a location.

So why do these two Lawrences exist? Why would two completely separate streets have the same name?

My theory: patriotic exuberance and poor planning.

In 1813 Albany's surveyor and engineer, Evert Van Alen, was looking out this way. He plotted about three miles of land stretching away from downtown and divided it into "great lots"—parcels for future development. My street appears on this 1813 map, a century before any of today's houses were built there.

Along the Great Western Turnpike Van Alen penciled in one paper street after another, mapping a vision of a much-expanded Albany: west of Erie Street was Main Avenue, then Lawrence, then Allen; and then, marching westward, were Burrows, Ludlow, Brookes, Pike, Covington,

Decatur, Hull, Bainbridge, Chauncy, Warrington, Porter, Wayne, Gates, Putnam, and Magazine Streets.

Most of these streets never bore these names, but, nonetheless, they point the way to the Lawrence of West Lawrence Street. Thanks to Google, even someone as ignorant of military history as I am can discover in two minutes that all of these people were war heroes. Covington was General Leonard Covington of the War of 1812, which was still being fought when Van Alen made his map. Pike, of course, would be Zebulon Pike, killed trying to take Toronto. And Allen? Before seeing this map I had wondered if Allen had been named after Van Alen himself. But the name's inclusion here, in the company of Revolutionary War generals Israel Putnam, Horatio Gates, and Anthony Wayne, suggests the street is probably named for Ethan Allen. We finish out Van Alen's street roster with 1812 naval officers Hull, Decatur, Bainbridge, Porter, Chauncy, Ludlow, Warrington, Burrows—and Lawrence.

Captain James Lawrence had achieved hero status just months before Van Alen started work on his map. My knowledge of the War of 1812 doesn't go much past "The Battle of New Orleans"—yes, the Johnny Horton song, not Andrew Jackson's victory—so I'll give you only the short version of Captain Lawrence's moment of glory. In June 1813, the thirty-one-year-old captain of the *USS Chesapeake* challenged a British ship blockading Boston Harbor. It was a daring move, done at midday with flags flying, but the Americans were no match for the force that opposed them. A musket ball struck Captain Lawrence, and as he was carried below deck, he said to his officers, "Tell the men to fire faster, and not give up the ship!" It was no use. The British took the *Chesapeake*, and Lawrence died of his wounds. The entire skirmish was over in eleven minutes.

Captain Lawrence's friend, Commodore Oliver Hazard Perry, had a flag made with the words "Dont give up the ship" (sans apostrophe; it was war and no place for such niceties); he flew it as he fought to victory in the fall of 1813 in the Battle of Lake Erie. (His flagship in that conflict? The *USS Lawrence*). Today, "Don't give up the ship" is still a motto of the US Navy.

The War of 1812 was a defining moment for our young nation. In the years to follow, its heroes lent their names to forts, roads, villages, and other civic projects. As for the bold young Captain Lawrence, towns and counties in a dozen states were named for him. And, in Albany, a street. Maybe two.

Two years after Van Alen made his map, Albany expanded northward. It took in part of Colonie, including a Lawrence Street. So why was *that* street named Lawrence? Well, I don't know. But my guess is that it was named for the same brash captain. I've seen a map of the area dated 1799 that includes this Lawrence Street, which sounds rather definitive except that it isn't: 1799 may have been the date of the original surveying, but the map includes data added later. The area, for example, is referred to as part of Albany's Fifth Ward, which in 1799 it wasn't. Also mentioned on the map is "John Fonda Junior deceased"; he was a prominent colonial-era resident who died in 1814. So since this map contains data from after the War of 1812, it doesn't prove that the northern Lawrence Street predates the war.

Of course, it doesn't prove it *doesn't*, either. Perhaps the street was named for some other guy named Lawrence or for St. Lawrence, like the river. But on Dutch land, I doubt it.

For the next fifty or sixty years Albany had two Lawrence Streets. Since no one lived on my street yet, there was probably not much opportunity for confusion. An 1857 Albany map shows Lawrence in the North End and Lawrence uptown. But at some point in the mid-nineteenth century, as development inched its way westward, someone noticed. By 1876, my street had been renamed West Lawrence. And Lawrence and West Lawrence streets coexisted into the mid-twentieth century, when the former was rechristened North Lawrence. And there you go.

This is an imperfect answer. Why didn't city planners just change the western Lawrence Street's name to something else? Why did they keep Lawrence as a street name, when they ignored so many of Van Alen's other choices?

One person who objected to the double Lawrences was a common council member named James G. Cummings. In 1891 he was alderman of the Sixteenth Ward, which contained West Lawrence at that time.

Cummings proposed that it be renamed Fifteenth Street and that nearby Erie, another street with a doppelganger, become Thirteenth Street.

Why Fifteenth and Thirteenth? Because, going west from the top of State Street hill, we have:

1. Eagle
2. Hawk
3. Swan
4. Dove
5. Lark
6. Knox
7. Lexington
8. Robin
9. Lake
10. Quail
11. Ontario
12. Partridge
13. Erie
14. Main
15. West Lawrence

It takes a bit of imagination to pick out this pattern on the quilt of the modern city, since some newer roads disrupt the grid, and others, like Erie, have been nearly wiped out. It's a little easier to see if you compare the modern map to the one Simeon De Witt made in the 1790s. De Witt, New York's surveyor-general, prepared maps of the city that included plans for its post-Revolutionary expansion. His was an orderly layout, not the jumble of lanes and angles at the heart of the colonial city.

The east-west running streets in De Witt's grid were named for animals: Hare, Fox, Elk, Lion, Deer, Tiger, Buffaloe (sic), Wolf, Otter, and Mink. Of the animal streets, only Elk has kept its name. Most of his north-south streets, the ones he named for birds, fared better, though not all: Pigeon, Snipe, and Swallow became Lake, Lexington, and Knox. A couple of streets were renamed for sexier birds: Turkey became Quail, and Duck changed to Robin, proving that birds, too, are victims of fashion.

So if you extend the western grid as originally conceived by Simeon De Witt, then Erie is the thirteenth north-south street above the State Street hill, and West Lawrence is the fifteenth—which makes a pretty compelling explanation but a pretty lousy street name.[1] The common council didn't go for the idea, either, though they did agree to appoint a Special Committee on Changes of Names of Streets, with Alderman Cummings among its members. I'll share a quote from the committee's report, because it highlights Albany's long history of crazy. A pair of Lawrence Streets was the tip of the iceberg:

> [W]e find two streets named Centre, having no connection. Two streets named Erie, one in the Ninth Ward and one in the Tenth and Sixteenth Wards. Two streets named First, running parallel and only a short distance apart, and First avenue. Two streets named Second and two streets named Third, running parallel and only a short distance apart, each one farthest north being designated as North First, Second and Third, with Second and Third avenues. Two streets named Garden, one in the First Ward and one in the Sixteenth. Two streets named Lawrence, one in the Ninth Ward and one in the Tenth and Sixteenth. Two streets named Main, one in the Ninth and one in the Tenth and Sixteenth. Two streets named Maple. . . . Two streets named Martin. . . . Two streets named Park. . . . One of each of the last four named streets are called avenues, but your committee fail to see the propriety of such designation. There is also Pine street and Pine avenue. Two streets named Pleasant. . . . Two streets named Rensselaer. . . . Two streets named Jackson.

---

1. One Albany street did succumb to the grid-counting scheme, at least for a time: Nineteenth Street. Today it's Winthrop Avenue.

Cummings and committee recommended that the newer street of each pair be renamed. The council took no action on the report that year; by 1892 Cummings was out of office, and the issue lost its champion.[2]

A lot of these duplications got worked out over time. Many did not; among others, we still have an Erie Street, a West Erie Street, and an Erie Boulevard; a Clinton Avenue and a Clinton Street; a Pine Street and a Pine Avenue. First, Second, and Third Streets run parallel to First, Second, and Third Avenues. This is what happens when parts of different plans and separate communities are stitched together over centuries—a Frankenstein's monster of a city, a bit chaotic, sure, but alive.

---

2. That wasn't the last time someone suggested renaming West Lawrence. In 1910 some property owners on the developing street petitioned the Common Council to have its name changed to Euclid Avenue. Their request, "duly certified by the City Engineer, was received, ordered filed, and printed in the minutes." An alderman entered it for consideration at the next meeting, and that, apparently, is all that ever came of it.

6

First Footsteps

Five foot 11, fair complexion, blue eyes, dark grey hair: that's how John Scott was described on his passport application in 1918. In the photo, his eyes are tired, his smile a little dopey. It's the kind of face that translates easily to the modern age; I can picture him in a golf shirt or a ball cap. More than once I've imagined crossing paths with him on the sidewalk. "Hey, John. How's Mary? How're the boys? What are you up to this year?"

This man was always up to something: changing careers, changing houses; he moved every few years. His jobs ranged from mortgage company president to paper mill owner to Oriental rug salesman to tire retreader, and more. If I had been his wife I might have throttled him. Was he restless? Desperate? Or was it something else?

"First owner, John A. Scott" is engraved on the Historic Albany Foundation plaque on the front of my house, and John Scott was where my house research started. From his story I went forward and backward to fill in the rest of the picture. The Albany businessman brought me face to face with two of the tougher issues in writing about history. The first is that the paper trail can tell you *what* someone did, but it probably won't tell you *why*. And the other is a reminder: to me, John Scott was an interesting story; to others, he's family, and in every family there are wounds that may never completely heal.

The public story of John Scott's life—as recorded in the census, city directories, and the occasional news story—takes the arc of the American Dream: start small, work hard, make something of yourself. That's the story we'll begin with.

John Alexander Scott was born in Albany in 1867. His parents had immigrated to the United States from Northern Ireland. His father, Robert, was employed at the gas works. John was a middle child; his mother, Margaret, bore seven children, though only three were still alive by the turn of the century.

The Scotts lived in a multifamily house on heavily Irish Arch Street, just around the corner from South Pearl. In the late 1800s the street was a mix of middle- and working-class families and the industries that employed them. Robert didn't have far to walk to work: the Albany Gaslight Company was at the corner of Arch and Grand, not a block away.

John lived at home until he married Mary Ainsworth, a nice girl he knew from church, then he moved in with Mary and her parents. As a young man, John worked for Albany Perforated Wrapping Paper—started by Seth Wheeler, the man credited with inventing rolled, perforated toilet paper, bless him—and then John Scott and a partner went into business for themselves as wholesale paper dealers. Their ad in the 1896 directory read:

> Scott & Thompson, 46 Quay Street, Wholesale Dealers in Toilet Paper, Wrapping Paper, Paper Bags, Twine, Rope, Clothes Line, Butter Dishes, Washboards, Ice Cream Boxes, Oyster Pails, Pie Plates, &c. A LARGE ASSORTMENT CONSTANTLY ON HAND.

About 1901, John moved deeper into the paper trade, from wholesaling to producing. He founded Scott Paper Mills, which manufactured "paper, paper products, butter trays, and twine," according to a trade journal; and "toilet paper, roll and package," according to a trade directory. (No, it's not *that* Scott Paper, the one still making toilet paper today; that company hails from Philadelphia.) With John's career taking off, he and Mary established themselves uptown in Albany's new neighborhood, the Pine Hills. They rented on North Pine Avenue for a few years; then, about 1906, they bought a house along the bridle path on fashionable Manning Boulevard.

The Scott Paper warehouse was in north Albany, near the intersection of Lawrence (yes, that other Lawrence) and Broadway, in a former

Methodist Episcopal church. John was a Methodist Episcopal himself, but probably escaped any feelings of blasphemy: the 1860s church had closed by 1870, and it had been used in the interim years as a pork-packing plant. Talk about creative reuse.

The paper industry was a natural for Albany, which by the late nineteenth century already had a long history as a lumber town. The city was once one of the largest lumber markets in the United States, thanks to the Erie Canal, and for two and a half decades it was the country's most important wholesale source of white pine. Boat transportation hung on in the lumber industry long after the dawn of rail, in part because of fears that locomotives would throw sparks and start fires.

In their bicentennial history, Howell and Tenney noted that even in 1886, with the glory days past, there was "no branch of business in this city of more extensive proportions" than the lumber industry. They went on:

> While the receipts of lumber are greater at Chicago, the Albany market is none the less important. . . . All the foreign shipments are negotiated from this point. The lumber for South America, the West Indies and other foreign countries is assorted here, and much of it is manufactured here into doors, ceilings, etc., so as to be ready for use when reaching destination. The trade with Australia is very extensive, millions of feet of prepared lumber being sent to that continent from here every season.

The Lumber District was north of downtown and Arbor Hill, in a patch of land between the Erie Canal and the Hudson River. City maps from the nineteenth century show dozens of long slips jutting off the canal like the teeth of a comb; from these, boats could unload right into the lumber yards. On some maps they're marked with the names of the companies that used them: Fogg Patton & Co., Dalton & Kibbee, J. Benedict & Son, Sumner & Hascy. Many more. The district handled hundreds of millions of board feet per year. An 1898 labor union publication sang its praises:

> The conveniences for doing business in the lumber district of Albany are unrivaled. A street railway runs to and through it;

telegraph and telephone lines afford immediate communication, large planing mills are ready to quickly dress lumber in every way and to any amount, and good clean dining halls await the wants of customers. Hydrants at regular intervals, with a full supply and a heavy head of water, and hose for immediate use, are ready for the extinguishing of fires.

Albany got its timber from the north woods and, via the canal system, from western New York and Canada. Paper manufacturers helped fuel the clear-cutting of the Adirondacks: spruce and other young softwood trees, even saplings and trees unfit for other uses, could be mashed for paper pulp. It seemed, for a few lifetimes at least, that the trees would never run out.

But they did, of course. As local mills had to seek timber farther and farther afield, it made less and less sense to ship it to Albany. Before the twentieth century was a decade old, the Lumber District was sputtering; costs were skyrocketing and some yards suffered fires. In 1921, the *Albany Evening Journal* urged the city to fill in the slips and the "obsolete" Erie Canal and use the land for a new industrial center. Ten years after, the Lumber District was Jungletown, a Depression-era camp of the homeless and the desperate, near the dump.

Obscure Erie Boulevard is an unworthy successor to the Erie Canal. It traces its old path but for years it led nowhere and offered little. The biggest thing on Erie in recent times has been Huck Finn's Warehouse, a sprawling furniture discount store. In 2014 the store's owners bought out Hoffman's Playland, a beloved 1950s-era Colonie amusement park, and moved the rides to their property. It's given a spark of life to a thinned-out stretch of Albany, beckoning visitors back to an erstwhile nowhere land, a land that once glistened with sawdust, water, and sweat.

John Scott got out of the toilet tissue business as the industry collapsed, passing control of Scott Paper to one of his partners, Henry Streibert, who announced plans to build a Scott Paper factory in or near Albany. Given the state of Albany's lumber market it's not surprising that the project apparently fizzled—other than a mention in a trade journal I haven't found any other evidence of it. Streibert held on, though; he renamed the company after himself and ran it as a paper wholesaler until his death in 1942.

Where did Mr. Scott go next? After a one-year detour selling Oriental rugs—huh?—he got into real estate. From there, John Scott's story dovetails with Lorenz Willig's. Their names appear together in dozens of ads in the early twentieth century: one- and two-family houses for sale, plus a selection of "choice building lots" for those who preferred to start from scratch. Working together, the real estate agent and the builder hastened development in Albany's western reaches.

In 1912 Scott and Willig bought twenty acres of trees near the intersection of Washington Avenue and Nineteenth Street (the road that today is called Winthrop Avenue). It was a good time to invest; the city was just getting around to improving Washington Avenue out that far.[1] The developers called the project "Pine Hills Park." The name didn't stick, but they were right about the location. In a spring 1915 auction Willig and Scott sold every plot in two afternoons and doubled their investment, clearing about $15,000 in profits; run that through an inflation calculator, and it's somewhere near $350,000.

On the day in March of 1912 that the Scotts bought my home from Willig, its builder, they sold Willig their Manning home plus several other neighborhood lots. Why did they leave the boulevard for a smaller house on West Lawrence Street? I have no idea. Perhaps that's how Scott got the cash for his part of the "Pine Hills Park" investment, which he bought into a few months later. That's just a guess.

Another guess is that it had something to do with the construction of the Calvary Methodist Episcopal Church. The Scott family had long been members of Calvary's predecessor, Ash Grove Methodist Episcopal,

---

1. In the late nineteenth and early twentieth centuries, upper Washington Avenue was known as "the Speedway." People would race their horses and sleighs from Quail Street to Manning Boulevard. The Speedway Hotel, northeast corner of Washington and Manning, served as the finish line and then served up postrace libations. The hotel was gone before the "Pine Hills Park" development came around; the building suffered a fire in August of 1914. It was razed the next year, to the apparent joy of its neighbors, who had "often expressed a desire that the building should be torn down, as it was a detriment to that locality," the *Times-Union* reported in 1915.

close to where John grew up on Arch Street. But as its congregants moved uptown, so did the church. A church anniversary piece put it this way: "The city expanded westward, and it seemed both wise and necessary that the church should follow the people." Ash Grove leaders considered buying property at the intersection of Madison and West Lawrence, but they settled on something a little more removed: the northwest corner of West Lawrence and Morris Streets, land that had once belonged to Robert Harper.

I wonder if the Scotts' decision to live here, on West Lawrence Street, was related to the church's construction. Their involvement in the Ash Grove / Calvary congregation went back decades by that point, and John was on the Calvary building committee. He could have overseen the work from his front porch.

The Calvary Church's first service in the Pine Hills was held in a rented hall in the spring of 1912, about two months after the Scotts bought the West Lawrence Street house. The parsonage was built first, and parishioners worshipped there till the church was ready. The church cornerstone was laid in 1913, the building dedicated in 1914, and by the time the 1915 city directory was printed, the Scotts had moved on—to Nineteenth Street, where John Scott would be near the development of all those lots he and Willig were about to sell in "Pine Hills Park."

Calvary Methodist Episcopal, by the way, is now Emmaus United Methodist Church. A lively multiethnic crowd converges on Sundays; their hymns bring a cheerful peace to the neighborhood on summer mornings, when the church doors are open. A refugee assistance center occupies the old parsonage, and language classes and after-school programs are held in the church basement. In summer the lawns are brightened by the colorful skirts and headcoverings of women, many from Burma and Bhutan, chatting there before lessons begin. The church itself went on the National Register of Historic Places in 2008.

When the Albany Real Estate Board was founded in 1914, John Scott was elected to its inaugural Board of Governors. He also served as a commissioner of deeds for the city of Albany, a position similar to a notary public. You'll find his name and certification on scores of property sales in the early 1900s. Along with his involvement in his church,

John Scott was a YMCA secretary and a Mason. Like Willig, he spent most of 1918 in Europe, doing charity work with the YMCA. Also like Willig, he was a founding director of the Central New York Mortgage and Home Building Company. And the story of their firm's rise and fall offers a glimpse into New York's financial world in the years before the Great Depression.

During the urban growth of the 1920s, Albany and other cities needed a quick, workable development plan. Central New York Mortgage and Home Building, with its program of investment, construction, and mortgage offerings, wanted to be the company that built affordable houses across upstate New York. Their ads were stirring. "The greatest need of America is homes," one read. "So great has been the demand for homes, so limited the supply, that real suffering has resulted." They evoked "the patriotic necessity of taking care of our people" and added, almost humbly, "In response to this call, we have acted."

Central New York Mortgage's directors were financial and political insiders, and the company's advertising made a point of listing their credentials. The officers included William Grattan, former state senator and county clerk; John B. Hauf, Albany businessman and president of the Central Bank; and William J. Brennan, Albany's city treasurer. John A. Scott, the mortgage company's vice president, was touted as former president of Scott Paper Mills and a "large property owner." And at the top was their gilt-edged calling card: Mayor Hackett,[2] president of Central New York Mortgage and of the Albany City Savings Bank.

When Scott, Willig, and the other representatives made their sales pitch to upstate cities, Hackett often accompanied them. In a 1922 news story on their meeting with Mechanicville leaders, the mayor hit all the right notes of civic and financial stability. "He gave a splendid argument for community progress and betterment," the paper reported,

---

2. Hackett's association with Central New York Mortgage predates his tenure as Albany's mayor, barely. The company was incorporated in 1921, the year Hackett was running for his first term. In an editorial shortly before the election, the *Times-Union* highlighted Hackett's association with the company as a reason to endorse him: "His leadership in this plan of home building is illustrative of the type of administration he will give in the office of Mayor."

and said that he became interested in home building because he saw the great need of clean, wholesome homes in which the young manhood and womanhood of the country should be reared. . . . He said that he hesitated to lend his name on account of his bank connection to this new company but that he became satisfied that the men had a sincere desire to benefit the capital district and to make Central New York the banner section of the state and he was exceedingly proud of the fact that he was president of the home building company, in which he had great faith.

It was a multifaceted operation; a subsidiary company, Central New York Title Guaranty Co., was formed to purchase mortgages and issue titles and bonds. The subsidiary had all the same directors as its Mortgage and Home Building parent. To sell shares, they organized the Great States Securities Co., which also had the same group of men as its directors. Scott served for a time as president of Great States Securities as well as vice president of the mortgage firm.

These men knew how to trade on reputation, and as they expanded, they followed the same pattern. When they opened an office in Troy, they chose a former Troy mayor to head it. In Schenectady, they recruited the head of the Board of Trade.

But if the company's political connections enhanced its reputation, they also brought it attention from Hackett's enemies. In October 1925, a Central New York Mortgage shareholder named Florence Holmes filed a lawsuit against Hackett and the company's other directors, asserting that they had given themselves thousands of shares of the company's stock without paying for them. Holmes was the wife of the Republican leader of the Albany County town of Bethlehem. Hackett, running for reelection as Albany's mayor, called it "a political pre-election scheme to attract votes"—and it may well have been.

The *Schenectady Gazette* noted that the action followed "a so-called exposure" story by an Albany newspaper "now controlled by Republican leaders in that city."[3] However, though the accusers may have been politically motivated, the investigation that followed seemed to support the allegations. And this was just the sort of case that the state attorney general was itching to pursue.

New York had been one of the last states in the country to pass a law targeting securities fraud. When the legislature finally drafted one—called the Martin Act—in the early 1920s, the state's financial power-houses used their political muscle to make sure it was largely toothless. But in 1925, new attorney general Albert Ottinger pushed for amend-ments to strengthen it. He used the Martin Act to secure injunctions against hundreds of individuals and corporations. Ottinger targeted not just small-time swindlers and bucket shops but also larger corporations that used deceptive stock practices.

In December 1925 Ottinger accused Central New York Mortgage and Home Building and the Great States Securities Co. of violating the Martin Act. He sought and received an injunction against the companies. Since Mayor Hackett was the company president, the story went statewide.

The court filings accuse Hackett, Scott, and partners of playing fast and loose with the facts in order to sell more stocks. Ottinger's first claims echo those of Mrs. Holmes: that the directors had issued some ninety-four hundred shares to themselves without paying for them—effectively giving themselves control of the company. Of all the directors, Hackett and Scott had received the most, according to Ottinger—twenty-five hundred shares each. Lorenz Willig received two hundred shares.

Some of the attorney general's accusations touched on money, claim-ing that the company's books didn't quite balance out or didn't meet legal requirements. But what Ottinger focused on most was the sales pitch. He called them out on dozens of points, asserting that Central New York Mortgage's promotional materials and advertising were full of statements that were "false, misleading, and calculated to deceive." A few highlights:

- to help spur sales, the directors had told the public that they had "bought and paid for" their stock, investing their own money in the company;

---

3. The Albany newspaper was probably motivated by something less noble than watchdog journalism. The papers of the day were political mouthpieces that made no attempt to hide their biases. The *Albany Evening Journal*, for example, was a Republican newspaper; the *Times-Union* glowed with reports of how Democrats were improving the city. Stories that didn't fit a newspaper's version of the truth just wouldn't get into print. Even when the papers did report on the same event it would often have a very different spin, depend-ing on whether the editors were trying to protect the city administration or impugn it.

- the company claimed it "ha[d] the endorsement of the Albany, Troy, Syracuse Chamber of Commerce, Schenectady and Amsterdam Boards of Trade"—when it did not;
- in its literature the company tried to persuade potential investors that it was something similar, "in its operations and margin of safety," to a bank—which it wasn't;
- the company's promotional materials contained wording "which, to the careless or uneducated reader, would make it appear that the said Issuer was 'Officially Recognized by the Federal Reserve Board' "—which it wasn't, nor was it eligible to be;
- the company traded on the directors' reputation to convince the public that Central New York Mortgage "would be a safe and wise investment," suggesting "that when such men as William S. Hackett and John A. Scott were at the head of the Issuer, it could not fail."

Ottinger even took a jab at the company's democratic rhetoric:

> They stated that the "business of lending money . . . is the most difficult to become interested in, because it has been so largely controlled by the wealthy men in each community, and that it is considered a rare privilege to be invited to participate in a 'ground floor' way in the banking business," thereby intending to convey to the prospective purchaser that the invitation to purchase securities in the said Issuer was in fact an invitation to participate in a ground floor way in the banking business, when in fact and truth, all the "ground floor" opportunities had already been allotted to the officers and directors of the said Issuer, and the business of the said Issuer was not, and is not, a banking business.

Central New York Mortgage and Home Building had a lot to answer for. But Ottinger's investigation was not the only thing that would complicate the company's future.

In February 1926, a couple of months after the injunctions were granted, Mayor Hackett took a trip to Cuba. On his way to dinner one evening, the car he was riding in struck something in the street. At the impact, the car door flew open, and the mayor was thrown from the vehicle, striking his head. He lingered for two weeks in a Havana hospital, where infection set in, and he died there on March 4, 1926. His political star was still rising; some say he would have been tapped to run for governor in 1928.

Accompanied by a Masonic delegation, Hackett's body came home to Albany to be mourned and buried. John Boyd Thacher II took over as mayor, and John Scott became president of Central New York Mortgage.

Ottinger's legal proceedings against the company ended a year later, on March 8, 1927, with an agreement signed by all the company's directors, plus Ottinger and his deputy. The directors made no admission that they had violated any law, but they pledged that in the future they would never engage in any of the acts of which Ottinger had accused them. They also gave up the shares they had received. John Scott signed twice, as both a director and as company president.

Throughout his tenure as attorney general, Ottinger continued to push against securities fraud. During a speech in February 1927, he predicted: "Unless greater safeguards are thrown around the investments of the public in the enterprises promoted by these concerns, big and little, a series of financial crashes that will stagger the business world is bound to ensue." How right he turned out to be.

Popular with New York voters for his antifraud campaign, Ottinger ran for governor in 1928. He was narrowly defeated by a Democrat named Franklin D. Roosevelt.

Central New York Mortgage hung on for ten more years, finally going bankrupt in 1937. But John Scott wasn't around to see that happen.

When I set out to write this book, my plan was to trace only the handful of people who built or lived in my house. Though I hoped to talk to their descendants as part of my research, I did not intend to write about the lives of succeeding generations, people who had no connection to this house. But stories don't always end where you want them to.

I'm not the first person to write a book about the Scott family. I'm not even the second. And to write about John Scott without acknowledging those stories would be a lie of omission.

Sisters Catherine Scott and Beryl Scott Glover never knew John A. Scott, their grandfather. He died before they were born. But it was more than time that separated them from their father's father. Though John Scott's 1935 obituary says he died at home on South Main Avenue, whispers in the family tell a different story, and John's burial records at Albany Rural Cemetery confirm it: he died in a state psychiatric hospital in Poughkeepsie.

John Scott's mental illness "was a source of shame in those times," said Catherine Scott. "My grandfather was a verboten subject in our family so I never learned much about him. My mother would only say, 'He was a martinet,' by which she meant harsh disciplinarian."

Beryl says she knew her grandfather had been a smart businessman who made and lost a lot of money. Her mother had talked a little about how difficult he was toward the end of his life: "He became a bit violent, and very argumentative." But Beryl got the impression that she shouldn't ask questions. "He just wasn't spoken of," she said. "When things weren't positive, they just weren't discussed."

What was the nature of his illness? None of his living relatives knows. Whatever he suffered from, it was only one part of who he was. But the irony is that because of the silence surrounding him, his descendants know little else about him.

In her book *Booze at Breakfast*, Catherine Scott goes head-to-head with that legacy of silence. The youngest child of J. Ainsworth Scott— John Scott's older son—Catherine grew up watching her father struggle with alcoholism and saw the affect it had on every member of the family. As an adult she became an addictions counselor. Her 2013 novel, which she calls "fictionalized autobiography," tells the story of a family's efforts to break the cycle.

In the book, Ainsworth becomes Carlos Mendoza, a talented Albany real estate man with three children: Cassandra, Pete, and Anika, the youngest, through whose eyes much of the story unfolds. In Carlos's drinking and outbursts, Catherine sees a reflection of his upbringing. Carlos watches himself turning into his own father, remembers the fear and anger he felt "when his father drank and got mean," but is unable to find any other path.

Carlos's father, the man who in real life was John A. Scott, is imagined not merely as an abusive parent but also as a man shaped by his times. Anika asks her mother, Sally:

> "Mom, what was Grandpa Mendoza like?"
>
> Sally cautioned herself to choose tender words and not vent her troubles on this undeserving child as her mother had done.
>
> "He was a hard worker, honey, a quiet man. He expressed his love for his family by providing. Those were hard times. It was a lot just to keep a roof over their heads."
>
> "Did he drink too, like Dad?"
>
> Anika always went straight for the truth, figuring she was best at deciding for herself what was what.
>
> "Not so much as your dad, honey, just on holidays. He kept to himself, always working. But in all fairness, that was the way most men were back then. Not much in the way of family life. Women ran the families. My dad was the same way when he was there, silent behind his newspaper. 'Dad who?' we kids called him. I'm sorry to tell you your family was this way, hon, but I know you always want to know the truth."

"I learned to love us all more by writing the book," Catherine wrote me. "Growing up in a family that 'kept its secrets' . . . I think I became a therapist because I felt and saw the pain that terrible silence engendered. . . . I think it's the stuff that's swept under the rug that does the most damage."

Another reason Catherine wrote *Booze at Breakfast* was to honor the life of her brother. John committed suicide in 1983. The novel does not include his death; Catherine ends the story in an earlier era, with the family at a Thanksgiving dinner, sisters, brother, mother, and extended family together, hopeful and strong, as no doubt Catherine wished they could always have stayed.

Booze at Breakfast is not an easy book to read. But the sorrowful understanding Catherine shows for both Carlos and his father infuses the story with compassion.

John's other sister, Beryl Scott Glover, also turned to writing as a means of healing. Three weeks after John's suicide, Beryl's daughter took her own life. With *The Empty Chair*, published in 2000, Beryl tries to light a path through grief that others might follow. Though her pain is tangible, she tells the story with a clarity that feels like faith.

That, to me, is the real legacy of the Scott family: their strength to endure.

Every life has at least a few stories to share. Most pass with their narrators. Some get written down. Once in a while, one gets clipped out, filed in a basement box, and found by the person who wouldn't have dared hope for that very thing.

And that brings me to Mary Ainsworth Scott.

John Scott may have been the first owner of my house, but he wasn't here alone. Other than the census, few public records paid heed to women in the nineteenth and early twentieth centuries. But I was determined to learn what I could about Mary, his wife, despite the indifference of her times. The census gives us blessed little: Mary Ainsworth was born in 1871. Her father was a railroad man. She married and had two children. That's about it. Fortunately, she left at least two paths for me to follow: a strong relationship with her oldest granddaughter and a lifetime of service to her church.

"My grandmother was a remarkable role model," said Beryl Scott Glover. "I think about her a lot. She was a superb human being."

As a child, Beryl saw a lot of her grandmother, because her mother would take her on regular visits. "I was expected to go, and then in due time I enjoyed going," she said.

> We called her Nanny. She was a very pleasant person to be around. She made it clear that she was interested in what you were doing. She didn't talk about herself much. She was smart and kind and a remarkably good listener—a remarkably

good listener. Most notably, we never heard her say anything unkind about anybody. If there was anything negative she kept it to herself. She was always interested in you, and what you were doing. . . . That's why she had so many friends. It was a remarkable skill.

Nanny talked so little about herself that Beryl couldn't recall any stories she ever told about her own childhood—except that as a young lady she declared that she was not ever going to ride in a "horseless carriage" because it was "too dangerous."

Mary Scott was sharp and witty, and she loved to laugh. "She loved a good joke—a good joke, not a dirty joke," Beryl said. "She was a devout Christian. No cards on Sunday and no alcohol whatsoever."

Catherine, Beryl's younger sister, does not remember their grandmother being "warm or fuzzy or loving," but she does remember her intelligence and her sense of humor—along with her remarkably long earlobes. Both granddaughters stressed Mary's involvement with the Calvary Methodist Episcopal Church and how much it meant to her, so that's where I headed in the hopes of learning more.

The Calvary Church had ceased to exist years ago. But records are usually *somewhere*. The pastor of Emmaus, Calvary's successor, put me on their trail, which led to the basement of the local Methodist conference. A nice lady rifled through a storage room and brought forth two boxes of baptismal books, programs, photographs, Sunday school essays, and newspaper clippings for me to explore.

A search mission like this is hit and miss. This time was a hit: Mary Scott's name was everywhere. She'd spent her life in that church, from its Ash Grove days through its move to the Pine Hills. She served on countless committees, hosted meetings and luncheons, gave lectures on the history of the congregation, and eventually was honored as the oldest member. Then, in a file, in a box, in another box, there in the basement, I found treasure: an interview.

The feature article, from 1974, ran in a church paper and marked the occasion of Mrs. Scott's birthday—her *103rd* birthday.

"I'm nothing special," she said. "I'm just old."

The wide-ranging memories Mary Scott shared in the yellowed clipping touch on the personal, the cultural, the political. It wasn't much—a pencil sketch, not a portrait—but compared to knowing nothing about her at all, it was something extraordinary.

"I was never a believer in women's suffrage," she said. "But some of my friends said that if I could vote I should, so after that I did. But I didn't think women should come forward so. I thought they should leave it to the men."

Mrs. Scott said she never wore slacks in her life. Hoop skirts and bustles, yes. She talked proudly of once meeting President Coolidge.

She said longevity ran in her family, and she also credited her age to the fact that she neither smoked nor drank: "I heard as a girl that poor Grant died of cancer and they said it was from smoking so much, so I never smoked."

When John Scott was courting her, he and she would read the *Ladies Home Journal* together. She told a funny story of his losing a horse that eventually turned up in someone's basement.

The first mistress of my house, reflecting on her life in her own words—what are the chances? Sitting there in the church conference offices, I was grinning from ear to ear.

The archivist photocopied the newspaper clipping and then placed the copy in the folder in the box in the box. "Acid-free paper," she noted. "We always replace newsprint when we come across it." She handed me the original. "You can have this if you want it."

I sent it to Mary's granddaughters.

At the family's camp in Averill Park, Beryl Scott Glover showed me a photograph of her Nanny, taken perhaps when she was in her nineties: a petite woman, frail but smiling behind large glasses. I noted that her earlobes were indeed remarkable. What struck me most, though, was how familiar the photograph was. The picture reminded me of those I'd seen of my own great-grandmothers and the framed mementos in other friends' homes. I'd like to think that somewhere in our past, we all have a grandmother to cherish.

Mary Ainsworth Scott died the day after Christmas in 1974, age 103½. She was sharp-witted and keen to the end.

My house is the one in the middle. This photo was taken by the Elwoods, the house's second owners, so that would date it between 1915 and 1921. Courtesy of Olivia Raffe.

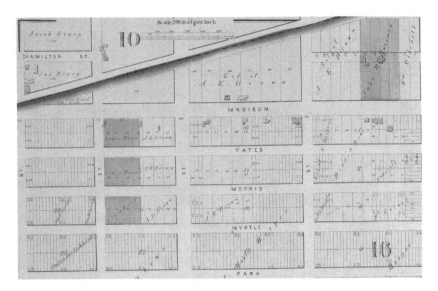

Not yet the Pine Hills, but not empty either: This detail from Plate O of the *City Atlas of Albany, New York* (Philadelphia: G.M. Hopkins, 1876) shows the upper Madison area as a mix of paper streets and existing routes. The north-south running streets here are South Allen at the image's left edge, then West Lawrence, Main, and Erie. The large "10" and "16" are ward numbers.

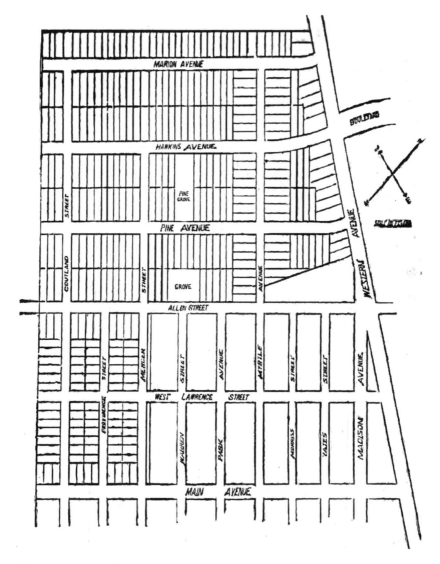

This map ran in the Albany Sunday Express on January 29, 1888, alongside one of the first newspaper accounts on the Albany Land Improvement and Building Company. It shows the developers' early plans for the Pine Hills neighborhood—so early, in fact, that the name "Pine Hills" isn't mentioned, and the subdivision didn't yet cross Western Avenue.

In Ancient Times Albany Was a Walled City!

THE GATES WERE CLOSED EVERY NIGHT.

Perhaps the limited extent of the territory within the stockade accounts for the very compact way in which the city was built up. The modern city has a tendency to crowd together a good deal. We cover less territory to-day than any city of our population in the country.

Come out in the fresh air! There are no Indians or wild beasts at PINE HILLS! You needn't shut yourself up in a flat or a stuffy block house. We have plenty of room for you at the WEST END. And only a couple of miles from the centre of the city. We have mapped out the lots at

PINE HILLS

On a large and generous scale, 200 feet deep. The lots are selling so cheap that you ought to buy at least two and own a little villa plot, 50x200 feet, a quarter of an acre! Come to the sale next Saturday afternoon and select two fine lots on South Allen Street.

The lots are very choice, and the fourteen lots to be sold should certainly be taken in pairs, making seven superb villa residence sites. Go up early and make a selection.

THE SALE WILL BE

HELD AT 3 O'CLOCK SATURDAY AFTERNOON,

At the Corner of Allen Street South and Mercer Street.

EXCURSION TICKETS, MAPS and further information may be obtained of Messrs. J. H. SIMMONS & SON, Auctioneers and Real Estate Brokers, 92 State Street, or of PRATT & LOGAN, 42 Tweddle Building.

One of the Albany Land Improvement and Building Company's advertisements for Pine Hills lots. This one ran in the *Albany Evening Journal* on July 28, 1891.

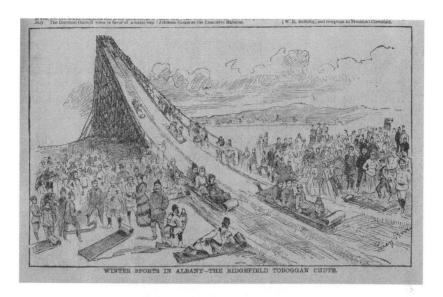

WINTER SPORTS IN ALBANY—THE RIDGEFIELD TOBOGGAN CHUTE.

Oh what fun it was to ride! Tobogganing at the Ridgefield Athletics Grounds. Illustration from the "Official Programme" as printed in the *Souvenir of the Albany Bi-Centennial Celebration, July 1886* (Thurlow Weed Barnes, ed. Albany: The Journal Co., 1886).

Lorenz Willig, builder of my house and many others. Undated family photograph. Courtesy of William Willig.

Postcard image of the Point, alias the Junction, alias the place where Madison Avenue merges into Western. My copy of this card has a 1908 postmark.

John A. Scott was the first owner of my house. Undated portrait. Courtesy of Beryl Scott Glover.

Robert Hamilton Scott and companions on West Lawrence Street, ca. 1913. Young Mr. Scott was one of the first two children to live in my house. He grew up to become a policymaker with the Michigan Department of Corrections and a professor of criminal justice at Michigan State University. His focus was on developing programs to reduce recidivism among youthful offenders; a prison in Michigan was named after him. Courtesy of Susan Scott Galbraith.

Mary A. Scott, first owner of my house, in her grandmotherly days, ca. 1964. She sits between her sons: Robert, the younger of the two, is on the left. On the right is J. Ainsworth Scott, who followed his father into the real estate business, building a long career as an agent and appraiser in the Albany area. Courtesy of Beryl Scott Glover.

School 16 on North Allen Street, which opened in 1906. This photo is from the *Annual Report of the Board of Education and of the Superintendent of Schools of the City of Albany, N.Y. for the Year Ending July 31st, 1906* (Albany: Argus, 1907).

Everett S. Elwood holds Barbara, his youngest, ca. 1917. Courtesy of Olivia Raffe.

7

House, Home

Gary and I rang the old brass doorbell, just because we could, and through the door we could hear it echo in the empty rooms. We put the key in the lock for the first time and went in.

The house looked bigger now that it was cleared of strangers' possessions.

Maybe too big.

Maybe we'd better sit right here, near the door.

The baby scooted around the bare floors through the angles of unfiltered afternoon light. We sat there with our backs against the foyer wall, cradling a little footed clock the real estate agent had given us as a housewarming present. We felt slightly ridiculous. We sat there thinking, Now what?

Now what, indeed.

Buying our house had been a whirlwind romance. It was the only house we looked at. We were the only people to tour it. The first day it was on the market in the summer of 2003, we viewed it, bid on it, and found ourselves betrothed.

It wasn't as impulsive as it sounds: Between the two of us, Gary and I had lived in nearly every neighborhood in Albany. We knew what was out there, and we knew what we wanted: an early twentieth-century house in the Pine Hills. We had been living nearby for two years, renting a flat on North Pine Avenue, and had fallen in love with the neighborhood. It was urban without being too dense, stable without being too clannish. We loved walking along the tree-shaded streets, noticing the details that made each house different from its neighbors. A recent Madison Avenue streetscape renovation, and neighbors' enthusiasm over it, had impressed us: people were here because they loved being here, and they wanted to work to make the neighborhood better. Within just a few blocks were a library, a post office, a grocery store, a coffee house, a movie theater, a bowling alley, several restaurants and pubs, a park, a children's theater, a pharmacy, two banks, a dry cleaner's, a barber shop, and a police station. If you tried to make up a neighborhood like that, people would say you were exaggerating.

At the same time, we wanted out of our flat. We were tired of watching the beautiful old place crumble while the landlord shrugged. We were tired of having upstairs neighbors. We'd had a baby the previous winter. All the signs told us that now was the time to buy.

Our real estate agent sent us just an address by email with the note: "Let me know." West Lawrence Street, huh? Oh yeah, that's the one near the Price Chopper. We walked over and checked out the house from the sidewalk. I seem to recall a bit of happy bouncing on my part. Double back porches! Diamond-pane windows! We made an appointment to tour it the next morning, but in truth we were sold before we'd gotten past the foyer.

While the owner was considering our bid, he called our agent. "Who are these people?" he asked her.

"You're not allowed to know anything about the buyers," she reminded him. "It's against the law."

"Yes," he said, "but I just want to know: Will they *love* this house?"

"They love the house," she told him. "They *love* it."

The day he accepted our offer, Carl Patka and his twelve-year-old son came over to our Pine Avenue flat. It was clear Carl had mixed feelings about leaving West Lawrence Street. He'd put a lot of time and sweat into renovating this house. When you walk away from that, you leave part of yourself behind.

He invited us to his—our—house and walked us through the place, describing the ceilings he'd fixed, the rooms he'd redone over the nine years they'd lived here. The upstairs bathroom was his baby, gutted and rebuilt as a 1920s showpiece. He pointed out the coat closet's original mirror glass and the pipe holes in the dining room floor from its brief tenure in the '70s as a separate apartment.

When we took the house in September 2003, Carl gave us an accordion file stuffed with all his house repair records, all the appliance brochures, and a list of recommended handymen, plus a seasonal, room-by-room guide to upkeep. It was four pages long, single-spaced. In tone it reminded me of the instructions we give the pet-sitter when we go out of town—"Here, love this for me while I'm gone." Carl ended with: "We have been very happy in this house. It has good karma, and good energy flow. We hope you will be just as happy in our house, for many years. If you have any questions, please call us anytime."

The first thing we did when we got the keys? We went exploring, of course.

We hadn't been inside the place in more than a month, and anyway, now that it was ours we saw it with new eyes. Look at the old button light switches! Look at this odd little window, maybe fourteen inches wide, between the kitchen and dining room! (*Dining room? We didn't even own a real table.*) On the plate rail Carl had left a scrap of wallpaper he'd found while renovating: paisley with yellow flowers. This niche with the big window: space for my desk, or a reading nook with a comfy chair?

The kitchen stairs were long gone, coming out in favor of additional counter/cupboard space. On the landing, where they would have joined the front stairs, were now built-in shelves (*stereo! games!*). In the upstairs hall I was disoriented for a moment, unsure which door would lead where.

The best one of all opened to a surprise. The closet to the left of the stairs was built like a staircase—well, like half a staircase. It took seven steps to a landing and then stopped. The design took full advantage of the space over the first-floor stairs. It was a stairway to nowhere! It was quirky and confusing, and I loved it.

Down in the basement, in the far corner, stood a cast-iron oven range thick with cobwebs and rust. It had been the house's original, Carl told us. Of course, we had no way to know for sure; it could have been some yard sale find that a previous resident had dragged down the cellar stairs, but I doubt it. Made by the Estate Company of Hamilton, Ohio, it's the right age[1] for this house. What's more, the range is the right size and height to fit the space in our kitchen where the range originally sat, next to the brick chimney. Like other original fixtures in the house, it's an appliance that straddles two eras: unenameled cast-iron but fitted for gas. It needed to be *blacked*, for heaven's sake. Cleaning the old piece brought a rolling series of discoveries: the knobs are wood; the fittings, brass; the decorative sunburst on the front, chrome. Under all the dust, it was very pretty.

Elsewhere in the basement, the coal furnace still lurked, along with a more recent oil tank and the modern gas unit. We could host an exhibit on the history of Northeast home heating. Hanging in a side room were heavy, mysterious tools: brushes and cranks for the coal beast, as best we could tell.

Up in the attic the name "Georgie" was scrawled between the rafters in capital letters, in something like white crayon. Another note showed where the *Life* magazine stash used to be kept.

And then there was this:

Emily lived here
for 10 years
and loved every minute of it

Emily was Carl's fourteen-year-old daughter. She wrote that inscription, very small, on the wall of her bedroom closet. You have to be standing in the closet to see it. I smiled. It was the sort of thing I would have done at fourteen.

Emily's little brother also wrote a goodbye message to the house, but it warmed my heart somewhat less. He wrote it in ball-point pen in the middle of his bedroom floor.

---

1. Actually, according to what I've learned, this model's the right age to have been installed in the Scotts' previous house, the one on Manning Boulevard. I wonder if Mary Scott used it there and then had it brought here. Eventually, when our kids were old enough to leave it alone, we brought the range upstairs to our living room, where it took a place of honor as kind of a rusty side table. It probably looks a little silly.

There was more to discover. We lived in this house for seven years before I found what, in my eyes, was the most incredible treasure of all. But we'll get to that later.

During our renting days, a friend of ours had told a story about troublesome neighbors—property maintenance, noise—that ended with: "But they're renters. They just don't feel the same." Being a renter, I bristled a bit: You're going to tell me I don't care about how I live just because I'm not paying a mortgage? I'd grown up in rented houses. *We* cared. But you know what? At least in my case, my friend was right.

Owning made me realize there's more to being a neighbor than just keeping the grass trimmed and the stereo turned down. It didn't happen all at once, but after we bought our house my relationship with my community changed.

Whenever a problem would arise with my house or with a neighbor, renting had allowed me to think, I can ignore this. I can outlast it. If it doesn't go away, then *I'll* just go away. Now that I'm not going away, and neither, probably, is the problem, I need to take steps to solve it—and to remind myself, again, that movement isn't progress. Owning reminds me to be a grown-up.

Despite all the houses I'd lived in as a child and young adult, I could count on one hand the neighbors whose names I'd known. What can I say? We were a family of introverts. But there was something else at work, too: We never thought of ourselves as part of a neighborhood. We were a unit unto ourselves. That fueled in us an independence, a fierce, protective closeness—and yet now, I can see that for all the strength it brought us, other possibilities were lost.

Of course, owning a house wasn't the only thing that prompted this change in me. Living with Gary, who is as much of a people person as I am a loner, was bound to draw me out of doors. He loves the idea of community, and it's contagious. And I had also become a parent to one, then two, little girls. Whatever its source, on West Lawrence Street I had a revelation: Here is a community worth preserving. And here, too, are others who feel the same.

When we moved in, two of the eight homes on our block were owned by college professors, and three, counting ours, housed journalists. The balance shifted a few years later when a journalist, headed to suburbia, sold her home to professors—a pair of them. The remaining three houses are divided into rental units, occupied by young families and graduate students, usually. Compared to many other streets, I suppose you'd call our block diverse. We are American-born and immigrants. We are Christian, Muslim, Jewish, atheist. We range in age from toddler to grandparent.

It's a good mix, our block. We watch each other's children, feed pets when someone's out of town. We have broken bread on Thanksgivings, Easters, and Christmas Eves. Not to say we're *all* that close; there are neighbors whose names I do not know. But it's a friendly-nod-and-a-wave sort of block, a block where you go out after a snowfall and find your walk has already been shoveled. Geography binds us together, however loosely: the place, and our respect for it.

For years, the police union's bagpipe troupe held Thursday summer evening practices over in the parking lot of the Elks Club hall, a block away. We would open our windows to the stirring notes of one or the other of the only two pieces ever written for bagpipes (if more than two bagpipe arrangements exist, apparently no one's ever told the PBA). I never used to care for bagpipes, but I liked those Thursdays. It sounded like *here*.

The neighborhood isn't perfect. We've had our jack-o-lanterns smashed and a couple of bicycles stolen. Trying to make it through both stoplights on their rush to the Price Chopper, cars hit the gas and run the yellows on their way past our house. Napkins and wrappers snag on our front slope—being a block from Dunkin' Donuts, Gary has pointed out, puts us at exactly the spot people will be walking past when they finish the last bite of their Boston creme. There are no driveways on this stretch of West Lawrence Street, and if you don't follow the parking signs you can expect a ticket to appear on your windshield pretty fast. Our block's absentee landlords do a spotty job of shoring up a sagging fence or mowing down the weeds more than once a season. Other neighbors and I have gone to the city to push back when we felt we needed to. On a few occasions we've called the police to report a loud party next door, or a screaming match.

Walking home from the store one evening I saw a young guy pacing the sidewalk in front of my neighbors' house and another kid walking up their front stairs. For a moment I hesitated, thinking, You never know, maybe Casey and Rachael have teenage friends in backwards ball caps? Nah, it didn't look right to me. A call to 911 brought the cops and scared off the kids, who returned the next afternoon and got into the house through the back, where the fenced-in yard protected them from the prying eyes of neighbors like me. What'd they make off with? A Mason jar full of pocket change.

I like it here because it isn't the kind of block where people are immediately sure of who does and doesn't belong. I don't want to live where I know everybody, where everybody knows me, and where we think we know who should be here and who shouldn't—even if that means, once in a while, the stranger on the sidewalk might be casing the place. That leaves us a little more open, I guess, a little more out of control. But it's better than living an insulated life.

When I work in my yard, I wonder: Did Ludwig Marx and his sons battle the creeping buttercup?

Probably not. The waxy little blossoms that stage an annual takeover attempt on my garden more likely escaped from a flower bed sometime in the past hundred years. But is there *anything* here anymore that the Marxes would recognize? The blue clouds of forget-me-nots that lighten the grass every spring? The darting and whistling of the chickadees? The heavy buzz of the carpenter bees?

Maybe yes: Maybe the pine trees on Oak Ridge.

It's a name that means nothing today, but to hear Henry Slack tell it, Oak Ridge was a Pine Hills landmark, the summit of the neighborhood. Slack was a local man who led a nature study class in the early years of the twentieth century, publishing some of his observations in a little book called *Pine Hills Bird Notes*. It's a portrait of a fragile world, a rural district on the path to becoming a city.

Oak Ridge was just west of the intersection of Myrtle and Pine Avenues. It had been so named, Slack wrote, because the view from its rise reminded visitors of the view from the top of the Gettysburg battlefield's Oak Ridge. The hill was crowned by a group of trees he calls the Seven Pines. "All of Pine Hills, a large part of the city, and much of the surrounding country can be seen from these Seven Pines," he wrote in 1908: "The Seven Pines are a beacon pointing back many decades before the intrusion of streets to days when our hill was marshaled by their tribe. A lone group, storm beaten and weather worn, yet like chieftains that were strong to endure the wild wrenching of other years."

Slack's writing has a nineteenth-century blend of formality and dramatics, but he was a keen observer, keeping notes on what lived here and when. He catalogues the neighborhood birds: sixty-one species in 1910. One chapter details the daily trials of robins building a nest in a cherry tree on South Allen Street. Some of Slack's wild neighbors are here still today: woodpeckers, robins, wrens, chickadees. Others in his list of Pine Hills regulars are birds I can't recognize, so I can't say if they're still around: nuthatches, phoebes, catbirds, bobolinks? Some I'm sure are gone: red-winged blackbirds, meadowlarks, bluebirds, sandpipers, little green herons, whippoorwills. These are birds of the meadows, wetlands, forests. Not here, not anymore.

Slack's world is like an old photograph, almost identifiable, almost unfamiliar. Most of his Pine Hills landmarks are foreign to me: Willow Run, Oak Ridge, Holler's orchard, Holmes's woods, the Tunnel Path. Others I recognize: Manning Boulevard, the Aurania Club, the Madison-Western Junction. He mourns the old trees "felled by progressive men" and laments the way the "ravaging hand of civilization" has transformed the neighborhood. He implores homeowners to keep their cats inside at night to lessen the number of bird deaths.

I've walked through the area Slack calls Oak Ridge many times— it's just a few blocks from my house—without realizing I was on a hill at all. Not that it's been graded that drastically; it's just me, as always, painfully unaware of my surroundings. So I went there one crisp May morning to look at it with new eyes. And what do you know? From a spot beyond Pine and Myrtle the ground *does* slope downward in every direction. These days, the shoulders of the hill are too thick with houses to offer much of a view. But in the backyards on the crest of the ridge stand six thick, towering pine trees. Maybe some of them are among the original Seven Pines, maybe none of them. But they're right where Henry Slack said they would be.

Slack had argued for Oak Ridge to be made into a park, to "leave for the generations to follow a chance for grateful remembrance of their forbears." He advocated the protection of habitat and urged parents to instill in their children an appreciation of nature. He spoke eloquently for living in balance with the natural world, not only for the peace it brings to the soul, but also for the long-term benefits to farmers and businesses that a healthy ecosystem could provide.

At the same time his eyes were open to the rush of change around him. "We fold our hands in sleep," he wrote in 1914, "and are awake only to the deceptive notes of an overstrained social life." Slack was witness to the Pine Hills' last wild moments, and he knew it. His book was a love letter to a disappearing world.

In 1912, the year my house was built, Slack wrote that for birds,

> the rolling fields and ravines east of upper South Allen, past Seven Pines to Willow Run and beyond . . . has been a favorite district; but the builders have sighted an opportunity and the birds perforce must move out. Seven Pines, Willow Run and the fields above lie in the direct line of march, and soon we that know them now shall know them no more forever.

Today, the Pine Hills makes a different music. It's lovely. But just the same, it's right to note that some voices are forever gone.

I was on South Pine Avenue one spring day when a white-faced bird hopped into view and studied me from the knot of a sidewalk tree. I looked him up in my phone; he was a nuthatch.

Olive White Elwood and her children, Margaret, Everett Jr., and Barbara, sit on the window bench in our—their—West Lawrence Street home. Barbara was born in May 1917, so I expect this photo was taken sometime late that year or early the next. Courtesy of Olivia Raffe.

8

The Newcomers

I know the place immediately: the diamond window panes, the two radiator pipes running up the corner wall. But the people? I have never seen them before.

The woman and her three children sit on the bench under our front window. The mother, tall and slender, has a narrow face, good eyebrows, full lips. A double collar of white lace lies against her dark dress. The children around her are all in white. The oldest, a girl of perhaps four, has bobbed hair topped by a bow half as large as her head. Behind her stands her brother in a sailor suit. He's part blur, a natural state for two-year-olds, which is what I'd guess him to be. One of his hands clutches the folds of the sheer curtain; the other is curled around the back of his mother's neck. On her lap, a baby with shining eyes looks poised to cascade into giggles. They all have the same alert eyes, the same purse to their lips: just one click of the shutter away from a smile.

This is how I met Olive Elwood and her children. The Elwoods were the second family to call our house their home.

The January day I received this photo, my five-year-old was sprawled out on that wooden bench, reading a comic book as the afternoon light spilled over her through the same window in the same way. The boards are thicker now, and rougher, from repeated layers of varnish. The window rattles a bit in its frame and always lets in a draft, but it's a favorite spot in our house: there's a radiator under that bench. Most winter mornings will find a child there, snuggled up with the couch blanket and a library book, waiting for breakfast.

To see the Elwoods sitting on our window bench, watching us with their lively eyes, seemed affirmative, somehow: quiet and ordinary and beautiful. They looked at home here, because they were.

Everett and Olive Elwood lived in my house for about six years, from 1915 to 1921, while Everett was secretary of the New York state Hospital Commission. He was the closest my house has come to an "important" resident, I guess: a policy maker who helped change New York's mental health care system. But I'm equally drawn to how familiar their story is, even though they lived here a century ago. Thirty-somethings who relocated to Albany for a state government job, they embraced the city—finding a church, neighborhood involvement, a place for their young children—until the job market moved them on again. The city has always had its lifers, its deep-rooted families, but it has also always had an ebb and flow of people who came from elsewhere to work in government, industry, academics—people like the Elwoods, people like my husband and me. It doesn't feel right to call them—us— "outsiders." We've always been part of Albany's story.

It was one of life's little injustices: Olive White Elwood never liked olives. She didn't much care for being called *Olive*, either. There wasn't anything she could do about her name, but she wasn't about to let a—vegetable? snack food? condiment? what *are* olives, anyway?—get in her way. "She was teased so much about it that she got a bottle of them and taught herself to 'like' them," her granddaughter told me.

The granddaughter's name is Olivia G. Raffe, child of the sparkling-eyed baby on Olive's lap. She's the lady who sent me the circa 1917 photograph, along with others that showed the family's brief time in Albany, long before she was born.

Olivia was named after her grandmother, with the older lady suggesting the variation as a nicer name than her own—"and I have thanked her ever since." As a child Olivia lived with her grandparents in Philadelphia for a while, and recalls Olive Elwood as an intelligent lady who pursued many interests—botany, reading, needlework—"when she wasn't busy running the house." She taught her namesake how to embroider and do needlepoint, and she drew her own patterns "because she said the flowers didn't look real in the commercial ones."

Mrs. Elwood was born Olive White in the Mohawk Valley hamlet of Sprout Brook, New York, in 1884. The oldest of three children, she taught school before marrying Everett Elwood in 1908. Her wedding announcement called her "an accomplished young lady, well known and popular."

Everett was from Starkville, a Herkimer County hamlet about eight miles away from Sprout Brook, where the road into town still bears the Elwood name. A few years older than Olive, Everett was the son of a nationally renowned expert on the diseases of bees, which is exactly the reason I don't write fiction: Why bother, when real people are so surprising? Everett taught school for a while, too, before heading to Syracuse University, and afterward he took a job as a school principal in Penn Yan. It was in 1910 that his career really took off: that's when Everett and Olive moved to Yonkers, where he had been hired by a nonprofit agency, the State Charities Aid Association (SCAA).

The SCAA kept tabs on conditions in state institutions and poor-houses and lobbied the state to provide better care. Its Committee on Mental Hygiene was launching a statewide educational campaign "for the prevention of insanity"—back to that in a minute—and Elwood was to be the committee's assistant secretary.

The twin upheavals of the nineteenth century, immigration and industrialization, brought a shift in the relationship between the government and its people. Few laws protected health or regulated work hours or conditions. Slums in New York City and elsewhere were nests of desperate poverty, high infant mortality, overcrowding, and illness. Traditional lifelines like family or village—such as they were—frayed thin. Advocates for the poor, many of them women inspired by religious teachings, used their social standing to call attention to the questions: What role should better-off citizens play in helping the destitute? What role should the *government* play? Reformers concluded that if poverty stemmed not from personal failings—laziness, entitlement, inferiority—but from social conditions, then society had a responsibility to try to help.

The push for greater government protections for the poor had many fronts. One of them was mental health treatment. Until the 1840s, most sufferers in New York state had two options: be kept at home or endure unimaginable conditions in county poorhouses. Social reformer Dorothea Dix visited Albany's almshouse in 1842 and demanded to see what the man in charge called "the crazy cellar." What she found in the dungeons was a horror:

> In the cell first opened was a madman; the fierce command of his keeper brought him to the door—a hideous object; matted locks, unshorn beard, a wild wan countenance, yet more disfigured by vilest uncleanness, in a state of entire nudity, save the irritating incrustations derived from that dungeon reeking with loathsome filth; here, without light, without pure air, without warmth, without cleansing, without *anything* to secure decency or comfort, here was a human being. . . .
>
> A woman, of what age one could not conjecture, so disfigured was she by neglect and suffering, occupied a dungeon on the right. The keeper harshly summoned her "to come out," but she only moved feebly amidst the filthy straw which was the only furnishing of the place; her moans and low cries indicated both mental anguish and physical pain.

In 1843 New York opened the first State Lunatic Asylum in Utica, in the hopes of moving people considered "curable" out of the poorhouses and leaving only the "incurable" cases in county care. To say it didn't work is an understatement. The asylum was flooded with more patients than it could accommodate; when others were built, they filled up, too. There was no cure available there, only misery, deprivation, and allegations of abuse. In 1887 newspaper reporter Nellie Bly feigned madness to get admitted to New York City's asylum on Blackwell's Island. The conditions she found there caused a public outcry:

> Take a perfectly sane and healthy woman, shut her up and make her sit from 6 a.m. to 8 p.m. on straight-back benches, do not allow her to talk or move during these hours, give her no reading and let her know nothing of the world or its

doings, give her bad food and harsh treatment, and see how long it will take to make her insane. Two months would make her a mental and physical wreck.

In 1890, New York took on full responsibility for caring for its impoverished mentally ill. It was the first state in the nation to do so. The state's mandate soon expanded to include any sufferers, regardless of ability to pay, but those who were able were expected to reimburse some of the costs. The State Charities Aid Association was a force behind the 1890 State Care Act, also pushing the government to make twice-yearly inspections at both state and private institutions and to require competitive exams for the institutions' medical officers instead of filling those positions by patronage. The powerful reform group approached the asylum problem from another angle, too: Was it possible to keep people *out* of institutions, by preventing them from going insane in the first place?

This was where Everett Elwood came in.

Teamed with noted social worker Homer Folks, Elwood created a media campaign aimed at health care providers, officials, and members of the public. Its goal was to curb mental illness before it required institutionalization or to help people avoid its onset altogether. A keystone of the project was a pamphlet, printed in several languages and distributed—to the tune of five hundred thousand copies—across New York state. Its title: "Why Should Anyone Go Insane?"

From a modern standpoint, many of Elwood and Folks's beliefs about mental illness may seem naïve at best, misguided at worst. But the work of the SCAA is an interesting snapshot of a period when reformers saw the interconnectivity of personal and social problems and tried to use public policy to solve them.

Insanity, their pamphlet explained, can be caused by identifiable factors: "immoral living" (translation: syphilis); the use of alcohol or other drugs; the ravages of physical disease; and poor "mental habits."

How about heredity? No, it's "undoubtedly wrong" that insanity can be directly inherited, wrote Elwood and Folks—though a *tendency* to insanity might be. "Disposition is not something fixed, like the color of our eyes. . . . As a weak constitution may be built up by healthful habits, so may mental instability be made stable by good mental and physical habits."

Mental health depends less on a person's circumstances than on how they respond to life's troubles. "The average person little realizes the danger of brooding over slights, injuries, disappointments, or misfortunes, or of lack of frankness, or of an unnatural attitude towards his fellowmen, shown by unusual sensitiveness or marked suspicion," they wrote.

> Yet all these unwholesome and painful trains of thought may, if persisted in and unrelieved by healthy interests and activity, tend toward insanity. Wholesome work relieved by periods of rest and simple pleasures, and an interest in the affairs of others, are important preventives of unwholesome ways of thinking. We should train ourselves not to brood, but to honestly face personal difficulties.

So buck up! And don't drink.

Alcohol received attention not only in the pamphlet, but also in a great many of Elwood's writings and lectures. It was his belief that "at least 20 percent of all insanity" had its roots, directly or indirectly, in alcohol use. Directly, because "the drink evil" degenerates both brain and body—and for people with a tendency toward mental defect already, alcohol makes it worse. Indirectly, because one person's use of alcohol can also lead to mental breakdowns in other members of the family. What's more, alcohol is expensive for the government, which gets stuck with the cost of institutionalizing the inebriate.

So what should be done? Simple: Support Prohibition. As Elwood wrote in 1914:

> When we consider the mental defect, the poverty, the crime, the physical suffering and disease caused by alcohol, we should hesitate to boast of our belief in the brotherhood of man, of our high state of civilization and our great philanthropies if at the same time we cling to the pleasures, the privilege, and the so-called personal right of indulgence in the use of alcohol.

Over the next few years, Elwood echoed many of the pamphlet's views in his other writings and speeches. He was acutely aware that mental illness came at high price for the state—not only the costs of institutionalization, but also the effect on the economy when workers are incapacitated and the strain that put on other state programs: one man unable to work might lead a whole family to seek assistance. Elwood began to speak of a link between poverty—its "privation, mental anguish, and physical diseases"—and mental illness. It's clear that he felt the influence of his boss, the pamphlet's coauthor, Homer Folks.

Folks is worth a book of his own. A pioneer in the field of social work, he spent more than fifty years at the State Charities Aid Association pushing issues of infant mortality, child labor, juvenile delinquency, and health care onto the state and national stage. Folks worked behind the scenes to enact several landmark laws, including New York's 1913 Public Health Law, a wide-reaching reform that created the first state public health council with the power to set sanitation standards statewide. He served as an advisor to Franklin Delano Roosevelt during his governorship and presidency and was instrumental in the 1929 overhaul of New York's "poor laws," replacing them with the landmark Public Welfare Law. The Public Welfare Law marked a philosophical shift: rather than treating poverty as a crime, with the threat of the poorhouse as punishment or deterrent, New York acknowledged that helping its most desperate citizens get the skills and resources they needed to support themselves was an act of *public welfare*—ultimately, better for society as a whole.

The government safety net continued to expand, of course, during FDR's presidency and beyond, but if you're looking for its origins, Homer Folks is one of the people to credit—or blame, depending on your point of view.

Both Folks and Elwood believed that a government's job was to assist its people, with the goal of making them productive citizens if at all possible. Folks believed small, community-based approaches were best: foster homes over orphanages, family residences over the poorhouse, outpatient care instead of institutionalization. Elwood did too.

"The medical profession and all those engaged in the care of the sick have become slowly but firmly convinced that the individual patient is not entirely an 'individual case' but that very often his family 'needs doctoring' as much as he," Elwood wrote in 1913. "It is now a well known fact that sending a patient back to the environment which was largely responsible for his broken health very often means sending him back to a relapse rather than to a recovery." A social worker or nurse who lived in the community could develop relationships with patients, see the troubles in their everyday lives, and suggest changes—leading, Elwood argued, not only to better mental health treatment but maybe even to prevention. Homer Folks had helped form "volunteer committees" at state mental hospitals to help discharged patients with aftercare, a practice that the state took over in 1911. A good idea, Elwood said, but one that was developing far too slowly. By 1913 only four hospitals had a social worker on staff to provide aftercare. He wanted every hospital to have them, and to put as many of its patients as possible "on parole"—that is, sent home.

For several years Elwood argued that it would be better for patients—and cheaper for the state—to move to a system of community-based care, one that focused on outpatient treatment and prevention. Soon he'd get a chance to put his ideas into practice.

After four years with the Committee on Mental Hygiene, Elwood was tapped by incoming governor Charles Whitman to be secretary of the state Hospital Commission, the part of the Department of Health that oversaw asylums. (From 1895 to 1912 the Hospital Commission had been called the "New York State Commission in Lunacy," which must be the most sought-after government letterhead on eBay.) Elwood learned on New Year's Eve 1914 "that this plum had fallen to him," according to a newspaper report, and that he was to begin his duties at once, for the tidy salary of $5,000 per year. This is the job that brought him to Albany, and to my house.

How'd the Elwood family end up on West Lawrence Street? I credit the Calvary Church.

The Elwoods were Methodist Episcopals. It's enough to imagine they wanted to live across the street from a new, growing church of their faith, but there might be even a closer connection. My house's first residents, John and Mary Scott, were founding members of Calvary, remember. John Scott attended regional and state meetings as a church officer; so did Everett Elwood. Perhaps they met at such a conference, or perhaps they were introduced by a mutual acquaintance who heard Elwood was looking for a place in Albany. In any case, Elwood made arrangements to rent my house from the Scotts.

The family embraced the Pine Hills. Olive took an active role with the Home Missionary Society and the Ladies' Aid Society at the church. Everett sang tenor in the church choir and helped organize its first Sunday school. He joined Albany's exclusive Fort Orange Club. They sent their oldest child, Margaret, to School 16. Their little boy was too young for school yet; and one more child—Barbara, Olivia Raffe's mother—was born while the Elwoods lived in this house. Indeed, according to both family lore and the *Albany Evening Journal*, Barbara was born *in* this house. I don't know why, but that makes me happy.

Thanks to newspaper society columns—the Facebook of their day, listing who was on vacation, feeling sick, having the ladies in for tea—we learn that the Elwoods traveled regularly to visit their parents in Central New York and that Everett headed up to go fishing in the Adirondacks whenever he had the chance. They hosted the Syracuse University Alumni Club in the house. And Olive was active in a neighborhood institution: the Pine Hills Fortnightly Club.

Founded in 1898 as a study club for women, it offered a kind of "continuing education" to the middle-class ladies of the Pine Hills. More than a book club, it gave women, most of them stay-at-home wives, an opportunity to engage publicly on social and political issues. Every year the Fortnightly Club would select a topic; members would each research and write a paper that touched on that theme, to be presented to the others at one of the meetings. Held in the Aurania Club building on South Allen, the gatherings would also feature guest speakers, music, poetry, and tea. Their motto: "Nothing but the best is worthwhile."

During the five years when Olive was a member, the club explored topics like "Present Day Conditions and Problems" (with papers on the effects of the Great War, women in the workforce, child labor); China (poetry, education, politics, "Exit Opium, Enter Beer"); and "Women of Shakespeare." Olive served on the Fortnightly Club's social committee and program committee, and she presented one paper during her membership: "Health: The Part of the Individual, the Part of the State," with the added consideration of "housing problems and health insurance." It was certainly a subject she would have contemplated at length. I wish I could hear her thoughts on it.

The Elwoods weren't the only ones who moved into my house in 1915. Living here with them was a child named Esther Hansen.

Esther's place in the household was noted by the state census enumerator, who came by some time after June of 1915. Her occupation: domestic servant. The census recorded little else: she was fourteen years old; she was born in the United States. By the 1920 census, Esther was gone.

Who was she? Where did she go? I do not know. The accounts of her leisure time weren't recorded in the society pages. I cannot find her in future city directories. I haven't been able to locate her in other census years. In the 1915 census, Esther appears alone, without any family, giving me few threads to follow. Tracing someone in old documents means navigating through misspellings, age errors, incorrect house numbers, and illegible handwriting. Too often, any single record could be suspect, so it's important to try to establish a context and put together a picture over time. There are just too many variables: Esther may have moved to Albany with the Elwoods, or she may have been local. My census searches of local Hansen families haven't turned up a likely child of that name,[1] but she may not even have been an Esther, or a Hansen. Hester or Essie? Hanson or Anson? Perhaps she was with the Elwoods only a

---

1. There was an Esther Hansen in the 1905 state census who caught my eye. Four years old, she lived in Schaghticoke, the sixth child of Danish immigrant farmers. Then, in 1910, the farm wife was a widow renting a flat in Troy, mother to eight living children, the ages and names all matching up. With an older brother's factory paycheck the only wages in the family, I began to wonder if this might have been how it started, the choice to send a child out into the world, bed and board in a stranger's employ better than uncertainty at home. But no, the 1915 census shows this Esther still with her mother, still in Troy, still in school. Not the same girl. How illogical my relief at finding her there, not knowing anything about her life or what may or may not have been best for her at that time. And still there is this other Esther Hansen, who wasn't in school, who wasn't at home with her mother, who did the chores and slept under my roof a century ago.

short while, helping out when the children were babies. Perhaps she lived with the family for years. Perhaps she moved out of town, or married, and where do I look for her then? So many ways to slip out of the beam of the searchlight. It troubles me that I haven't been able to learn more.

> The admission of all insane persons, whether rich or poor, to excellent medical care and treatment is, next to public education, the greatest task of a quasi-social nature yet to be undertaken by any State government.
> —*Everett S. Elwood, 1913*

A decade into the twentieth century, New York had thirteen institutions for the so-called "civil insane," two for the criminally insane, and two more under construction. Elwood inherited a system that had thirty-five thousand patients in February 1915. It was the largest state hospital system in the country. Elwood believed it was right for government to bear the expense of mental health treatment. He called it the state's "conservation of its natural resources." But it vexed him that the money wasn't doing enough to ease the suffering.

"We are deeply concerned in [sic] the enormous cost of mental disease to the State of New York to-day," Elwood told the first state conference on mental health, held in 1915. "We are even more disturbed when we attempt to comprehend the enormous amount of human suffering occasioned by the 35,000 cases of mental disease under treatment in our State institutions."

What could be done? Prevention and community-based care: that was Elwood's answer. For both, outpatient clinics were the key.

"Every city and many of the larger towns should have an outpatient department of a State hospital or a mental hygiene dispensary to which the public might have access for advice and treatment of mental disease," Elwood urged. By making early detection easier, the social workers at the clinics could identify and correct problems before they required institutionalization. What's more, they'd be a source of information on how to prevent mental illness.

With the "hearty approval" of Governor Whitman, Elwood dove in. Mental health clinics were opened around the state, offering free diagnosis, advice, and treatment. By 1917 New York had thirty clinics statewide. By 1921, there were forty.

These clinics also made it possible to send more institutionalized patients home. Elwood believed it was better for many patients to be "on parole," as he called it, but that would only work, he argued, where there was a social worker to monitor the case and make sure the home environment was a supportive one. Social workers would counsel the whole family to improve conditions that might lead to relapse and teach the family how to care for a loved one at home. Treatment had the best chance of success, Elwood believed, if caregivers could look at each client's life in context, treating sufferers as the individuals they were. And after all, he pointed out, "Six patients at home on parole represent a saving to the state equivalent to the salary of one social worker."

For patients still within the hospitals, Elwood urged occupational therapy: putting patients to work and getting them ready for self-support. He agreed with a state hospital superintendent who said: "The doctors on the staff and the board of managers should be imbued with the idea that about the worst place for a patient . . . is the ward of a state hospital. . . . [T]he more time spent 'off the ward' each day by every patient, the better for the institution and the patient."

The number of patients sent home on parole had grown from 861 in 1913 to 2,283 in early 1920, and Elwood was pushing to add still more social workers so he could increase those numbers. Outpatient care was still just a small part of the Hospital Commission's work; it would be decades still before the institution system was dismantled. But it was a step toward the modern era, and Elwood was one of those who pushed New York to make that step. And since New York state was a pioneer in public health policy, changes made here rippled throughout the country.

All the houses on my block of West Lawrence Street were built after 1910, making 1920 our first US census. A walk up our street via the census records tells us a thing or two about the Elwoods' Pine Hills.

Here, on the corner with Myrtle, lived Frank and Grace Hoyt and their two teenage daughters, Helen and Elinor, plus elderly maiden Aunt Ellen. (I love the way a name echoes within a family.) Frank was a superintendent at an express company. Next to them lived a railroad engineer, James Gilkerson, with his wife, Julie. Their twenty-two-year-old daughter worked as a stenographer down at the secretary of state's office. Next, the Mardens, Walter and Lillian, with their sixteen-year-old son, Paul. Walter was a civil engineer engaged in bridge-building work. Then the Elwoods, who lived here with their three little ones, ages eight, five, and two in 1920. And on the corner were the Suttons, a couple in their late fifties. Walter was a newspaper foreman.

The whole block was like that: mostly middle-class professional men—a college professor, a company president, a few state officials. Everyone was white. All but two were American-born. The wives, unsurprisingly, did not work outside the home, but three unmarried women did. Two were stenographers, and one, a fifty-nine-year-old widow named Isabelle Brown, was a servant in a house across the street—the only live-in domestic on the block.

One house out of eight with live-in help: that's consistent with other homes nearby. In 1920, of the 235 households in my district (census info is divided by wards, and within wards into districts), 37 had one or more live-in servants. It's something I've always been curious about. These houses were built with back stairs and maid's rooms—they're labeled as such in the building specs—but between 1910 and 1920 a shifting economy and slowing immigration brought a drop in the number of domestic servants. Builders like Lorenz Willig constructed these houses based on an older definition of what it meant to be middle class—a definition that was already changing soon after the first residents moved in.

One of West Lawrence Street's residents in 1920 was Ronald Kinnear, president of an Albany manufacturing success story, the Albany Billiard Ball Company. The brains behind the company belonged to John Wesley Hyatt, inventor of celluloid, the first commercially viable plastic. Ronald Kinnear's grandfather Peter Kinnear had been the money man: he gave Hyatt space in his machine shop to conduct his experiments, and later he drummed up funds to build a factory. Eventually Peter Kinnear became the majority owner of the company, founding the family fortune even as Hyatt went on to other projects. Albany dominated the market for a century, saving the lives of countless elephants by making balls that were better balanced, more durable, and cheaper than ones made of ivory. When it closed in 1986, it was the last remaining billiard ball manufacturer in the United States.

Ronald, who was thirty-three in 1920, had been the company's president since his grandfather's death in 1913, a title he held until his own death in 1954. He and his wife, twenty-seven-year-old Marguerite, were the youngest householders on the block. Within ten years they had moved on, to a row house on State Street between Lark and Dove. Most everyone on my block, in fact, would be gone by the time the 1930 census taker came through. Of these eight houses, only one had the same occupants in 1930 that it did in 1920.

And the Elwoods? They rented this house from John Scott for five years. Then, in February of 1920, they bought it—and within a year they sold it and left Albany. Why? Why rent? At least, why rent for so long and then buy—and then sell? Maybe they'd made some kind of rent-to-own arrangement? Maybe they didn't plan to stay? Maybe they *did*, at last, plan to stay and then their plans changed? I don't know, and there's no way to find out. So it goes.

In 1921 Elwood resigned from the state Hospital Commission. He accepted a job as executive secretary of the National Board of Medical Examiners, a six-year-old institution pushing to standardize the licensing of physicians. The board reorganized its management structure to create a position for Elwood, a nonmedical administrator, who signed on to guide the creation of a new medical exam and seek ways to get more states to accept its licensing.

The *New York Times* ran a story July 21, 1921, on Elwood's farewell dinner. His colleagues gave him a traveling bag and praised his work, "particularly in obtaining free clinics for mental and nervous disorders." The *Times* wrote: "It was said that the State now operates forty clinics for mental and nervous disorders, and that 3,000 persons were treated at the free clinics last year. Direct credit was given to Mr. Elwood for the establishment of this branch of State medical activity."

Everett and Olive Elwood moved their family to Philadelphia, where they would live out the rest of their lives.

In the nine years since my house had been built, two families had called it home. And in 1921 it came into the hands of the family who would live there for the next half-century.

9

Marguerite

Let's go upstairs. No, higher.

The maid's room: What's above it? Well, yes, the roof. But something else, too.

For us, the third-floor room is something of a library—shelves for music and books, a workspace away from the kids. It's where we hide all the junk when guests come over: open door, toss crap on stairs, shut door quickly, pray they don't ask for a house tour. From this room, doors on the left and right lead into unfinished attic storage space. The attic facing the street has diamond-pane windows that let in a little low, dusty light. The other attic has no windows at all, but there's a bulb on the wall near the door: enough light to find what you came in for, but the corners stay dark.

After we'd lived in this house for about seven years, I decided to reorganize the shadowy side of the attic. The craft supplies were too jumbled to use, and the contents of the costume chest had been strewn on the floor since the previous Halloween. I brought in a work lamp, ran its cord to an outlet, hung the light on a nail in the attic wall, turned around.

And saw a ghost.

There was a face in between the rafters. A woman's face, in profile, with bobbed hair and pouted lips—a flapper, sketched in pencil.

My heart thumped for a moment. Then it soared. Even with nails from a 1990s roofing job piercing through it, the drawing was beautiful. Had this been here all along?! Is it as old as it looks? Who drew it?

Who else has seen it? The previous owner had affectionately shown off the house's quirks to me after we'd bought the place, but this face wasn't on the tour. Did he not know about it? Or, if he had, how thoughtful of him to leave it to me to discover for myself.

I carried the light into the other corners of the attic; in between another set of rafters was a second face, only half drawn. And as I surveyed the room in—literally—this new light, something occurred to me: there was one place in my house that I had never seen.

These storage eaves are roofed only by the rafters, which continue up to the peak of the house. This left a space above the third-floor room's ceiling. I got a ladder, took the light, and climbed up for a look. The air at the top of the house was heavy with dust, and the "floor" was covered with two layers of Owens Corning's finest. I rolled back a corner. Underneath was another type of insulation, that crumbly, powdery stuff. Oh, great. I pushed a handful aside, and there, poking out, was another pencil drawing, just a fragment of a face on a scrap of paper.

Then I found another drawing, another face, and then a brittle Oh! Henry wrapper and a colorful cardboard Valentine inscribed "from Georgie to Joanie." Those were names I recognized. I had just started to research my house's past, and I knew Georgea and Joan had been children here in the 1920s. I'd gotten as far as looking up their obituaries, and that was about all I knew of them.

I dug further. Underneath the insulation was as much stuff as I could grab:

> church periodicals with stories and poems for children, dated in the 1920s;
>
> homemade paper dolls with the pout and bobbed hair of Louise Brooks;
>
> wrappers from Touraine Chocolate and O.K. Perfect Gum, Beeman's Pepsin Chewing Gum, and Wrigley's;
>
> handmade puzzles cut from newspaper comics, photographs, and their own drawings (one piece of a comic strip showed a date on the back of 1927);

empty cartons of English Ovals and Herbert Tareyton cigarettes—and more than a few gold-tipped cigarette butts;

and more: a broken necklace of black beads, a homemade
knitting spool, a little tin spoon, a wooden domino, a
piece of shingle with "JOAN" scratched on it.

Then there were the old letters. Most of them were folded and
torn into bits. The only intact one was dated April 25, 1928, and is
addressed to "Dearest Joan" from a friend in Nassau, Rensselaer County.
("I suppose you have forgotten all about me since you went to Albany
but let's hope you haven't. You make me think you have because you
don't write.")

Some of the papers had what appeared to be poems on them,
printed out in fountain pen. One turned out to be the lyrics to "I'll Be
Blue Just Thinking of You," a song Ruth Etting had a hit with in 1930:
lost love lightened by jazz stylings. On the back of the copied lyrics is
written "2 mo. 3 week." Ah, adolescence.

Unearthing these papers left my lungs full of dust and my hands
coated in powdery insulation, but just by standing on a ladder at the
attic's edge, reaching in, I had a handful of treasures. They were only
scraps, yes. But they were scraps that told the story of a childhood
hideout, preserved for nearly ninety years: love notes and cheap novels,
chocolate and cigarettes, growing girls clambering up to the top of the
house and indulging in a bit of hedonism out of Mother's reach.

How marvelous that no one ever bothered to get a broom and
clean up all this junk. Lazy or hasty, the workmen who just rolled out
insulation over the messy attic floor had left me a wonderful gift. I was
dying to know: Who *were* these children?

Their names were Joan, Georgea, Sylvia, and Cornelia, and there
was more to their story than I could have imagined.

In 1921 the Elwoods sold their Albany home to a woman named
Marguerite Stickles. She and her daughters went on to spend most of
their lives here on West Lawrence Street. In many ways, they are the
soul of this house. And, thanks to Marguerite, we have a chance to
know them as something more than a list of names.

Marguerite was nearly sixty when she typed up a forty-three-page, single-spaced document for her children: her life story. I received a copy from her grandson. The memoir, written in 1937, details her 1880s Albany childhood; her twelve-year career with the telephone company; her travels around New York as a fun-loving, independent young woman; and, finally, her marriage in her early thirties and the start of her family life—including how she purchased and moved into my house. It has never been published, but it should be. She was an engaging storyteller with an affectionate sense of humor. Her writing calls to mind that of Huybertie Pruyn Hamlin, a lady from a wealthy family who grew up on Elk Street and whose memoirs were published as *An Albany Girlhood*. Marguerite's was an Albany girlhood of another strata, as rich and as full in experiences, if not in privilege. Marguerite and Bertie were contemporaries, in fact, and comparing their Albany childhoods would be an interesting project. Let's linger on Marguerite for a while, because her memoir lays the foundation for all that came later.

The story of how the Stickles family ended up on West Lawrence Street begins on Clinton Avenue, and it takes us to Nassau village by way of a moonlit night on Kinderhook Lake.

Born in 1879, Marguerite Claffee was the daughter of Irish immigrants. Called Dotty by her family and friends (her mother was also named Marguerite), she was the only child in her family to live to adulthood, herself barely surviving scarlet fever at age three. Dotty grew up on Clinton between North Lake and Ontario, living in several rentals before her parents bought a two-family house at 603 Clinton in the 1890s, where they rented out one flat and lived in the other.

Her father, Marguerite wrote, owned a wine and liquor store. "Please don't confuse this with a beer saloon," she says—but if we *were* to feel confused, we wouldn't be the first. The census lists Morris Claffee as a "saloon keeper"; and in the Albany business directories for 1884 and 1885, his establishment is *not* listed under "liquors, wines, etc.," either wholesale or retail, but it *can* be found under "refreshment saloons."

Daughter of a barkeep or a wine merchant—either way, Dotty had fond memories of her childhood. Her memoir gives a lively picture of a nineteenth-century family neighborhood: dancing school, close friendships, and endless hours spent practicing the piano; strict parents, silly games, and an unsettling familiarity with sickness and death.

Clinton Avenue, Marguerite writes, was a German neighborhood; her playmates had surnames like Henckel, Bohner, Zimmer, and Schmidt. "Little German bands" would make the rounds about once a week in their gold-braided coats, stopping at each house to play a song from the old country on horn and drum and then knocking on the door for some change.

"All the houses had their high wooden fences in front, protecting their flower-filled front yards from the passerby," she wrote. "In the evenings, the front 'stoop' would be filled with the mothers and their 'broods,' the mother usually knitting socks, or stockings or mittens or mufflers, or wristlets. Always four needles were used, and inches of knitted material would grow under my amazed eyes as the 'knitter' would continue laughing and talking with us children, never once glancing down at her flying fingers."

Marguerite's mother did not knit, but she did sew all of Marguerite's clothes, with great skill. "My, my, what a particular woman my mother was. Everything had to be just so. . . . Each morning I sat on her lap to have my teeth brushed and my nails cleaned. (Not a child I knew ever touched their teeth, the result being 'pale green grins' when they smiled.)"

She remembered one coat in particular her mother had made for her:

> The color that winter was called "Pigeon Drab" and that little coat was always spoken of by that name. It had a little ladder of braid the same shade, up the front and back, and a tiny cape of the same, edged with loops of the braid. This was topped off with a little bonnet of grey, with tiny pink rosebuds around the face. Black button "French" kid shoes and black lisle stockings and little tan gloves—this was Dotty Claffee in the year 1884.

During Grover Cleveland's presidential run (probably his 1884 campaign, though Marguerite's dates are fuzzy), her block was evenly divided: about half the houses hung a picture of Cleveland and his running mate in the front window, and the others pasted up pictures of their opponents.

> Each afternoon small groups of children would march up and down with sticks in their hands and going up to the windows showing these faces would point the sticks and call loudly—if Democrat, "Shoot the cat, shoot the hat, shoot the dirty Democrat"; if on the other side, "Shoot the can, shoot the pan, shoot the dirty Republican." As we had no pictures in our windows, and my father would not tell me who he favored, it made no difference so I was always quite ready to shoot all four.

Behind their row house, her father planted grapevines that grew, in time, to curtain the back terrace; from their porch chairs Marguerite and her friends could reach out their hands and pluck the ripe fruit.

"Dell Henckel and I were the best runners on the block," she wrote. "Beat you down to the Home of the Friendless!" was their challenge to each other each day after school; and when they reached the home for old ladies at the corner of Clinton and North Lake they would frighten the poor souls inside by walking atop its rickety wooden fence.

After graduating from Albany High (and winning a prize and a set of tools for the Dutch hall chair she had decorated in woodcarving class), Marguerite decided "to go out to business" at the telephone company. She worked her way up the ranks from telephone operator to switchboard teacher, then became a quality-control officer who traveled around the state observing work at other exchanges. Finally, she was made information desk supervisor in Albany. "I can't recall the number of times I was going to walk out of that office, but the work held me," Marguerite wrote. "I loved it, and I stayed for 12 years."

She remembers the day in 1905 that the Myers Department Store on North Pearl Street collapsed: how all the telephone boards were swamped for three hours, every light ablaze, every operator working, and still all the calls could not be answered, and the church bells outside sounding alarms. Thirteen people died, and a hundred more were injured, as the store pancaked into its own cellar.

Her childhood friend Harry Flanagan was her sweetheart. "You can't see anyone but that Number 11 of yours," her best friend Winnie McCormack teased her—"Number 11" was what Win called him on account of his being "tall and slight." (How can one person look like an 11? Wouldn't "Number 1" make more sense? Eleven, though, is what Marguerite wrote.) But in 1905 Harry complained of a terrible headache and died a week later. "A hospital full of doctors, and not one can stop the pain in my head," he told Marguerite as he lay on his deathbed. Marguerite never says in her memoir that they had been engaged, but family stories suggest it was so. "I was utterly lost for a time after his passing," she wrote.

Through her twenties and into her thirties, Marguerite lived with her mother, by then a widow, at their home on Clinton. One of the things that makes her story so compelling is that Marguerite did not seem confined by her times. Her job required her to spend five nights a week alone in hotels and boarding houses, and in her free time she would go to the theater or go boating out at Thompson's Lake. She and her girlfriends traveled often to New York City to shop, visit museums, and see shows. She had a lively sense of humor and liked to have a good time, though she didn't like crude language and wouldn't laugh at coarse jokes. Dealing with difficult supervisors at the telephone company had taught her self-control, and if she needed to she would look someone in the eye and make sure they heard what she had to say. She was independent, unafraid, and in charge of her own life.

And that's how she ended up in 1912 at a friend's Labor Day weekend house party out on Kinderhook Lake, where she met a well-dressed, heartbroken man twenty years her senior. In less than two weeks, they were married.

Dr. George Stickles had been born in 1859 in Nassau village, Rensselaer County. The son of a farmer, he grew up to become a gymnast. Yes, that's right. Hold on for a moment to that mental image of a mustachioed man in a leotard. . . . Now let it go.

The first time I saw Dr. Stickles listed as a "gymnast"—it was on his marriage license down at the Hall of Records—I thought I was seeing things. *G-Y-M* . . . I went letter by letter to see if I could make the cursive handwriting say anything else. But he was a gymnast indeed: Dr. Stickles was a practitioner of a form of nineteenth-century medicine known as medical gymnastics. He would guide a patient through a series of exercises and assist them with passive movements—massaging and stretching muscle groups—intended to improve the person's health or provide strength training. Medical gymnastics was a precursor to modern physical therapy.

Massage was a central part of "the movement cure," as it was also known; it commanded respect as a health treatment in the late nineteenth century. Dr. Stickles worked in Manhattan and was well known up in Saratoga Springs, where he provided his services in massage and medical gymnastics to several spas. His practice left him quite well off. He bought a lot of real estate and played the stock market.

He married young, had two children, then divorced (the marriage had "gone on the rocks," he told Marguerite later); the wife went back home to her parents in Milwaukee and represented herself in society as his widow. Dr. Stickles married again, in his midthirties, to a Swedish-born lady named Charlotte Anderson. They had a daughter, Eva, with blonde hair and a saucy little pout, and for nearly two decades they divided their time between New York City, Saratoga, and Nassau. Their names appeared from time to time in the newspaper society columns. It looked like a lifetime's worth of family comfort and companionship.

But it wasn't. His daughter and his wife died within weeks of each other in 1912, leaving George Stickles alone. Eva, eighteen years old, passed away first. I don't know the cause. Charlotte, her mother, died a few weeks later, at their home in Nassau. She was blind, and according to her death certificate she had been sick for some time. She hung on just long enough to outlive her only child.

After the deaths of his wife and daughter, George closed up his house and moved into a hotel. He roamed the Capital Region, visiting county fairs, going to the Saratoga races, anything so as not to be alone. It was just a matter of weeks after Charlotte's death that his wanderings brought him to a Kinderhook Lake house party held by friends of friends, where he met thirty-two-year-old Marguerite Claffee, a telephone company supervisor who had endured her own share of loss.

Their romance began with a bit of snark. There was another fellow in attendance who didn't like Marguerite much; she never laughed at his jokes, and he thought her a wet blanket. When she went upstairs "to tidy up a bit" before dinner—she'd just come back from a motorboat ride—he quipped to the others, "Well, I suppose we will have to wait for Miss Primper to get all primped up."

George hadn't paid Marguerite much attention before that, but the remark caught his ear. When she came downstairs, George checked her out. He liked what he saw—and he realized she was unattached. Marguerite came into the dining room to find everyone else at the table, already passing dishes around (apparently, they didn't wait for Miss Primper after all). She noticed the widowed doctor "looking at me with a whimsical expression in his eye." After dinner, George asked if he could take Marguerite and her friend Ella out motoring in his four-cylinder Buick. She had already committed to a canoe ride, but Ella pressed her, and she agreed to come along.

They drove to Electric Park, an amusement park on the other side of Kinderhook Lake. Electric Park is one of the Capital Region's forgotten wonders, "a place where ladies and children can go unattended" (or so their advertisements claimed) and find amusements galore: bowling, boating, shoot the chutes, daily concerts, and a dancing pavilion, plus, as Marguerite remembered, "out-door movies, a Ferris wheel, merry-go-round, and roller skating rink." The park was owned and operated by the Albany & Hudson Railroad Co., which ran an electric train from (wait for it) Albany to Hudson. Admission was free with a round-trip train ticket. "The place was always crowded," Marguerite wrote.

The three of them stayed there till after dark. When they returned to the summer house, George cast his line.

"Let's you and I stay out here for a little while," he said.

Marguerite couldn't think of a reason to say no, so she and George ended up, a little awkwardly, standing together at the porch railing, "in full view of the occupants of the living room," and Marguerite found herself thinking more about what the others were thinking than about making conversation with the doctor.

But her ears pricked up when she heard him say, "I was much impressed the minute I saw you."

"Well, this made me pay attention," she wrote in her memoir, "and I heard some very nice things. (Did I say it was a beautiful moon-lit night? Well, it was, and shining on the lake made everything very romantic.) But I did not put much stock in what I was hearing, as the acquaintance was only a few hours old."

Sure enough, everyone teased them when they went in the house— "The doctor is an awful jollier," they said—and Marguerite laughed along with them. But the next day, George was back to take everyone out motoring again, and he asked Marguerite to sit beside him.

The following day was Labor Day. "Everyone had it 'off' but me," wrote Marguerite, who was due for a shift at the telephone company, so she had to head home Sunday. George volunteered to drive her back to Albany in the bucketing rain.

"How it did pour that night," Marguerite wrote, "and how the car would skid. . . . At different times the car would almost twirl around; he would say he had the car under perfect control, which I doubted very much." The doctor remarked that he was glad she wasn't the "nervous type"; he didn't know Marguerite was reciting silent prayers.

George detoured into Nassau village on the way back to Albany, saying he wanted to show her his house. "He backed into a driveway from the street and pointing across said, 'There it is,'" wrote Marguerite. "All I could see were shadows of trees and trees and trees, not a house, but rather than admit it—this man might run the car right up on the sidewalk to give me a good view of it—I said, 'It's lovely.'" They made it back to Albany, where Marguerite's mother was waiting up for her.

The next morning—of course it was right after Marguerite had finished shampooing her hair—the doorbell rang. She looked out the window: "There was the four-cylinder Buick, and I was in a quandary, to go or not to go (and me looking like this) but I went, and there stood the doctor, with a 'Danker, Florist' box, the longest I had ever seen, and containing the most beautiful 'American Beauties' that ever entered 603 Clinton Ave., with stems two feet long."

Dr. Stickles, Marguerite said, "looked like a million dollars": "A light grey suit with blue tie, socks, and breast-pocket kerchief all matching, and a most becoming automobile cap with a peak." He'd come to take her for a ride—she didn't work until that evening—and they motored up to Saratoga for lunch. He told her of his background, the deaths earlier that summer of his wife and daughter, his long-ago first marriage that had ended in divorce. She was impressed by how many people in Saratoga knew him. To get back to Albany for her five o'clock shift at the telephone company they flew home at a "breath-taking pace"; and when her shift ended he was there, outside, waiting to drive her home.

That's how George was: when he wanted something he went after it. And with Marguerite he felt he had found a way out of his grief, a way back into life. Marguerite wrote years later that George always made decisions like that. "There was no weighing of matter, no pro and cons," she said, "and I never saw one to make so few mistakes."

George Stickles, twenty years Marguerite's senior, came by every night that week, bringing flowers and boxes of Huyler's candy to her Clinton Avenue row house. Their mutual acquaintances were miffed about the developing romance: the doctor was no longer interested in taking his other friends out motoring, and they had so enjoyed his automobile. One was overheard saying to another, "You can thank yourself for bringing that woman around."

George proposed to Marguerite before the week was out. She accepted, and they went to Washington Park and heard the band play "Moonlight Bay." "My, my, I sure was happy," Marguerite wrote.

There was one problem: Marguerite's mother.

"How much longer are you going to keep this up?" Mrs. Claffee asked her daughter after one date. "We'll be the talk of the neighborhood." She thought the doctor was a "man about town," and she told her daughter that his type couldn't be trusted. "Why, you know nothing about this man!" she warned.

Marguerite reassured her mother that she'd like him once she'd had a chance to know him. George, for his part, was pressing Marguerite to let him meet her mother, but she kept stalling him as she tried to warm Mom up to the idea of this fifty-two-year-old well-dressed stranger sweeping in to take away her only child.

One day, when Marguerite was at work, the doorbell rang at 603 Clinton Avenue. Mrs. Claffee, in the middle of her ironing and a little disheveled, opened the door, and there was her daughter's suitor with a big bouquet of garden flowers. "My elusive mother had been caught," wrote Marguerite. "She was furious for the first few minutes, but Dad's charm and manner soon dispelled the cloud." He told Mrs. Claffee that he had fallen in love with her daughter and "had to declare himself." (Scoffed Marguerite, "This old-time gallantry went out with the turn of the century.") The doctor sweetened up Mom by asking her to accept a box of produce from his Nassau farm, "so down in the cellar went apples, Bartlett pears, beets, potatoes and other vegetables." And that night, when George came to call for Marguerite, Mrs. Claffee came out to greet him. Victory, thy taste is crisp, and in season.

Marguerite and George were married at the minister's house in Nassau on September 11, 1912, twelve days after they first met. George called for her at ten that morning in a dark blue suit and a white straw hat, his car all polished up. Marguerite wore a white linen suit she had bought that spring at Wanamaker's in Philadelphia. When she ran back into the house to fetch her engagement ring, her mother threw a slipper after her, and a handful of rice.

As Dr. and Mrs. Stickles enjoyed a honeymoon in New York City, Mom back in Albany had to deal with reporters on her doorstep.

"It seemed that marrying a person after such short acquaintance was NEWS," Marguerite wrote. "Two men and two women called at different times. . . . The papers for two or three days had something to say about it." "WIDOWER ONLY FEW MONTHS," read the headline of one clipping. "Dr. Stickles to Marry Clinton Avenue Telephone Girl." "NASSAU HAS A NICE ROMANCE," read another.

Marguerite later collected the newspaper snippets into a scrapbook, noting with amusement facts the reporters got wrong—their ages, the details of their courtship, where they spent their honeymoon—but who can blame them for trying? Everyone loves a good "happily ever after."

The newlyweds moved out to George's hometown of Nassau and got to know each other. They had four children, all girls, in the next eight years.

In between babies, they loved to travel, and exploring the countryside in the Buick, or the Apperson Jackrabbit, or whatever George was driving that year, was part of their daily routine. "I guess every road that radiated out from Albany knew us," wrote Marguerite.

"The attire for the autoist in 1913 was a long linen 'duster' worn alike by men and women," Marguerite wrote. "Men wore caps and women usually had yards of veiling swathed around their heads, to prevent their hats from blowing off. . . . [George] wore long leather 'gauntlets'—gloves with cuffs reaching to the elbow, and everyone wore 'goggles'—glasses edged with tortoise-shell rims."

She herself never wore a veil, and she tells the story of the time the wind blew off not only her hat but also her braid of false hair. They couldn't catch their breath from laughing.

George gave Marguerite driving lessons, but she didn't really take to it. He teased her for never knowing east from west; she marveled at his sense of direction, how he could always find his way on unfamiliar roads. "Watch me beat this car" was one of his catchphrases.

George retired from his medical gymnastics practice before 1920, but he kept busy as a country landlord. A Nassau history booklet notes that George Stickles owned so much property in one part of the village that people called it "Stickleville." He would be "up at six every morning in summer building houses, looking the picture of the typical workman," Marguerite wrote. "At one o'clock, after lunch, he would take a bath, dress and we would go for a ride. Now he looked like a million with his Panama hat, grey suit and white silk shirt; socks matching tie in color."

George had hired men to repaint and wallpaper his Nassau house before bringing his new wife there, but echoes remained of Lottie and Eva, the wife and daughter George had lost just months before. Marguerite recalls soothing baby Joan to sleep in Eva's old doll cradle.

Still, her writing brims with jolly memories of the late teens and early 1920s: George singing in the mornings, sitting up in bed paring apples for the children; teaching the girls to ice skate in Washington Park; the endless country drives. Marguerite's mother and aunt both came out to Nassau to live with them and helped nurse their daughters through all the childhood sicknesses. The girls were beauties, all four of them, with bobbed hair and intense eyes. They were charmers, too. Proud Papa carried their picture with him everywhere in a leather wallet.

Born and raised in Albany, Marguerite never really got used to small-town life. In her eyes, Nassau offered nothing to do, nowhere even to take an evening stroll (the sidewalks were "treacherous with broken flagstones"), and people were far too interested in each other's business for her taste. As she and George would walk down the street she would notice "front room curtains moving slightly" as they went by. "To attract so much attention amused me greatly," she wrote; "in Albany no one ever looked at you, only with a passing glance."

"Poor little Nassau," she called it, "with so little to talk about."

The family frequently found reasons to travel to Albany; George was there all the time to visit with his stockbroker, and they used to take the kids in every Saturday to see a movie at the Strand. Some years they even spent the winter in the city. So it's not too surprising that George decided, in 1921, to buy them a place of their own in Albany. And he did it in typical George fashion: without telling Marguerite what he was up to, he bundled her into the car and took her to the Pine Hills. To my house.

As she told it in her memoir: "Alighting from the car, we ascended a terrace. Dad then said, 'I want you to look at this house and see what you think of it.' A nice-looking woman answered our ring and showed us through. Then we visited two other places and Dad asked which one I liked best. Of course it was the first one. Then he said, 'I thought you would. Well, I am going to buy it.' And that was that."

It's a story the family heard many times over the years. "He told her to pick out any house in Albany that she wanted," including houses on fashionable upper Madison, said George and Marguerite's grand-daughter, Lynn Devane. "And she would say she chose this one because she liked the hill."

It *is* nice, having a house on a hill. We're a little removed from the noise and the traffic, and we can leave the curtains open with-out feeling we're on display to every person who walks by. (*Take that, Nassau,* Marguerite might have thought.)

No doubt there was something else, too, that sweetened the deal: Marguerite's best friend, Winnie McCormack, lived just down the street.

The McCormack sisters are a story unto themselves—or maybe the setup for a sitcom: seven of them, six unmarried and one a widow, lived together in a big rambling corner house on West Lawrence Street. Marguerite had loved the whole family since her days at the telephone company. The noise and activity in a house full of kids: what a contrast to her upbringing as an only child! Dotty and Win were travel companions and confidantes. "She was a born wit," wrote Marguerite. "I know I will never meet a person again as funny." Her family still has photos of the two posing together in a photographer's studio, young women with proud chins and improbable hats. And Winnie's greatnieces have the hand-drawn postcards, peppered with inside jokes, that Marguerite sent her best friend over the years.

So in the fall of 1921, my house became home to the Stickles family, changing hands for the third time in its nine-year existence. One of the first things Marguerite did was take out the telephone installed on the stair landing, which wouldn't stop ringing with friends calling to welcome her home.

The Pine Hills in the 1920s had a lot to offer. Between Main and Allen Streets there were four grocers, a creamery, and a delicatessen. Up on Madison, George and Marguerite could go to the pharmacy, get a haircut, and drop clothes at the cleaner's or the tailor's. There were doctors, a dentist, and a filling station. The West Lawrence Street house had no garage or driveway, but on the corner of West Lawrence and Madison was a garage where George could stable his beloved automobile. Behind it, facing West Lawrence, was the Pine Hills, a silent movie house where the Stickles family became regulars, at least until the Madison Theatre opened—with talkies!—in 1929. Calvary Methodist Episcopal Church was a stone's throw away; George was a Methodist, and the family joined the Calvary congregation for a number of years before Marguerite and her children returned to the Catholic Church.

"Albany at night seemed an enchanted city," Marguerite wrote, "with all the homes lighted up and no shades drawn; after poor little Nassau, so dark, with few streets to walk at night. . . . You were not going to peek in any Nassau house in your rambles, no sir."

Mr. and Mrs. Stickles kept their Nassau place and used it as a summer getaway for years to come, but Marguerite settled in to make my house her home. Next to the back porch, she planted grapevines to form a cool, green curtain, just as her father had done on Clinton Avenue. The wall between the window bench and the staircase was the perfect fit for her upright piano. She was a skilled player thanks to years of childhood lessons, and from the foot of the stairs her music would have filled the house. Her mother, Mrs. Claffee, joined them here and did most of the cooking. Marguerite had her beloved Albany, her children, her husband, her mother, and her best friend all at arm's reach.

It was the end of a chapter. But they didn't know it yet.

Some time after they bought the West Lawrence Street house, George Stickles started to worry about a small growth on his tongue. It had been there for a long time, but he hadn't paid it any mind until it started hurting. It was cancer.

George went to New York City for treatment, where doctors injected radium into his tongue. No anesthetic was available to ease the pain of the needle, Marguerite wrote in her memoir. "The agony suffered lasted for four hours." The treatments also left him unable to eat, and he lost a lot of weight. But it looked, for a time, as if it had worked: George's cancer appeared to go into remission.

His doctor had recommended that he come back to New York City every two years for a preventative dose of radium. In one of these sessions, in 1925, he was given an overdose. It caused him three months of suffering, and when George recovered, he told Marguerite, "I can never go through with that again."

But the next year, his cancer returned. The doctor recommended an aggressive course of radium treatment. George came home to Albany to think about it.

"We talked about it for days, weighing the pros and cons," Marguerite wrote. "One morning while shaving, he called to me and said, "I am not going to New York.""

They knew what that meant. Nonetheless, George felt as if a weight was taken from his shoulders.

"We might as well have a good time while we can," he told his wife.

It turned out they had three perfect days.

They set out doing what they loved best: traveling. They rambled through western Massachusetts, exploring different towns, with the goal of eventually reaching Boston. But on the morning of the fourth day, George awoke in terrible pain.

Mr. and Mrs. Stickles returned home, where George's condition deteriorated quickly. Morphine eased his suffering—he called it God's Own Medicine—and allowed him restful sleep, but they knew there was no recovery. George told Marguerite, "Don't feel sorry for me; I have had a good time."

Shortly before he died, he said to his wife, "There is nothing to life, when your time comes, it seems the things that seemed so worth striving for, are of no worth at all."

George died at nine in the morning on October 14, 1926. He was sixty-seven years old, and they had been married for fourteen years.

Marguerite sold their car to a man who, she learned later, coddled it and drove it only on Sundays. "I was glad, as I would hate to have it belong to someone who would wreck it," she wrote. "It seemed part of us, almost."

She and their daughters returned to Albany from the Nassau funeral to find their house had been broken into and many things stolen: a mere insult on top of the greater loss they had suffered.

The next six months were a terrible time. If Marguerite cried, the children cried too. "So when I felt a 'spell' coming on I would gather a few things together and hasten to the bath-room and do a little washing, let the water run and cry and cry."

When George died, his four daughters were thirteen, eleven, eight, and five. There was a lot of life yet to be lived in the West Lawrence Street house.

The Stickles sisters, lined up oldest to youngest in the back yard of the West Lawrence Street house sometime in the 1940s. From left: Joan, Georgea, Sylvia, and Cornelia. Courtesy of Crystal Wortsman.

10

The Flappers in My Attic

Greg Spencer is one of those people oral historians dream about. To start with, he's a great storyteller, with warmth, timing, and an eye for detail. More than once my coffee went cold as I got lost in his memories of growing up in Albany in the 1940s. But he has much more to offer: He has kept in touch with everyone, it seems, from the past chapters of his life, and can provide a wealth of contacts. He has scores of family photos and actually knows who's in them. And all his life he has kept scrapbooks. Themed by subject matter, they're full of clippings, pictures, and other mementos. Some of them span decades.

Most of all, Greg believes in the power of stories. For him, sharing stories—even, or maybe especially, the difficult ones—is a source of connection, strength, and healing. That's a belief he inherited from his grandmother, Marguerite Stickles. Her oldest girl, Joan, was Greg's mother.

I first met Greg not long after we moved into our house, though I didn't know it at the time. The timing could have been better: my husband and I had just finished loading the car for a vacation, and we were buckling our toddler into her car seat when a man walked over and said he had grown up here. He reminisced a little, and I asked him if he knew who Georgie was—the name written in white on the attic ceiling. That was, he told us, his aunt Georgea. Greg gave us his business card, and we made promises to connect; the card got lost, of course, and it was several years before I tracked him down again.

Greg said he'd be happy to tell me stories about life in the house. He had three generations' worth: his own memories, the tales he had heard from his mother and aunts, and his grandmother's memoir. Over the course of a year or so, he led me on tours of my own house and neighborhood, lent me hundreds of photographs and other documents, and, best of all, entrusted me with some difficult truths about his family and the struggles they had faced. Telling their remarkable stories would be impossible without him.

Joan, Georgea, Sylvia, and Cornelia—the little girls who had hidden from Mom above my attic ceiling, drawing pictures of flappers, copying down song lyrics, and sneaking cigarettes and candy—grew up to be lovely, flirtatious, clever, and wild.

When their father died in 1926, the oldest of the girls was just entering adolescence. Raising four daughters was a tough job for Marguerite to do alone. Her mother, Mrs. Claffee, lived with them here on West Lawrence Street for a time, helping with the girls and preparing the meals—Marguerite had never learned to cook—but Mrs. Claffee passed away in 1929. Her granddaughters encountered her ghost, once, afterwards, on the third-floor stairs, chiding them for misbehaving. Please don't tell my daughters that.

"I think she tried to keep the lid on the girls," Greg said of Marguerite. "She tried to bring them up to be ladies." But their mother, Joan used to say, "couldn't control us."

With access to money and very little discipline, the Stickles girls didn't take too much to schooling, and only one of the four, Cornelia, graduated from high school. The Great Depression didn't seem to put a strain on the family: George had bought the house outright, and he left Marguerite with enough money to raise the girls and not have to worry. Family photo albums from the 1930s show the young women vamping in swimsuits, attending boat races, skiing in the Adirondacks, and clowning around at picnics and clambakes. They enjoyed trips to Ocean City, North Carolina, and Miami Beach.

One of Greg's scrapbooks has the program of events from the 1932 Olympics in Lake Placid. Another contains a program from the Madison Theatre's opening night gala. It's not too surprising that one of the Stickles girls—or maybe even Marguerite herself—was there that night in 1929. They loved the cinema. Greg remembers his mother's carefully preserved movie magazines from the '20s and '30s, and Joan's teenage sketchbook was filled with drawings of the bobbed and pouting starlets. They look just like the flappers in my attic.

In the twenties, Marguerite and the girls had been regulars at the Pine Hills, a silent movie house that sat along West Lawrence where the Price Chopper parking lot is today. It was a relief to escape, for a time, from their sadness, but other than that they didn't like the place much: "What a crude place that theater was," wrote Marguerite in her memoir, "with its uncarpeted floors, its cheap seats and its awful piano." But they so loved living "in the picture," as Marguerite put it, that for a time they went there every night.

The Madison was in another class entirely. Designed by Thomas Lamb, the architect also responsible for Proctor's in Schenectady, the Madison Theatre cost a quarter of a million dollars to build. It was one of the first theaters in the nation built to show that marvelous new sensation of the 1920s—talking pictures. While older theaters were scrambling to retrofit for talkies, the Madison had the latest equipment and a building made for sound: Balsam wool was sandwiched between the theater's inner and outer walls to deaden the noise of traffic on Madison Avenue. No cheap seats and bare floors here: the lobby featured an Art Deco chandelier, the hall held fourteen hundred upholstered seats, and the walls were hung with special draperies fashioned to enhance acoustics.

The theater opened on May 29, 1929, with a gala attended by Mayor Thacher, neighborhood association president Judge James Nolan, and a host of other dignitaries. From time to time, it has been reported that Al Jolson, star of the early talkies, was there to act as master of ceremonies that night, but the opening night program indicates that he performed his emcee duties by way of "a special Vitaphone dedication film." Sorry, Albany, but the sound equipment, after all, was the real star.

Even without the World's Greatest Entertainer, there was plenty to enjoy at what newspaper ads promised would be "the most brilliant event in the annals of Albany"—including the feature film *The Desert Song*, a Mickey Mouse cartoon, and a musical performance of a piece called "At the Madison" played on the Wurlitzer organ.

The summer after it opened, the trade magazine *Motion Picture News* called the Madison "one of the finest residential theatres in New York State." Within the next few years, the Pine Hills movie house on

West Lawrence was shuttered, then converted to a grocery store: farewell to the silent screen.

Maybe the Stickles girls entered the 1930s with visions of those flapper starlets still in their heads. The free-spirited daughters loved to go downtown and hear the big bands play. They drank a lot and had handsome, athletic boyfriends.

"The girls were all party girls. . . . My mother and Georgie, they were like '20s girls in the '30s," Greg said. "Downtown Albany in those days, it really jumped, and they started hanging out with a real upscale, fast crowd."

One family story tells of the time Cab Calloway put the moves on cute, blond, underage Georgea down at Keeler's Restaurant. Cab was in town to perform, and when Georgea's mother stepped out of the dining room, the singer came sidling up to Georgea at their table. "Grandma came in at the nick of time and pulled her away," Greg said, and Marguerite scolded Cab: "She's 16 years old!"

After years of summering in George's old house in Nassau, the Stickles family got a seasonal place on Lake George, where the girls ran around with prominent families like the Freihofers (baked goods) and the Simmonses (machine parts). Later, Marguerite bought a house in Miami, where she and a daughter or two would spend the winter months. The girls grew up, paired off, started families of their own. Georgea married Harold Page Evans—his friends called him "Chick"—in 1937, but he couldn't stand her drinking, and he left. Joan married a talented minor league ball player named Fred Spencer. Marguerite remarried in 1939 to Chick Evans's father—Georgea's father-in-law—but the elderly gentleman passed away before the year was out.

The 1930s also saw the establishment of one of the neighborhood's most unusual landmarks: the glass school at Vincentian Institute.

Vincentian, a parochial school operated by St. Vincent de Paul parish, had begun as an elementary school in 1917 in a building at the corner of Madison and Ontario. It added a grade per year until the school offered K–12 education, with the first high school class graduating in 1925. The school grew with the neighborhood, and in 1934 the parish bought one of those sprawling nineteenth-century Madison Avenue estates.[1] Its home, grounds, carriage house and two large conservatories all became part of Vincentian. For the conservatories, VI founder Father William Charles had something special in mind: He converted them to classrooms for the primary grades.

There is, of course, this question: Why put a school in a greenhouse? The answer has its roots (ha, ha) in a health craze that was enjoying popularity in the 1920s and '30s: therapeutic sunbathing. According to this school of thought, exposure to sunlight would promote general health and help cure all manner of ills. In the words of one early 1930s text: "Sunlight causes the bones to grow. It develops muscles and brain. It strengthens and invigorates the skin and increases its resistance to infection. It prevents and remedies disease—not merely rickets, tuberculosis, anemia and the like, but all disease." 1930s photographs of the VI Child Culture Division, as it was called, look like something from a sci-fi "School of the Future": rows of children in identical sunglasses and sleeveless white v-necked tops sit, hands folded on desktops, under a flood of blinding light.

The children, at least, had those short, sleeveless uniforms. Most of the glass school's teachers were Sisters of Mercy, teaching in black habits that, according to Vincentian lore, would get bleached out by the sunlight.

And of course there's the delightful image of children tromping to school on a freezing February day to trade their wool mittens and boots for sun suits and sunglasses. May childhood ever be home to such absurdities.

---

1. The house, at 994 Madison Avenue, had belonged to a man named George Hawley, and before that to his in-laws, the Amsdells. George married Theodora Millard Amsdell in 1892. Beer made the family fortune: Theodora's father, Theodore Amsdell, had been co-owner of Amsdell Bros. Brewery; later, he and George bought the Dobler Brewery. George and Theodora shared a love of gardening and would send flowers from their greenhouses to Albany hospital wards. Upon his death in 1928, George, having no children, left his estate to the Albany Hospital, which sold it to St. Vincent's. Today, the house is the College of Saint Rose's Huether School of Business. The Amsdells, by the way, were the house's second owners; it had been built for Charles J. Peabody, Pratt and Logan's partner in early Pine Hills development.

"I didn't know how it would work," Father Charles told the *Knickerbocker News* in 1938. "I didn't know what effect the sun would have on the children nor what the heat bills would be in the winter. But the experiment has turned out beautifully. The children wear uniforms which permit as much exposure to the sun as decency allows. They have a fine tan all winter and it does them good. And we have found that, even in zero weather, the heat often can be turned off because we get enough heat from the sun."

He was so pleased with the results, in fact, that St. Vincent CCD added two more steel and glass school buildings by 1936.

The love affair with sunlight faded after Father Charles's death in 1944. We'll return to Vincentian later. For thousands of Albany children and their families, it was an anchor of neighborhood life—and, eventually, a bellwether of change.

Fred and Joan had two kids, both boys, before the war, and two more, both girls, after it. Fred was playing for a Dodgers farm team in North Carolina when Pearl Harbor was bombed, and instead of finding glory in Brooklyn he ended up in England with the army. Georgea's second husband, Howell Kase, went to the Philippines with the 4th Engineer Special Brigade. Don Henderson, the husband of Cornelia—or Nini, as they called her—became a supply officer for a navy flight squadron. Sylvia never married.

The war changed everything, from what you ate and where you worked to how many places you set at the dinner table. When the sirens went off up at the old Steamer 10 firehouse, you turned off the lights and pulled down the shades. The air raid warden, Greg remembers, was a man named Madigan. He went house to house to check for compliance, and he'd pound on your door if even a sliver of light was visible from the street. Also going house to house, at least along Morris and Myrtle Streets and around Ridgefield Park, was mail carrier Bill Gannon, who always rang the doorbell three times when he had a letter from a faraway son or husband to deliver. And if he spotted a long-overdue letter at the post office after hours, he'd telephone the family right away, so they wouldn't pass another night wondering when they'd hear from their soldier.

Pine Hills residents planted victory gardens and queued at School 16 for their ration books. Of course, even if you had your ration stamps and a fistful of cash, you could still be out of luck, because the stores might be sold out of what you needed.

At the Pine Hills Food Market, 1096 Madison Avenue, butcher Pete Girzone did what he could to help folks he knew were hurting. Staples like Carnation milk and Karo syrup, used to make baby formula, were in high demand. When Pete got some, he would save them to sell to the families who needed them most.

"He always favored families," his son, Ed Girzone, told me. "He took care of customers who had children. They were primary."

Pete would add a little extra food to the orders of folks who he knew needed more, or quietly cut the prices for families who couldn't afford much. Pete knew a thing or two about feeding a family: by the middle of the war, he and his wife had nine kids.

But that didn't stop Uncle Sam. Pete got his draft notice in early 1944. And he wasn't the only man drafted that year who had his hands full: Albany's iconic mayor, Erastus Corning II, was called up, too.

"We joked that they had finally reached the bottom of the barrel when they drafted us," another 1944 draftee, Stanley Zimmer, told Paul Grondahl, writer of Corning's excellent biography. "The war was almost over by then, we were older guys with families and we knew they must have been reaching way down to get us."

The mayor wouldn't take a deferment or seek a commission; he left City Hall in temporary hands and signed on as a regular grunt, just another of the Albany boys. He himself had two children. But people found it hard to swallow that a fellow with nine kids all under age fourteen was the government's best remaining candidate for army service. Pete Girzone became a bit of a cause célèbre, and his story ran in newspapers in the Capital Region and beyond. "Why draft him?" read one headline. "He's got an army of his own." A *Knickerbocker News* editorial used his situation to criticize FDR's draft policy.

A man of strong faith, Pete accepted this turn of events. God, he said, will take care of my family. Certain he was about to be inducted, he sold the Pine Hills Food Market.

Ed remembers his father coming into his bedroom early in the morning of the day he was to report.

"Be good to your mother," Ed remembers him whispering. "Do as she tells you. Don't disobey."

"Where are you going?"

"Shhh, go back to sleep."

A little while later, Ed got up and went into the kitchen and found his mom there, crying. "Say a prayer for your father," she told him.

Down at the induction station, the doctor informed Pete he had passed his physical and was on his way to the army. At that moment, Pete's own doctor entered the room.

"What are you doing here?" the doctor asked the butcher.

"I've just been approved."

"Like hell you have!" said his doctor. "Who approved you?" And to the other doctor, he said: "You approved him with that ulcerated varicose vein in his foot? That's criminal!"

Pete Girzone's feet and legs were in bad shape from years of standing behind the shop counter. His own doctor failed Pete on his medical exam and sent him home.

With the Pine Hills Food Market sold, Pete got a job at Williams Press in Menands, working nights, but lost it when he fell asleep in a boxcar. So he took himself and those painful feet down to the Port of Albany, joining the pool of day laborers hoping to get picked to work each morning.

Pete and his wife went on to have three more children. In 1947 he opened his market again, this time around the corner on West Lawrence Street.

Greg Spencer was a boy during the war, living with his mom, Joan, and baby brother, Keith, in his grandmother's house—my house. In one of his earliest memories he is walking along Madison Avenue, passing shops near the theater, holding his mother's hand. It didn't seem to him to be an unhappy time; they'd go for ice cream at Stittig's candy store, and as they walked home, she'd sing to him. Because the Stickles girls still liked to have their fun, their house "was almost like a clubhouse for returning servicemen," Greg remembered. "These were all people they went to school with, people they partied with before the war. They would sit around playing Glen Miller records, having beers and mixed drinks, and talking. There'd be maybe eight or ten people, sitting around in a circle, laughing." Young Greg would sit in a chair in the corner of the living room and watch.

On a clear night when the front windows are open, we can sometimes hear trains from over in the West Albany yards. One time, Greg was sitting in the living room with his mom, his aunts, and a handful of servicemen when the sound of a train whistle floated across the night. "And all of a sudden I remember a guy jumped up," Greg remembered, "and he said, 'What time is it? Holy shit, I have to get on that train!'" The soldier grabbed his bag and ran.

Childhood is childhood, and for Greg and the other kids on West Lawrence Street there were movies to see up at the Madison and baseball games to play. The brick intersection of Ryckman, West Lawrence, and Park was their diamond. Gerry Conway, one of Greg's childhood friends, stood with me in that intersection one spring day and told me this story: Wartime gas shortages meant lots of deliveries were still made by horse-drawn wagons. Boys used the inevitable manure piles as bases. After the manure had sat for a day or so it was dry and dusty—"but when you slid in it a day early," Gerry remembered, "your dungarees, as we called them, would get a little bit . . . stinky?" Angry mothers, scrubbing out the stains, would scold their sons: "I told you not to slide!" A trifle, indeed, compared to a shot at streetball glory.

Gerry, by the way, grew up just down the street from Greg in a house full of maiden great-aunts. One of them was Greg's grandmother's lifelong friend, Winnie McCormack.

In the 1940s, the Pine Hills was part of the Thirteenth Ward, which had given twenty-five hundred men to the armed forces by the middle of the war, according to one newspaper account. When the neighborhood wanted to erect a monument to its service members, it reportedly received a donation of at least a dollar from every single household in the ward—all forty-five hundred of them. Fourteen feet of Vermont granite, the monument was dedicated on November 11, 1944, up at the old Madison-Western Junction, with a priest and a rabbi in attendance, and members of the American Legion, and the Fort Crailo Band playing patriotic standards.

Chosen to unveil the memorial was an Albany woman who had seven sons in the service. Mrs. Josephine Ravida—the newspaper called her Mary, heaven knows why—had given Jerome, Joseph, Sebastian, Angelo, Charles, and Michael to the army, and Dominic to the navy. A 1946 *Knick News* article noted that the Ravidas had set the Capital Region record for "one family's contribution to the military service."

It was a heavy honor to bear, said Mrs. Ravida's son Thomas. "It was a great concern," he told me. "Especially since they were all *in* the war—they weren't stationed down at Fort Dix."

Mrs. Ravida had eleven children in all. The baby of the family, Thomas attended the monument's unveiling with his mother when he was eleven years old. Today, he's the only one of the Ravida children still living.

How did his mother hold up during the war years? "She did all right," Thomas said. "She did all right. It was kind of tough for her, but she did all right."

All seven of Mrs. Ravida's sons made it home safely. So did the Stickles girls' husbands.

On August 14, 1945, when the news of Japan's surrender came over the radio, "Everybody came roaring out of their doors," said Gerry Conway. Revelers poured into the streets of the Pine Hills, banging on pots with big metal spoons and crying, "We won the war!" The firehouse sirens blared and all the church bells rang. It was the same all over the city: downtown streets were choked with people cheering, honking horns, setting off firecrackers. Office workers poured makeshift confetti out of upstairs windows, and banks and businesses closed to let the people celebrate. "Peace Bursts Like a Bomb Over Albany As Entire City Explodes Into Celebration," a *Knick News* headline read. Wartime metaphors would take a little time to unlearn.

Greg remembers the day his dad came home: "We went down to Union Station, me and Mom and Keith," he said. Keith was Greg's younger brother. "Mom went running up; she hadn't seen him in two and a half years."

When they got to the house, Dad took the chair in the living room corner, the one Greg liked to sit in. "He had his duffel bag; he opened it, and he started taking things out. He had a German helmet in there, with an eagle on it. I can still remember the smell of the leather around the brim. I never forgot that smell."

"I remember sitting there not really knowing who he was. I mean, I knew he was my father, but I didn't know him."

All over the neighborhood, the city, and the country, families were getting to know each other again. It was a bittersweet celebration, and they had earned every moment of it.

Marguerite "Dotty" Claffee was born in Albany in 1879. Here, she poses with her father, Morris Claffee, in 1885. Courtesy of Crystal Wortsman.

Dotty and Win—Marguerite Claffee and Winnie McCormack—travel companions, best friends, and eventually West Lawrence Street neighbors. Undated image from the days before Marguerite's marriage. Courtesy of the Spencer family.

The newlyweds: George and Marguerite Stickles, 1912, in front of one of George's beloved automobiles. Courtesy of the Spencer family.

This is the photo of his lovely girls that George carried with him in a leather wallet. Clockwise from the top: Joan, Cornelia, Georgea, and Sylvia. 1925. Courtesy of the Spencer family.

Here they are again, perhaps 10 years later, in the same places. Courtesy of the Spencer family.

Cover of the program for the Madison Theatre's opening gala, May 29, 1929.

It's no Ridgefield toboggan run, but at least you're close to home when your toes get cold: The four Stickles sisters are poised on a sled atop the rise of West Lawrence Street, just outside their front door. From left, Sylvia, Cornelia, Joan, and Georgea. The photo's dated 1932. Courtesy of the Spencer family.

Looking east along Madison Avenue, south side, from the corner of West Lawrence, 1934. Courtesy of the Albany County Hall of Records Archival Collection.

For students at the Vincentian Institute's Child Culture Division, also known as the glass school, the future was bright—and usually, so was the present. This *Knickerbocker News* photo was taken September 11, 1936. Courtesy of the *Times Union*.

Traveling again: Marguerite Stickles poses with her daughters at the train station in 1939 ahead of a trip to Canada. Courtesy of the Spencer family.

Madison Avenue at West Lawrence, looking west. The photo is undated, but the mix of businesses here puts it at about 1940–41. Courtesy of the Albany Public Library.

Joan Stickles Spencer and Fred Spencer sat for this portrait sometime in the late 1930s; they were married in 1934. Courtesy of the Spencer family.

"The Bowling Show Place of AMERICA!"—and it's right here in the Pine Hills: The Playdium opened on Ontario Street on November 10, 1940. This advertisement, which ran in the *Times-Union* the previous day, promised all-night bowling, "a most unusual restaurant," and a separate wing for afternoon teas and Mah Jong parties.

Joan and youngster Greg in the back yard of the house on West Lawrence Street, 1942. Courtesy of the Spencer family.

UNCLE SAM BECKONS—The fact that he is the father of nine children, ranging in age from two to 13, was no barrier to placing Peter J. Girzone in 1-A, and shortly the Madison avenue meat market proprietor will appear at the Albany Induction station for a physical examination. Left to right are: James, 11; Loraine, four; Margaret Mary, five; Mrs. Girzone; Cecelia, two; Mr. Girzone; Mary, three; Joseph, 13, and William, 10, Eleanor, eight, and Edward, seven, are seated on the floor.

—Times-Union Staff Photo.

"Uncle Sam Beckons," read the cutline on this *Times-Union* photo on February 3, 1944, after Pine Hills butcher (and father of nine) Pete Girzone got his draft notice. Courtesy of the *Times Union*.

Madison Avenue between South Allen and West Lawrence. Undated, but the businesses shown here put it after 1940. Courtesy of the Albany Public Library.

The Hard Road

The day I brought a light into my attic and discovered the flapper sketch between the rafters, I found something else, too.

At first it looked like just a smear of white, maybe chalk or crayon. Remembering the other side of the attic, where the ceiling is tagged "Georgie" in white block capitals, I shifted my lamp to give this smudge a closer look. I could make out blurred letters, in some places only a waxy shadow: *Sylvia*, it said. It *was* a name, but it had been rubbed out.

At that time, I hadn't known about Sylvia at all. I had just begun researching the history of my house and its previous residents, but I had seen Joan and Georgea's obituaries. They mentioned only each other and their sister Cornelia as siblings. Where was Sylvia?

It was my first glimpse of the trials the Stickles sisters faced in the years after World War Two.

Housing was scarce after the men came home, and for a time Marguerite and Sylvia took everyone in: Joan and Fred and their growing family, plus Nini and Don and their son. This is a five-bedroom house, but that crowd would have pushed it to the limit. "Oh, the fights over the bathroom," recalls Greg.

Georgea and her husband moved into a place of their own. Eventually, so did Cornelia's family. Sylvia, still single, stayed on with her mother in the West Lawrence Street house. Joan and Fred Spencer and their children did too.

Fred remained in the service after the war, first overseeing the installation of gyms and athletic clubs on military bases and then becoming one of Albany's top recruiters. "He was very proud of his work," Greg said of his father. And he was very good at it. Fred was popular with the other men, and he liked to have a drink or two with them after work. "He was a great drinking buddy when he was out in the bars," Greg said. "Not so much when he got home."

Fred was an alcoholic. So was Joan. And so were Greg's aunts, Georgea and Sylvia.

The 119 Club on Dana Avenue was Fred's favorite watering hole, a place with cold cuts, eggs, and beer, and Campbell's Soup behind the bar so you could tell the bartender to heat you up a can. It was run by two brothers, John and Charles Leonard, one an ex-boxer and the other a veteran of both world wars. Greg remembers heading downtown one morning with his dad to buy shoes. They never made it: Greg sat and waited while his father stopped off to tip one back at the 119 Club. He waited until the daylight drained from the sky.

Sometimes, Joan would go out with Fred. More often, she drank alone. She'd send Greg, seven or eight years old, out with a five-dollar bill to fetch her a bottle from the store on the corner of Madison and West Lawrence.

It was not an easy way to grow up.

"I knew she was a drunk," Greg said. "Dad was a drunk. I kept trying to hide it from all my friends."

Greg remembers watching his dad come home in a taxi. Still a kid, he was across the street at the Calvary Church, hiding in the bushes as his father struggled to pull himself up the sixteen steps to the house. "I was afraid someone was going to see Dad trying to get up the stairs, because he was so drunk. And afraid to go home because I knew what was going to be happening in there." It was a scene he'd witnessed more than once. Greg would just hope his father passed out right away. But often, Fred didn't. "And the screaming would start," he said.

There were some bad years. "That middle hall"—our upstairs landing, with the bedrooms radiating off of it—"it was like the ring at Madison Square Garden. People would come out of those rooms and start screaming and fighting." Once in a while the police would come, called in by the neighbors or even Marguerite herself. "Cops would come and get my dad periodically," Greg remembers. "But he knew all the cops."

One night in the mid-1950s, a teenage Greg couldn't take it any more. It was just another drunken rage, but this time it got physical. Greg stepped in, and he knocked his father down.

"I was a strong kid," Greg said. "I never realized that before. From that point on I wasn't afraid of him." He told his father, "Don't you ever touch anyone in the family again." And he never did.

This was in the small front bedroom, the one we use for guests. It's unsettling to know the space so intimately, the cramped room, the spot on the wooden floor where Fred fell, a scene in a rite of passage no kid should have to endure.

Georgea, the second oldest of the Stickles girls, didn't think she had a problem. She was just a beer drinker, after all, and she didn't drink every day. "I drank between drunks and seemed—what I thought—to get away with it," Georgea said in a speech recorded years later. "I wouldn't get in trouble, the cops wouldn't get into the act, I wouldn't black out or pass out."

But when she drank, she binged. In time, the blackouts caught up to her.

Georgea's first husband left her over her drinking. Her second husband did the same. "I didn't think I was all that bad," she said. "[My husband] had warned me, threatened me for a year, and told me I had to do something about this drinking or he'd get rid of me. And he did. And I thought, he had the nerve. He'll be sorry."

They'd been living down in Florida, in the family's Miami house, and she came back to her childhood home on West Lawrence Street. Her husband sent her plane fare, told her he would take her back—"The stipulation was that I would never get a glass in my hand again."

"I didn't love him that much," Georgea said. She stayed in Albany.

As the adults around them struggled with alcoholism, the children of the Spencer family had a stabilizing force: their grandmother, Marguerite Stickles.

"She was the glue that kept that place together, no doubt about it," said Greg.

To the kids, Marguerite was Bah, a nickname that came from her affectionately dismissive response to childhood nonsense: "Oh, bah," she'd say, smiling, as she waved their silliness away with her hands. Bah was gentle and kind, her grey hair pinned in a bun stuck through with pencils, and nothing ever fazed her. "She was a terrible cook," remembered Greg, smiling. "She was awful. She'd cook everything in a frying pan and burn it. Everything she ever made she burned." But she was a great storyteller (her riveting memoir makes that clear), and if she came across something funny, a joke or a news item, she'd clip it from the paper and add it to the pages of notes she kept under the oilcloth that covered the kitchen table. When a child climbed onto her lap and needed a story, she'd have her material ready. Marguerite could even be coaxed into playing "Chariot Race" for the kids once in a while on the upright piano in the foyer. Those long-ago lessons on Clinton Avenue were never forgotten.

"She was my savior," Greg said. "She brought me up. She got me over the hump, till my mother got sober when I was thirteen."

And just as his Bah had done decades before, Greg would escape to the movies. Georgea's third father-in-law ran the Madison Theatre, so Greg had a pass. "When things would get hairy at the house," Greg said, "I'd go up there."

Then there was Sylvia.

I've tried to get to know Sylvia, as best I could from all these decades away. The few fragments I've found suggest a young woman with a quick mind and a playful soul. As a kid she collected autographs and entered newspaper contests. Harry Neigher, a 1930s *Times-Union* cartoonist-columnist who did a "Believe It or Not"-style feature on local life called "Take It or Leave It," named young Sylvia "one of my best reporters" and featured her letters to him several times. In one, the twelve-year-old wrote to tell him she'd discovered that in Nassau village, a Mrs. Lyon lived across the street from a Mr. Lamb. The next month, she wrote him again with more Nassau neighbor pairings: Rowe and Fite, Bell and Clapper, Wood and Waters, Angell and Savage, Cook and King, File and Steele, Brown and Green.

It's her handwriting, I believe, labeling many of the photographs in the old Stickles family albums. In one, Sylvia stands out in West Lawrence Street, near its corner with Morris, in oxfords and a drop-waist dress. She squints in the low afternoon sun, hands joined loosely at her waist. Behind her, her shadow falls sharp across the brick pavers, stretching out until its head rests on the curb. The photograph is labeled, simply, "ME."

"I loved Sylvia because she loved music," said Greg's sister, Lynn. "She used to invite me in her room; she had a Victrola, and she'd play Mario Lanza." Sylvia's room was the smaller back bedroom, the one with the north-facing window that never gets enough sun. But it has one thing going for it: it's the room that opens onto the upstairs back porch.

Sylvia hid from life in that second-floor bedroom, sending her sister Joan out to get her quarts of Dobler beer, which she would keep out on her porch. She would drink four or five quarts a day. Greg remembers her making prank calls, playing a 78 rpm record of the radio play "Sorry, Wrong Number" over the phone at people and laughing and laughing. In those days, it seemed to him, "she lived in a fantasy world."

As an alcoholic Sylvia was barely functional. It's a wonder, Greg said, that she made it down to Florida at all in 1952. That fall, Georgea and her husband Howell Kase were living in the family's Miami house when Marguerite and Sylvia went down to pass the winter months with them. A canal ran behind the house. Sylvia, thirty-four years old, drowned in it on Halloween night.

Earlier that evening, she had hit the bars with a fellow she'd known in Albany. His name was John Gilleran, and he had gone to Miami in August to find work. "We must have had as many as 20 drinks of beer, wine or whiskey. I can't remember how many," the police said Gilleran told them. He was "so drunk," police told the newspapers, "that he could not remember the names of the bars he visited."

Gilleran told police it was Sylvia who suggested they take a swim when they returned to her sister's house around midnight. She left her skirt on her sister's back porch and jumped in the canal in her blouse and underwear. Gilleran stripped down and jumped in, too. When he vomited in the water, Sylvia helped him climb out. She didn't follow him. A few minutes later, a neighbor saw Gilleran running along the canal, calling, "Sylvia!" Then Gilleran ran to the house and woke Georgea and Marguerite.

"Sylvia must be hiding in the canal," he said. "I can't find her."

The police questioned Gilleran for days, trying to determine if he was responsible in some way for her death. The newspapers dredged up that he'd once been a mental patient in the Hudson River State Hospital down in Poughkeepsie. He'd been arrested for passing bad checks. He had a wife and four children back in Albany.

Sylvia's death was national news in the first week of November 1952. Papers around the country carried the story of the "attractive blonde," the "comely Albany girl" whose excesses led to her death. Nearly all of the stories pointed out that she had been clad only in her blouse, bra, and panties when she died. For them, a sensational story. For the family, the loss of a sister and daughter.

And a turning point.

Joan was the first to get sober after Sylvia's death, then Georgea, then Fred. That remarkable story will be their next chapter: how, for the rest of their lives, the Stickles and Spencer families devoted their energy to pulling others up with them.

12

Play

The last of the old tree is gone.

The guy with the grinder came and removed the ragged stump one day while I was out shopping. I got home to find the corner of my yard raked strangely smooth, as if the tree had never been there at all.

Our property came with just this one tree, a scraggly conifer of some sort. It was a very tall tree. It provided no shade, no aesthetics, no branches for climbing. Pretty useless, as far as human-tree interaction goes. About as interesting as a pole. Still, we hadn't planned to remove it—after all, it was our only tree. And we did wonder if it could have been one of the original pines of the Pine Hills, one of those that bird lover Henry Slack had said were preserved here and there in the backyards of the newly built neighborhood.

But some things change because you change them. Other things change with or without you.

The tree fell down some years ago on the night our new playhouse came in, a symmetry we appreciated. Their tales are woven together in the story of how our house became, little by little, our own.

When I was a kid I had always wanted a playhouse. I had a swing set in my yard, which was fun, but I was a story-making girl: a playhouse could be a log cabin, a school, a little shop, whatever I wanted. And the fun I'd have decorating it, with tiny everything! Well, since one of the side benefits of being a mom is the roundabout indulgence of your childhood self, I tracked down a playhouse on Craigslist from a Guilderland family whose girls had outgrown it. And I set my husband to the task of figuring out how to get it here.

The truck rental place told Gary that all the flatbeds had been reserved for the next two months, so he ended up with the largest moving van on the lot—it was the only vehicle tall enough to accommodate the seven-foot-plus playhouse roof. I was at work that evening, so I have no idea how Gary and his friends got that house into the truck. There was some rolling on logs, apparently, some heaving and ho-ing, a great deal of cursing. The thing might have been built out of scrap lumber, but it's solid. (And big! It easily fits two kids and a grown-up for a tea party, plus a toy oven, a little table, two chairs, some shelves, a tiny broom, a pantry full of miniature plastic food . . . but I digress.)

Anyway, into the truck went the playhouse. And then it hit: one of those sudden, violent summer storms. The guys were marooned in the trailer as it rocked and swayed in the wind, rain on metal a vibrating roar. When the sky calmed to an angry yellow-grey, branches and power lines lay everywhere. It took them forty minutes to travel four miles back to our neighborhood; street after street was blocked with debris.

When I think of Gary and friends inching that truck backwards between two rows of parked cars on Morris, our side street, and up our neighbors' driveway, then removing a fence so they could *unload a building*—by hand!—into our yard—well, it's a wonder any of our friends are still speaking to us and a wonder that I wasn't banished to sleep on the couch for a week. By that point, I think, it seemed bigger than my bad planning, more like a cosmic test: Gary stepped out of the rig to find our tree horizontal, the fence crushed beneath it.

The wind had snapped the tree trunk about six or seven feet above the ground. It fell away from our house, its scraggly top just brushing a 1920s garage behind an apartment house on Morris Street. There were no buildings in the path it chose, thank goodness, but parked behind our broken fence was a neighbor's car. Gary held his breath as he went to inspect the damage: the tree had sheared off the front license plate. Other than that, the car didn't have a scratch.

We couldn't have asked for a tidier tree removal.

After my shift I came home to a strangely dark and quiet street— the power was out across the neighborhood—and went straight out back.

The physics of the yard had changed: on one side, the new, heavy bulk of the playhouse; on the other, the oddly empty stripe of sky.

I reached up and felt the jagged edges where the tree had snapped and marveled at the length of it, all stretched out across the neighbor's property. I felt a little sadness. I'd never liked that tree, but it was old, and I respect that.

A friend helped us chop it down to stump level. I planted flowers inside it, and that's how it stayed for the next few years. I almost liked the stump better than I had the tree. My expectations for stumps are lower, I guess.

Since they had a playhouse, our daughters, of course, always pined for one of those swing/slide/play structure combos.

"Or how about a treehouse?" asked one. "Could we have a treehouse?"

"We don't have a tree."

"We used to."

"It fell down. It wasn't the right kind of tree anyway."

"We could plant a new one."

"By the time it grows big enough to hold a treehouse, *your* children would be able to play in it."

The part of me that lacks appreciation for irony has been caught thinking, Why can't you just be grateful for what you have? But the rest of me pricked up when friends offered us a tower, one of those wooden things with a rope ladder and long yellow slide. Their daughter had outgrown it. It was ours if we had a place for it.

And we considered that if the stump came out, we would.

Again with a crew of friends—okay, actually, they were my sister's[1] friends, because we can't ask anyone to move something for us, ever again—we carried the tower on our shoulders from North Pine Avenue to West Lawrence Street. Drivers gawked at the seven of us and our ridiculous load. Wise pedestrians crossed to the other side of the street.

So the tower became a two-story apartment, and the playhouse became the store where the kids did their shopping. Or the tower was

1. Seventeen years younger than I, she came to the Capital Region in 2008 to attend RPI, providing me, for a short time at least, with local family whose good nature I could exploit.

a boat in a sea of lava, and they could reach Superhero Headquarters only by leaping from slide to chair to bench.

When we set the tower in place, Gary and I climbed up in it and surveyed the lively chaos of the yard: the playhouse and the hammock, the picnic table and clotheslines and the mismatched fences overgrown with Marguerite's old grapevines. It's never going to be one of those manicured urban-hipster gardens I admire on Historic Albany house tours. But to us, it's something better.

The corner of the yard where the playhouse went in had been, in the Spencer children's era, a backyard dirt pile where they played trucks and made mud pies. One day in the 1950s Greg's sister Lynn and her best friend sat there together, spit into their hands, swore an oath to be blood sisters, and buried a box of—something. Lynn doesn't remember. "Treasure," she said.

I've tried to keep that story quiet; I don't think my daughters could stand knowing there could be buried treasure under the playhouse. I'd find them out there one night with a crowbar, trying to tip the thing off its blocks. And then, if I'm being honest, I'd have to admit my kids would probably have had just as much fun if I'd skipped the playhouse and just turned them loose in a pile of dirt.

Talk to people of a certain age and you can get dazzled by an image of Pine Hills in the golden era of childhood: a safe world of empty-lot kickball, Saturday double features, and staying out on your bikes until nightfall. I'm clear-eyed enough to know it wasn't that simple. But I can also recognize the truth in what they say: for good or ill, there was an innocence to a 1950s childhood, and it offered freedoms that my kids will probably never have.

Two places seemed to embody the best of that spirit: the Partridge Street Little League fields and the Madison Theatre.

In the 1950s the Madison belonged to every kid in the neighborhood. Public school and Vincentian, Manning Boulevard mansion and Ontario Street flat—they all met on Saturdays in the velvet hall. A couple of coins would get you a double feature, plus cartoons and a serial. Blown your allowance already? Join the group in the alleyway: one kid would pay admission, then he'd open the fire door and let ten more rush in. "Two or three would get caught," Greg remembers, but the others would make it—not a bad percentage. "The usher going around with his flashlight, the kids slinking down in their seats," Greg recalled. "But the place was so full of kids he couldn't find them."

Every Saturday Greg, Keith, and their pals would be at the Madison eating jujubes, leading, for Greg at least, to a standing Tuesday gig at Dr. McMahon's to get his fillings fixed. Others would spring for root beer floats or raspberry sundaes at Stittig's ice cream counter after the show.

Then there was the night in 1952 when some kid brought his older brother's gun with him to the Madison to show his friends. In the middle of Doris Day's *I'll See You in My Dreams* the gun went off, and the bullet went through the seat in front of him. Fourteen-year-old Theodore Wendell, a freshman at Albany Academy, was the kid sitting in that seat. The bullet pierced his left lung. Things looked dicey for him for a time, but he made it, and while in the hospital he received a telegram from a sympathetic Eddie Waitkus, first baseman for the Philadelphia Phillies. Eddie had been shot in the chest by a crazed fan in 1949, but he fought his way up to be declared baseball's Comeback King of 1950.

Greg wasn't at the Madison that night, but later he found Theodore's seat and stuck his finger in the bullet hole. Never would Greg sit in that chair. Never not ever.

The shooting happened at the back of the theater, where boys always sat. Up front, far left side, was where the older kids gathered on date nights. A big mixed group, guys and girls, would go on Friday nights, and again on Sunday afternoons because the movies had changed. After the show they'd all head up the street for snacks at the Madison Diner, then the guys would peel away one by one to walk their girls home.

That's how Chris Cohan remembers it, at least. Chris had been going to the Madison since—well, he can't remember exactly, but he does recall that the first movie he saw there was the cartoon version of *Gulliver's Travels,* which would put it about 1939, when he was in grade school. He still remembers scenes from that movie, though he's never seen it since. The Madison was one of the landmarks of his childhood: "Over the years growing up I must have spent hundreds of hours in there."

Chris was seven or eight years older than Greg, so by the time Chris was sitting up front with his girl, Greg was probably huddled in the back, chomping on jujubes and thinking about baseball, because movies were big but baseball was bigger, and if you were a boy in Albany in 1952 you were on the cusp of the biggest thing ever to happen in the Pine Hills.

Little League baseball debuted in Albany that summer, when the Junior Chamber of Commerce founded National Little League of Albany. For the first time kids would have a real place to play—not manure-pile bases in the intersection of Ryckman and Park, not some empty lot littered with broken glass, but a real diamond with real bases, with dugouts and even a clubhouse. True, there was a neighborhood ball field at the Ridgefield athletics grounds, but at that time Ridgefield was YMCA property, and high school and college teams had dibs.

"It was an exciting thing to have your own little ball park instead of having to sneak into Ridgefield to play baseball" when the teenagers weren't around, said Tom Whitney, one of the boys who played Little League ball that first season. "It was a great opportunity."

Many Pine Hills boys, Whitney among them, volunteered to help the Jaycees clear the land they'd chosen, a vacant lot at Woodlawn and Partridge that had become an unofficial dump. The volunteers built a grandstand and put in the diamond with its sixty-foot baselines. A donated railroad boxcar became the clubhouse. The field was christened Johnny Evers Memorial Park, after the major-leaguer of "Tinker to Evers to Chance" fame, who hailed from Troy and who had died in Albany a few years before, in 1947.

"We were excited," said Greg Spencer, who was another of the inaugural players. "This was a big deal. Everybody started reading up on Little League and the rules." A shop on upper Madison got in a stock of "official Little League shoes" and made a killing.

There were to be four teams that first year: the Patroons, the Clinchers, the Trading Ports, and the Red Sox (really? In Yankees territory?). It was the talk of the schools: The league would hold tryouts to fill the teams. There were spots for about sixty Albany boys.

The ones who made the teams were notified by telephone. Guys couldn't wait to share their news: "I'm on the Patroons!" "I'm on the Clinchers!"

But not Greg Spencer. "Everybody's sitting by the phone, and I don't get my telephone call," he said. "I *don't get a call*. I wasn't picked. I threw myself on the bed and cried."

Greg knew he was a good ball player, just as his dad had been. He wondered if he wasn't picked because his dad wasn't around to advocate for him. (Fred was stationed elsewhere that spring.) But if there's one thing Greg had learned, it was that if he wanted something, he was going to have to go after it himself.

Shortly before the season started, he showed up with his glove at a Patroons practice down at Ridgefield. "I went up to the coach and said, 'I'm better than these guys; I should have been picked. I want to be on the team.'"

"I'm really sorry," said the manager, Nate Boynton. "There's nothing I can do."

"I want to play," Greg persisted. "Should I go to one of the other teams?"

Right then, Greg said, "something clicked" with Boynton. "And he said, 'I just got a call about a kid on the team; he might have broken his ankle. Come back at the next practice in two days.'" Greg came back; the other boy's ankle was indeed broken, and Boynton put Greg on the team.

He started at third base. After six games or so he was put in as a relief pitcher and gave what the newspaper called a "masterful" performance: he held the Red Sox hitless for two and a half innings and allowed the Patroons to escape with the win. At the 1952 end-of-season awards breakfast, Greg won the trophy for Most Improved Player. He was a pitcher from then on—not only in Little League, but on through a stellar local sports career at Vincentian and then Siena College. And he still remembers Nate Boynton for giving him his first break.

Greg's longtime friend Gerry Conway felt he just *had* to make the team, too—but he had a big problem: his family had moved out to McKownville. So he registered using his old address, his grandmother's house on West Lawrence Street. He shone at the tryouts—he was fast and he could hit—but his fib caught up to him. "Someone turned me in," Gerry said. "I got bounced."

Later that season, a bitter Gerry was down at the field watching a game through the fence when a foul ball came right down on him.

Then, as now, the league asks for foul balls to be returned, but Gerry didn't feel he owed them anything. When he caught that ball he took off running. He sprinted away from the field, but as he ran he realized he could hear footsteps behind him, and they were gaining.

"The next thing I know there's a hand coming at me from behind," Gerry said. It was Jake Dalton, manager of the Clinchers. Dalton brought Gerry back to the ball park and made him hand in the ball in front of everyone.

"It was humiliating," Gerry said. He added with a rueful smile: "I hated Jake Dalton."

People came from all over the city to watch the Little League's Saturday opener on June 7, 1952.

"The place was mobbed," Greg said, "and all the dignitaries were there. It was a really big deal." He wasn't kidding: Nearly a thousand people turned up to watch the double-header, according to the papers. They filled the grandstand and lined the fences. Mayor Corning was there, of course, and a marine corps color guard and a band from Menands. John Boyd Thacher, the former mayor and judge, threw out the ceremonial first pitch.

The local newspapers covered not only the opener but the whole Little League season pretty thoroughly; the sports editors of the *Times Union* and the *Knickerbocker News* had been made league commissioners, a canny move on somebody's part. Those two-paragraph game write-ups make me smile, the line scores and the boys listed by last name: kind of small town but also kind of big time, as if these games meant something, which of course they did.

It wasn't all smooth that first year. Take, for example, the infield, which coughed up debris from its corner-dump days that whole first season.

"It was still rough," Greg remembered. "There were still a lot of rocks and brick chips. You took your life in your hands" out there. Before each game they'd send the players to pick rocks out of the base paths. According to the boys of the Pine Hills, here's how you hit a triple at Evers Field: "Hit a rock in the infield, bounce over the infielder's head, hit another rock in the outfield and bounce over the outfielder's head."

Sixty years on, men still remember the talent of some of their teammates, like Alex Sokaris ("He was the toughest and the fastest"), Paul Ellenbogen ("When Paul pitched, we won") and Johnny Leonard ("By his third year he was breaking every record").

"Some of those guys were great athletes," said Tom Whitney, who was left fielder for the Trading Ports. "The rest of us were just going along and trying to have fun."

Greg can go face by face through the Patroons' team picture from that first year and tell the boys' futures: this one became a doctor, that one a lawyer, that one a banker, that one a judge. And then there was Freddie Neulander. Fritz, they called him. He grew up just down the street from Greg, on Ryckman. He became a New Jersey rabbi, and he was convicted of paying two men to kill his wife in 1994. Still serving a prison sentence, Neulander maintains his innocence.

All four teams ended the eighteen-game inaugural season with nine wins and nine losses. The Albany all-star team made it to the district semifinals, beating Rensselaer-Columbia County and Hudson before being shut out, 7-0, by Schenectady. Two years later, the boys from Schenectady would win it all, becoming 1954 Little League World Series champions.

The National Little League is still playing over at the Partridge Street fields. Nowadays it's a pretty sophisticated operation, with a pitching cage, a press box, picnic tables, and a concession stand that serves up anything that can be cooked in a deep fryer. About three hundred kids play every year, both boys and girls, learning sportsmanship and teamwork and maybe a little patience. Some years ago, my daughter was one of them. She didn't take to it—something about feeling uneasy with nine-year-olds throwing balls at her head—but *I* enjoyed the experience more than I expected. I'm not much of a sports mom; I'm no good at making small talk with the other parents, so I usually go off in a corner by myself and pretend to be on my phone. But the league's expectation is that the parents will pitch in, doing shifts in the concession stand. Somewhere during all those practices and all those games you start to see the other parents not as strangers but as neighbors, and one day you recognize them in the library or at the store, and you remember that there are some things we just can't teach, or learn, in our own backyards.

Late in the season, a boy on my daughter's team came up to bat. Things had not been going well for him at the plate, and frustration came off him in waves. The coach shouted encouragement: "This is your time." And wouldn't you know the kid hit it over the back fence. It was the only homer I saw anyone hit, all season. His dugout emptied as his teammates ran to meet him at home plate. And that, more than the hit or even the win, was the moment of triumph.

13

The Gentle Man with the Meat Cleaver

Remember the butcher with the army of kids and the bad feet? His story didn't end with the war.

Pete Girzone opened his second shop, Peter's Market, here on West Lawrence Street in the years after World War II. If the little cinderblock shop was still standing, I'd be able to see it from my front steps. It was tucked behind a Madison Avenue liquor store and right across the street—spitting distance—from the Miracle Market, the grocery store that moved into the old Pine Hills movie house in the early 1930s, after silent films died their silent death.

"It was a little two-bit store, only a postage stamp size," remembered Father Joseph Girzone, Pete's oldest son. "There were two big supermarkets right nearby—how could he open a store? He would say, 'I have my own clientele.'"

That clientele included state officials, judges, lawyers, doctors, and other well-to-do Pine Hills homeowners. Peter Girzone knew what they liked: high-quality meat cut just the way they wanted. But that wasn't all that kept them coming back. Pete was a man of powerful faith and a keen observer of human nature. Some of those same prominent Albanians whose iceboxes he kept stocked could be found sitting in his market late into the night, talking spirituality and politics with the butcher.

October 1947 was a terrible time to be opening a butcher shop. Meat shortages and record-high prices were front-page news. And there was more to come: President Truman was pushing for restaurants and homes to adopt "meatless Tuesdays" to help feed postwar Europe. Albany's meat

137

dealers told the *Times-Union* early that month that "sales are off so much anyway because of high prices that a meatless day won't make much difference."

And there was stiff competition for those dwindling sales. Albany's 1948 business directory lists nearly two full columns of retail butchers: 123 entries, some with more than one location. There were about two and a half pages of retail grocers—hundreds of little shops across the city, including five other grocery stores in the upper Madison area.

It was completely characteristic of Peter Girzone that he went ahead and opened his little shop despite these warning signs: he lived every day by the belief that the big picture was in God's hands, and he was just going to do what he knew how to do. And the butcher business was what Pete knew. As a young man he had worked for the Tobin Packing Company in West Albany, and later he took a job at Johnston and Linsley's, a grocer's on Madison Avenue in the block between Allen and West Lawrence. Around 1934, with a growing family to support, Peter thought he'd go into business for himself. He opened the Pine Hills Food Market, a combination butcher counter/neighborhood market in space that today is part of Junior's Bar and Grill.

That's the market that Peter Girzone sold during the war, when he got his draft notice. In 1947, after some hard years as a day laborer, he took steps to open another butcher shop, on leased land around the corner from his old place. It was a concrete building, painted white, with a big "Canada Dry" logo on each side since they paid for the paint job. Inside, Pete scattered sawdust on the floor and put a picture of the Holy Family on the wall. A "big white beautiful Tobin truck," his sons remembered, pulled up and filled the freezer. He hung out his shingle: "Peter's Market. Quality Meats."

Like specialty shops of today, Peter's Market set itself apart by offering superior products and excellent service. "He knew his customers, knew they were fussy, and knew how to handle them," said Pete's son Ed, who like Joe worked alongside their father as a youth.

Pete wouldn't sell beer, cigarettes, or "magazines that would lead people astray," Joseph remembered. "He loved kids. Didn't want that stuff in the store." But he did get a second-hand ice cream cooler, and next to it he put a cigar box for money. Kids served themselves and made their own change, and the butcher would never look over to see if they did it right. A generation of Pine Hills kids remembers buying their popsicles in the little shop with the sawdust on the floor.

Albany's uptown elite kept Peter's Market in business for the next twenty years. But the butcher's heart belonged to the families that were struggling to get by.

Father Joe related a story on his blog about meeting an elderly woman in Maryland and, while chatting, discovering she used to live in Albany. As he told the story:

"Where did you live in Albany?"

"On North Allen Street."

"Oh, my gosh. My father had a butcher shop on Madison Avenue right around the corner from there."

"What was the name of his store?"

"Peter's Market, then Pine Hills Food Market."

The woman was shocked, and burst out, "I can't believe this. At that time, it was during the war and the Depression and I had nine children and my husband was away, and we were so poor. Your father kept us in food during all those years. I will never forget that man."

Talking to my brother tonight, I told him that story, and he almost had a heart attack. "I know those people. I used to work at Daddy's store then, and every week two little boys came in with a note and an envelope with two dollars and a little change in it. The note said they needed the ends of cold cuts, and the ends of bacon, if they still had them, and few other left over pieces of meat that would usually be thrown away. When Daddy read the note he told me to get new loaves of bologna and other cold cut meats and slice off the ends with four inches more slices. And get a new slab of bacon and start at the end and cut off five inches of slices. And Daddy would get cans of other things and put them all in bags. He would then tell the kids, 'There's too much money here. There's still enough for a bottle of soda for the two of you.' The boys were so thrilled. That was routine every week."

The Girzone children remember their father filling many orders that way, slipping extras in the bag and ending with: "You've got a little more money than you need here. Better take something out of the ice cream cooler." And the shop would buzz with the excitement of a little kid picking out a treat.

Ed once watched his father refuse to fill a judge's order for cow's liver and butter during the years when such things were scarce. Others would come in, the butcher figured, who needed them more.

Peter's insights and his unwavering faith led people to his shop even when they weren't looking to buy meat. "People would come in and just pour their hearts out to him," Father Joe remembered. And more than once the boys fell asleep on an empty shelf, or on a white apron spread atop bags of sawdust, as the men talked into the night.

The bad feet that had kept Peter out of the army never got better. He went to work every day with his legs wrapped in bandages, and he had to cut the backs out of his shoes in order to get into them. The butcher wasn't the sort to complain, but his children saw that he was suffering. One Christmas young Ed asked Santa for a doctor's kit so he could treat his father.

Unable to put overshoes on his swollen feet, Peter wore burlap bags over his shoes when he had to go out in the snow. It wasn't the sort of thing that would faze him.

"He was not ashamed of looking poor," Ed remembers. "We were not technically poor; he made sure we were well dressed. But he never cared about taking care of himself."

His brother agreed. "My father was comfortable doing without. He believed in being simple, like Jesus."

Joseph remembers one winter's morning when he and his father arrived to open the store and found a prominent Albany judge already waiting outside. The son remembers feeling a flash of embarrassment to see his father, with his worn overcoat and his bag-wrapped feet, next to the nattily dressed official.

The judge mentioned it.

"Quite an outfit you've got there," he said.

And the butcher had a quiet reply, one his son never forgot: "Yes, your honor. You have to have dignity."

More than once the well-heeled people Pete knew tried to give him things. He turned down an offer of a car and even a house, his sons recalled. "He believed God would provide what was needed, and no need to have more," Father Joe said.

So when he had an old car Peter Girzone would drive it from his home (in North Albany and, later, in Rensselaer County) to the Pine Hills, and when he didn't he would take the bus. When there were customers he would cut meat to their specifications, no matter how long it took or how many people were waiting. When there were no customers he would stand behind the counter and recite the Hail Mary. There were times when getting all the bills paid came down to the last few coins coming in at the end of the week, but it always got done somehow. "Worry and faith don't mix," he would tell his kids.

That faith shaped his life, and the lives of his children.

Joseph and Ed related to me a favorite story about their mother, Margaret, a story the family also told the *Washington Post* in a 1991 interview.

Here it is, as it appeared there:

Margaret, . . . hospitalized during one of her pregnancies, became so sick that her physician telephoned her husband, Peter, at his shop and told him to rush over.

[Girzone's son] Jim, who was in the store at the time, said he listened in disbelief as his father said, "No, I'm not coming over. She is going to be fine." Peter Girzone took Jim home, gathered all the children around him and prayed.

His wife, meanwhile, appeared to have died, and the physician covered her over with a bedsheet. A few minutes later, a nurse went in the room and screamed. Margaret

Girzone had said straight up in bed, asking, "What is this sheet doing over me?"

"You couldn't have a conversation with him," Ed said. "He was always teaching. I don't want to call it 'preaching'; he was teaching. Many times he said, 'If you're willing to listen, you're willing to learn.' I remembered that. And I would hang on every word."

"My father always encouraged being of service to others," Ed recalled. "He told me people should not be less off for having known me." Ed took this message to heart. When he was a young man, he said, "It was a burden. It boxed me in a corner." But it was a burden Ed found a way to bear, embarking on a decades-long career in clinical social work.

Joseph entered the seminary at age fourteen and was ordained in 1955. After years of service in Capital Region communities and elsewhere, his health prompted him to retire from the priesthood. In the early '80s, he began writing stories of a man, Joshua, who moved through a complex world with a simple message that could change everything: *love thy neighbor*. Father Girzone's books have sold millions of copies worldwide.

To people who had known the Pine Hills butcher, Ed told me, the *Joshua* books had another dimension, too. More than one person had remarked to him: " 'When [Joe] wrote *Joshua*, he was writing about your dad.' It was Daddy," Ed said.

Ed loved his father's shop so much that at one time he wanted to take over the store, but Peter said no. "It's not a good time for that," he told his son. When the youngest of the twelve kids graduated, he said, that's when he was going to turn the key for the last time.

Peter's Market closed around 1970, and the building was razed soon afterwards. The butcher was a prescient man: the way people shopped was changing, and the era of the big chain supermarkets was about to begin. Remember those 123 butcher shops listed in the 1948 business directory? The 1971 directory lists nineteen.

That year, 1971, there were three places to shop for food in the upper Madison business district: the A & P, the Pine Hills Food Market—still holding on after all those years—and Central Market, a Schenectady-based grocery that had bought out the Miracle Market folks in the mid-1950s. By 1975, Central Market, which changed its name to Price Chopper in 1973, was the only place left to buy groceries on upper Madison Avenue. Today, the store and its parking lot fill nearly a whole block of West Lawrence Street, from Madison Avenue to Morris. And on the other side of West Lawrence, the spot where Peter's Market stood is a narrow patch of weeds and broken blacktop.

My guess is that Peter wouldn't care.

Father Girzone remembers, "He always used to say, 'It's not how much you make; it's how much you give away. My family are my treasures. And I can take them all to heaven with me.'"

14

Pioneers

In the decade after Sylvia's death, her sisters, Joan and Georgea, and Joan's husband, Fred, fought and won their battles with alcohol. They could have returned to private life, caring for their families and quietly sharing their strength with their peers, as so many in recovery do. Instead, they chose to spend the rest of their lives fighting for others who suffered the same way they did.

Fred, Joan, and Georgea's story is tied up with the story of the early days of modern addiction care. And it's a story I can't tell without the help of Father Peter Young of Albany, a trailblazer in alcoholism treatment in the Capital Region, the state, and the nation.

In the 1950s, Father Young was a parish priest at St. John's Church, looking for ways to help the needy, the jobless, and the addicted in Albany's South End. St. John's was one of the few safety nets in the neighborhood, offering a health clinic, beds for the homeless, and assistance with finding a job or housing. He also provided help for addicts.

Today, we talk of alcoholism as a disease. But in other times it was considered a sin—and a crime. People saw it as a moral failing or a bum's affliction. Certainly not something that happened in *good* families. If you were publicly intoxicated you'd go to jail. The same homeless men were ending up in the drunk tank night after night, and Father Young wanted to do something to break the cycle. He became a court chaplain, and at the police lineup every morning the judge would give defendants a choice: "Do you want to go with Father Young, or do you want to go to jail?" The priest would give the men a place to stay, try to stabilize them. But he knew it wasn't enough. "It turned out to be a journey and a half to figure out how to help them," he told me.

Two men were watching Father Young as he came into court day after day. They were lawyers, defending many of the same guys Father Young was there to see. They were also members of the recovery community. "How can we help?" they asked the priest. And they invited him to accompany them to an AA meeting.

"That started a new career for me," Father Young said. These homeless men, "they were turnstiles; I didn't see any hope. When I saw AA I saw hope."

And this is how formal treatment services began in Albany: a handful of men hitting the streets, "going around with the guys," as Father Young put it, "having coffee with them, trying to find one or two who might have a desire to stop drinking." They'd bring them to an AA meeting, try to find them a sponsor.

Alcoholics Anonymous had begun in the 1930s in Ohio. By the 1960s there were a few meetings a week in the Capital Region. It was a small but close-knit community of peers helping peers. At one of these AA meetings Father Young saw someone he recognized: Fred Spencer.

Father Young had known Fred many years before, when they were both involved in Albany's Twilight Baseball League—he'd come in as Fred was on his way out. "I knew him as a very competitive baseball player," Young said. "He hated to lose; he was a scrapper. He got in everyone's nose."

Now, decades later, Fred needed a job. At one time he'd been a top army recruiter. Father Young thought he knew how to put his talents to work: Fred Spencer's determination was just what was needed when you're trying to bring people into recovery—and keep them there.

"I see how someone plays a game, and I think that's how they're going to be in life," Young said. So he told Fred, " 'Hang around here and help me.' I began to see, this guy was dedicated. He was a good salesman. A persevering guy."

Fred Spencer was one of the first paid employees of what became the Albany Citizens Council on Alcoholism.

Other than those few AA meetings every week, there were very few local options for people suffering from alcoholism. Even the hospitals didn't want them.

"Hospitals considered (alcoholics) problems and usually wouldn't deal with them because they took up hospital bed space from those who were 'really sick,'" wrote Father Young in an unpublished memoir. "Alcoholism was not yet seen as a disease and society thought it was their own fault and all they needed to do was stop drinking."

Father Young knew there was more than enough need to support an Albany treatment center; he himself had made the five-hour drive to Wernersville, Pennsylvania, more than a hundred times, bringing local people down to the Chit-Chat Farm, one of the first alcohol care centers in the country. At the least, Albany needed a clinic—a place that could offer education, counseling, and other resources to addicts and their families.

Clinics did not meet with universal support from Alcoholics Anonymous. They were a culture change for the recovery community, with AA's strong traditions of anonymity and its belief that help should come peer-to-peer. Given alcoholism's heavy stigma, the general public did not always support efforts to help alcoholics either. But in the 1960s, the idea that addiction was a disease—and one that deserved professional help—was gaining steam.

The outreach being done by Father Young, Fred Spencer, and the others had been funded so far by the parish and private donors. To open a clinic they would need more money—and getting government funding for alcoholism treatment was a typical Albany power play.

Young had friends, he told me, among Albany County Democrats, but he also faced opposition from some key leaders. Mayor Corning's feathers had been ruffled by Father Young's social work in the South End, where St. John's parish was doing a better job than the city. "The political battles behind the scene were unbelievable," Young said. But there was someone with the power to end the tug-of-war: Dan O'Connell.

County power brokers went to Albany's longtime political boss to seek his support for Father Young's agenda. A South Ender himself, O'Connell knew about and appreciated Father Young's work in the neighborhood. He gave his blessing, the priest said—and he told Corning to lay off.

"Dan came in and trumped it," Father Young said, bringing the palm of his right hand down onto the back of his left with a smack of finality.

In May of 1967, the Albany County Board of Supervisors voted unanimously to approve a community alcoholism program based on the recommendations of the Albany Citizens Committee on Alcoholism, headed by Father Young; they appropriated $10,000 for its implementation, with further funds coming from the state. Shortly thereafter, the *Knick News* editorial board praised the plan, though complaining for the nth time that these decisions seem to come out of nowhere, with county Democrats sharing as little information as possible with the public.

Young never met Dan O'Connell face to face. But, he says, mutual acquaintances let him know that Dan thought he was doing the right thing.

In early 1968, the Albany Citizens Council on Alcoholism opened a small office in the South End. Its mission was to guide people to treatment and educate the public about alcoholism. Fred Spencer was the council's first executive director, and Father Young was its president.

A 1968 *Times-Union* article looks at the organization's early days, its mission, and its hopes for the future. It begins:

> A college student no longer able to cope with his studies. A construction worker in danger of losing his job. A well-to-do housewife watching her family fall apart. These are just a few of the some 50 people who in recent weeks have paid a visit to a small second-floor office in the new Albany County Health Building at 175 Green Street. They have come to seek help for a common problem—alcohol.
>
> . . . Fred M. Spencer, executive director of the Albany Council on Alcoholism, sits behind the metal desk to which these people with a problem are invited to pull up a chair. A short, wiry man in his fifties with close-cropped gray hair, he listens sympathetically. Having won his own battle with the bottle, he knows what drink can do.

"We have to correct an awful lot of distorted thinking on alcoholism," Fred told the newspaper. "People are afraid to come forward because they think their excess drinking is a sign of weakness, of failure. They think it can be cured by will power alone—like smoking."

In those early days, Fred Spencer counseled people on what course of treatment would be right for them. He sent them to psychiatrists, to hospitals, or to AA. In just a few years the profession of counseling would become more formalized, and, lacking credentials, Fred shifted to education—the determined salesman, selling the public on the need to accept and treat the alcoholics among us. He became director of the Council on Alcoholism's information office, appearing on television, doing talk shows, giving countless lectures at meetings and schools. When SPARC—St. Peter's Alcoholism Rehabilitation Center—was established in 1972, Fred went uptown and became its first director, a position he held until he retired in the late 1970s.

Fred Spencer was one of the Capital Region's first public voices of recovery. Right alongside him were two of the Stickles girls: his wife, Joan, and her sister Georgea.

In 1987, a halfway house for alcoholic women opened in the former St. Adalbert's convent in Schenectady. It was the second such facility in the Capital Region, and one of only a handful in all of New York state. The house was named in honor of Georgea Stickles Perrin.

"It is a dream come true to live long enough to see treatment for alcoholics, especially women alcoholics, made accessible and acceptable in this community," Georgea told the newspapers when Perrin House opened.

Back in the 1950s, when Georgea fought for and won her sobriety, treatment was neither accessible nor acceptable, especially for women. Alcoholics Anonymous was practically the only local place to seek help, and it was almost exclusively male. Joan used to say she hadn't even known a woman could be an alcoholic; she'd thought it was a man's affliction. And the disease's veil of shame was an extra burden for women to bear. Women like Georgea and Joan were standard-bearers of their generation, helping to change public attitudes toward alcoholism, but the sisters led by more than just their example. Soft-spoken Joan and tough, bold Georgea took different paths to the same goal: opening up treatment options for others who suffered as they had.

Joan, the oldest of the Stickles girls, was one of the first women to join AA in Albany. In the early 1950s you could count the group's female membership on one hand. After a few years, she brought in her sister Georgea.

Georgea remembered how Joanie had all but dragged her into sobriety in the late '50s. "I was *sick* of my *sister*, who was sponsoring the *hell* out of me . . . taking me to meetings. 'Come to the meeting,' she'd say; 'Get yourself dressed up and I'll take you to an AA meeting.' And I'd say, 'Big deal.'"

Georgea hadn't wanted to believe she was an alcoholic. But Joan refused to give up on her kid sister, though it took her five years to stop drinking. Once she did, Georgea became one of the most respected women in Albany's recovery community.

From the early days of her sobriety, Georgea embraced a leadership role in the AA peer network. She knew that women wanted a place to talk in confidence, and she went down to volunteer at a call center that Father Young had established in St. John's parish so people could phone in to seek help with a drinking problem. Then the woman who had dropped out of school in the 1930s as a freewheeling party girl went back to the classroom, and she became one of the first women in New York state to become a credentialed alcoholism counselor.

Feisty, funny, and outgoing, Georgea was an unforgettable lady. After I wrote about her on my blog, some of her counseling clients from the 1970s contacted me to tell me how much she had meant to them. One agreed to talk to me, provided I didn't use his name.

He and she had connected through the St. Peter's Addiction Recovery Center, where Georgea worked. "I would go up to talk to her, and I'd have one or two problems, feeling like I'm carrying the weight of the world on my shoulders. And she'd say, 'Things must be going pretty good for you if that's all you've got to worry about,'" he laughed.

Georgea spoke her mind and had a low tolerance for bullshit. "If you tried to make up stories, she would see through it," said her former client. "She was a wonderful, down-to-earth person, very well liked and respected by just about everyone."

Those who knew Georgea refer to her with words like "pioneer" and "legend." As a counselor, a public speaker, and a fellow alcoholic, she helped an untold number of women and men fight their battles. I'm told people still quote her at local AA meetings.

Georgea's sister Joan Spencer chose a quieter but parallel path. "She would say, 'I just like people,'" said Greg Spencer about his mother. "Where Georgea was a tough nut, my mother was total class: gentle, caring, and soft-spoken. Anybody who knew her loved her."

Joan became a longtime volunteer at St. Peter's Addiction Recovery Center, lending her strength to fellow alcoholics, just as she'd done for her sister. And she traveled around the region to help establish new AA meetings, with a focus on outreach to other women. "My mom was very much behind the scenes," Greg said. "She had her special place up on the 7th floor" of St. Peter's, where AA meetings were held. "She would go up to meetings all the time and carry a message of hope." She was recognized by the Albany Citizens Council on Alcoholism in 1993 "for her many years of dedication and countless contributions to those in recovery."

Georgea, too, received many accolades. The Perrin House dedication may be the one that touched her the most. I toured Perrin House one day in 2012 when its residents were elsewhere, busy with education and job-training programs. I just wanted to see a bit of Georgea's legacy, and I found the place warmly familiar. One of the curiously interwoven threads of my house's story is that I used to work in a rehab myself. I was the English teacher for a number of years in a Troy residence for teens. Perrin House reminded me very much of my old workplace, a place held together as much by hope as by budget, trying hard to be homey, doing the best it could with what it had.

Perrin House is one of three residences run by New Choices Recovery of Schenectady. It holds twenty-one women, most of them Capital Region residents, who stay for as little as four months or as long as a year. Their single and double bedrooms look like college dorms, a cheerful clutter of pillows, books, lotions, and makeup. The women cook their own meals and break bread together in the basement dining room.

I have great respect for people who work in addiction treatment. The pay is lousy—I know that from experience—and it can be much easier to focus on the failures than to remember the successes. But to offer dignity and warmth to people at their most vulnerable reflects a belief that everyone in our community has something to contribute.

Today, the Albany Citizens Council on Alcoholism is the Addictions Care Center of Albany, deftly keeping the same acronym. Its outpatient clinic on Ontario Street was dedicated to Fred and Joan Spencer in 1999. The plaque there reads: "To the Spencer Family, in grateful recognition for their many years of dedicated service to those who suffer from addictions."

Though Georgea, Joan, and Fred have passed on, the work continues, of course, and the family continues to be a part of it. As an adult, Fred and Joan's oldest son, Greg, fought and won his own battle with alcoholism. More than thirty years sober, he himself is an addictions counselor. His latest project echoes his father's early work with the Citizens Council: Greg's a founder of Substance Abuse Information Resources, a community coalition that offers free educational programs about addiction and prevention.

"It's amazing how God has taken our family," Greg said. "He has really turned things around. It was a crazy family in a way, but it's really been blessed too."

Through the programs they helped establish and the lives they touched, that blessing still radiates.

15

"Where Everybody Talked about the Good Old Days"

On November 6, 1967, Marguerite Claffee Stickles passed away at St. Peter's Hospital. She was eighty-eight years old. There were no viewing hours before the funeral at St. Vincent de Paul Church, and the family requested that no flowers be sent. One final car ride brought her out of Albany and across the river to Nassau, where George was waiting for her.

Marguerite had transferred ownership of her house to her three surviving children, Joan, Georgea, and Cornelia, earlier that year. After their mother's death, Georgea and Cornelia signed over their interest to Joan and Fred, who continued to live here.

In many ways, the neighborhood that Marguerite left was the same as the one she had moved into nearly fifty years before: Its big old houses sheltered big middle-class families, sending their children to School 16 and Vincentian. Up on Madison Avenue, every storefront between Main and Allen was occupied. People could still walk to see a movie, shop for groceries, and grab a bite to eat. In other ways, though, change was everywhere.

That year, 1967, the Madison Theatre got a facelift of sorts. Its old-fashioned "island" ticket booth came out in favor of a walk-up glass window, and the square marquee yielded to the V-shaped one that's still there today. Owners modernized the interior (Formica, vinyl, drop-ceiling tiles to lower heating costs), hung gold draperies, and installed new projection equipment. "It's a rave!" enthused the Pine Hills business association, taking out newspaper ads to offer congratulations on October's "gala reopening premiere."

Other neighborhood landmarks were changing, too. The Aurania Club, social doyenne of the Pine Hills, still hung on, but its headquarters on South Allen Street was gone: the rambling wooden building had burned down in a suspicious fire in 1964. The only part of the clubhouse that could be saved was its 1928 brick addition, which contained the ballroom. Club members rallied, though, razing the rubble and building a low, modern brick clubhouse that opened the next year.

The 1967–68 school year closed the books on School No. 4 at Madison and Ontario. Kids attending that year didn't know they'd have the distinction of being the old school's youngest alumni, but on a June Saturday shortly after school let out for summer vacation, a ten-foot section of the building's roof collapsed. Engineers declared the school (built 1922–24 to replace the one that had burned down, thankfully also on a Saturday, in 1922) to be structurally unsound, despite the fact that it had passed inspection just a few months before. The building was demolished in 1969.

In the late '60s, playgrounds and "pocket parks" were going in all over Albany, and in 1967 officials were in talks with the YMCA to buy the old Ridgefield athletics grounds and turn the parcel into a city park, a deal that was finalized the next year. The city razed the Victorian clubhouse, constructed in the days of the Ridgefield Athletic Association, because "the mayor said it might cost as much to renovate the structure as to build a new one," as the *Knick News* reported. So out it went, and a modest modern facility was put in its place. I don't know what's inside it because I've never seen it open.

In an April 1967 editorial, the *Knick News* was cautiously optimistic about the city's playground plans, but warned: "Playgrounds to which the gates are locked much of the time, playgrounds littered with broken glass, playgrounds that are not supervised and in which there are no organized activities are not playgrounds at all." They had reason to be skeptical: city facilities were in a shameful state. Consider Washington Park, at least as the newspaper described it in 1968. What should have been Albany's showpiece had devolved into a few nice flower beds surrounded by neglect: paint flaking from benches and broken lamp posts, pedestals missing their urns, lawns of knee-deep weeds, and swing sets without swings. At the boathouse, kids sat on a broken dock and counted rats along the shore of a trash-dotted lake.

Albany's long decline—shoddy parks and dirty, potholed streets, inadequate and uneven services—was a hot political issue in 1967.[1] Take trash, for example: Albany was the last big city in New York state not to provide municipal trash collection. Instead, its refuse was handled by a bevy of private collectors with erratic schedules, and residents paid rates that were some of the highest in the state. What's more, social justice groups found through surveys that people in Albany's poor neighborhoods had to pay much more for trash pickup—in some places, more than twice as much—than people in better-off neighborhoods. People across the city wanted better service, and they were calling for it publicly.

If there's a silver lining in the cloud of 1960s urban decay, it may be that it inspired residents to organize. Many preservation groups and neighborhood associations found their start in that era. That holds true for the Pine Hills. People seeking more control over their neighborhood and better services from the city reestablished the Pine Hills Neighborhood Association, incorporating it in 1971.

One of its founders was a neighborhood newcomer named B.J. Costello. A native Vermonter, he moved to Albany for law school in 1969 after serving as a navy officer in Vietnam. Though he knew no one in town, he found out pretty quickly how things got done here.

"The ward committeeman came to my third-floor walkup," which was on North Allen across from School 16, Costello remembered. "He told me, 'If you have any problems, let me know; I can take care of you. All you have to do is vote Democratic.' Well, *okay*, I thought; I can take care of myself, and it doesn't matter how I vote."

---

1. Crumbling neglect affected many parts of Albany life by the late 1960s. Other Albany chroniclers—Paul Grondahl, William Kennedy—have written of the city's downslide under the O'Connell-Corning political machine. See in particular Grondahl's damning assessment of this legacy in chapter 14 of his *Mayor Corning: Albany Icon, Albany Enigma;* he traces how Albany suffered for decades from its leaders' paranoia, empty promises, and determination to hold onto power at all costs.

Costello liked the Pine Hills neighborhood, but he didn't think much of Albany governance. Snow removal operated on the "God put it there, God'll take it away" model. Garbage pickup was sporadic. Ridge-field Park—surprise!—was fouled with broken glass and trash. "City services?" Costello scoffed. "Unless you called your committeeman and asked for a favor you didn't get any services." Even Madison Avenue, he said, was "treeless and depressing."

"This was the neighborhood where everybody talked about the good old days," he said. "It was a place way in decline but with a rich history."

There had been a neighborhood association here since the early years—remember the no-sand-on-our-piazzas crusade?—and it held on for a good long time. In fact, as far as I can tell, the Pine Hills Association was still kicking around in the late '60s—at least it was holding anniversary dinners and annual smokers, according to the newspaper society briefs. But if it was active in community affairs, or as anything more than a social club, Costello never heard about it.

So a handful of people set out to bring neighborhood advocacy to the Pine Hills once again. True to the spirit of community organizing, they were guided by the president of another neighborhood group, Harold Rubin of the Center Square Association. By day Rubin worked for the state Division of the Budget; by night he fought for things like code enforcement and historic preservation and thus earned the wrath of City Hall—and, over several decades, great acclaim as an influential Albany activist and watchdog.

The Pine Hills Neighborhood Association rebooted with neighborhood cleanups of Ridgefield Park, gaining support from the Department of Public Works. Then there were some tree plantings and some victories in zoning. "These little steps of taking back the neighborhoods began to happen, and they were very encouraging," Costello said. The group reached out to households across the neighborhood, sharing information and problem-solving strategies, listening to concerns and identifying issues that needed collective action.

"It's all just about empowerment," Costello said. Residents asked, "Yeah, why am I worried about offending that committeeman? I *deserve* these things." It was the opposite of the tit-for-tat, divide-and-conquer politics that helped keep the machine chugging along. Albany's neighborhood associations fueled—and were fueled by—a political culture change.

Despite its faded colors, the neighborhood had its bright spots, especially for young people. One of the "approximately two million children" roaming the Pine Hills in the 1960s was a boy named Gregory Maguire. The middle child of seven, he grew up on Lancaster Street near North Pine, and he remembers the neighborhood as "a green enclave of noisy children and genial parents," a place of quirky architecture and long winters, a good place to be from.

Maguire is a local-boy-made-good: today he's a best-selling author whose works include the *Wicked* series and *Confessions of an Ugly Stepsister*. We exchanged a few emails in 2012, as he and his siblings prepared to sell their childhood home, and I asked him if he'd write a piece about the neighborhood for my history blog. He did, reflecting on the landmarks of his childhood: Madison Theatre and Vincentian CCD, Clapp's bookstore and St. Vincent's Church. Standing tallest of all in his memory was the Pine Hills library, housed in a Victorian mansion at 1000 Madison Avenue.

"For me it was truly a mecca," he wrote, ". . . an archive of promise about all that lay beyond Pine Hills. It was my second home, intellectually; therefore, that the collection was housed in a great and noble building originally designed as a home seemed fitting and even holy."

That house, built in the late 1890s for the president of a cement company, served as the neighborhood's library branch from 1952 until the late 1980s. Many of the features that made the stately Victorian ill-suited to be a high-circulation library—its cramped spaces, irregular nooks, many stairs, round tower—are the very ones that made it such a delight for patrons, especially young ones. Maguire remembered:

> To pull open the heavy oak door of the library!—then to encounter, first, the silence; and slowly to note the creak of floorboards and the squeak of rubber soles on grey linoleum tacked down in heavily trafficked areas. Then to hear the clank of antique radiators and to smell the radiator heat. Then to

notice the pleasant odor of old lady clothes, and of those replacement library bindings, which seemed to be made of plastic chitin and gave off a noxious smell that provided a good buzz. Then, at the same moment, both to smell and to see the wood varnish on the golden lintels and rood screens and turned bannisters of the magnificent staircase. . . . It was a kind of heaven. The children's room was at the top of this great set of steps. One climbed with gusto much as a salmon returns, undaunted, to home. Nowadays no one would put a children's room up so many steps, but back then it seemed a happy enough penance, like that felt upon mounting the steps of an altar.

Pine Hills was one of the lucky places. For a twentieth-century urban neighborhood, it enjoyed remarkable stability. But it wasn't immune to the pressures reshaping American life. As the 1960s gave way to the '70s, as happened in so many urban neighborhoods, some of the Pine Hills' vibrant community faded and dispersed: businesses closed, old institutions folded, and people moved to the suburbs. It was a change felt especially keenly on the densely settled blocks along Madison and Western from, roughly, Lake to Main. And it's a change Albany is still struggling with today.

Childhood fun in the '50s: Keith Spencer and friends in the backyard "digging hole." Courtesy of the Spencer family.

Greg Spencer gets in a shot at brother Keith in a snowball fight on West Law-rence Street, 1950s. Courtesy of the Spencer family.

Butcher Pete Girzone stands at the front door of Peter's Market, 236 West Lawrence Street, in this undated family photo. Courtesy of Edward V. Girzone.

Joan Spencer and Father Peter Young share a moment at a 1982 memorial dinner honoring Fred Spencer. Courtesy of the Spencer family.

No, it's not "Invasion of the Body Snatchers;" this photo of School 16 students crossing Western at North Allen was doctored to accompany a *Times-Union* editorial from September 8, 1961. The issue: A proposal that would have built a gas station on that corner. The message: This is a plan that will cost children their lives. Courtesy of the *Times Union*.

A look west down Madison Avenue, ca. 1973. Photo by Jim Burns.

Early 1970s *Knickerbocker News* photo, with crop marks, showing the Central Market grocery store on Madison Avenue. Central Market stores were renamed "Price Chopper" in 1973. Photo by Bob Paley. Courtesy of the *Times Union*.

Students board a SUNY bus at the corner of Western Avenue and North Main, December 10, 1979. Photo by Bud Hewig. Courtesy of the *Times Union*.

Our house in the 1980s, during the years it was split into two apartments. Part of the front porch has been enclosed and a second entry door added. Photo from the family of Connie and Don Henderson. Courtesy of Crystal Wortsman.

Carl Patka and kids, former residents of my house, clowning around on the steps on the first day of school, September 1998. From left, Emily, age 8; Isaac, 5; and Sophie, 7 months. Courtesy of the Patka family.

The old School 16 building on North Allen was demolished in August of 2005. A modern building was constructed on the same spot; it opened in 2007 as Pine Hills Elementary. Photo by Ric Chesser.

Volunteers work to re-create the 1977 mural on the side of the CVS drugstore, corner of Madison and South Main, on July 14, 2012. Photo by Michael P. Farrell. Courtesy of the *Times Union*.

16

Kegs, Eggs, and Beyond

Who's responsible for turning a wide stretch of Albany's Pine Hills into the student ghetto, a place the *Times Union* has called "a neighborhood under siege" from deteriorating properties, trash, noise, and parking problems? Here's the short version.

It's the colleges.
It's the landlords.
It's the students.
It's the city.
It's social change.
Want the long version? Read on.

In the late twentieth century, sections of the Pine Hills were reshaped: flats filled up with university students looking for off-campus housing, and some owners split their properties into apartments to accommodate more of them. Any issue the neighborhood faces today—residential stability, aging housing stock, business development, public transportation, codes, zoning—must consider, for good or for ill, the presence of hundreds of rental properties and thousands of young residents.

This story has its roots in the way the neighborhood was built. The Pine Hills has long been two neighborhoods, or rather, it has had two personalities. In the original Pine Hills development, as planned by Pratt and Logan back in the 1890s, craftsmen built single-family houses on spacious lots with maid's rooms, "verandas," and the occasional turret: amenities meant to appeal to middle-class families. Pratt and Logan's

159

efforts were concentrated in the upper reaches of the city: Pine Avenue, Allen Street, Manning. As Albany fanned out along the streetcar lines, other builders filled in the blocks between the Pine Hills project and Washington Park. Some of these streets developed with similar dwellings; others, with houses intended for families of more modest means, who also needed homes during the city's early twentieth-century housing shortage. Enter one of Albany's ubiquitous housing styles: the flat.

I'm sure every person in Albany has at least visited one of these flats, if not lived in one at some point in their lives: the two-story, two-family house, built with one apartment above and one below, each running the length of the house. Hundreds of them were built across Albany from the late nineteenth century into the 1920s. As Jack McEneny points out in his city history, this type of housing offered an opportunity for working-class families to move into nicer circumstances: The owner could live in one flat and rent out the other, using that income to help pay the mortgage. Or, he writes, two related families would often acquire a house and each live in a flat: "Thus the extended family, by pooling its resources, was able to move up to a better neighborhood and greatly improved living conditions."

On streets like Hamilton and Hudson, a stable family neighborhood grew and flourished. At one time known as Paigeville, the neighborhood fanned out along streets near Madison and Western Avenues, on either side of Ontario and Partridge. Many blocks were settled by Irish and German families, who helped grow St. Vincent de Paul Parish and the Vincentian schools.

Michael Huber grew up on Hudson Avenue between Quail and Ontario in the early 1970s. He remembers a close-knit neighborhood of two-family flats up and down the block and a lot of kids to play with.

"It was very family-oriented," said Mike. "A couple of police officers lived on our block. You couldn't get safer. There was stability." The neighborhood kids would walk everywhere—down to the corner store for treats, or up to Madison Theatre to see *The Love Bug* and *Jesus Christ Superstar*. They walked to VI or to the public school.

Mike's family lived on the first floor of their house, renting their upstairs flat to another family, until 1978, when they moved to the suburbs "like everybody else did," he said.

The Hubers, in fact, were late to that trend: Albany's population had hit its peak in 1950, with nearly 135,000 residents; then, between 1950 and 1980, the city's population fell by more than 33,000. Families were moving out of Albany, and the Pine Hills took a hit. Many houses in the neighborhood lack off-street parking, so in the era when every family had a car—or two—side streets like Hudson, Myrtle, and Morris became crowded with vehicles. The convenience of a driveway was one reason for the Huber family's move. The chance for a larger yard and some newer housing stock also drew people out of Albany.

The city suffered, too, as commercial trends shifted away from downtown shops and neighborhood stores in favor of enclosed shopping malls. A *Knickerbocker News* article from 1977 evoked images of a city Main Street and the town park only to point out that their time had passed: the role of community gathering space belonged to suburban shopping centers like Clifton Country Mall and the Northway Mall. Said one mall manager: "Most people who come here steadily do feel this is 'our town.'"

Fred Ruff, a Pine Hills Neighborhood Association leader beginning in the early 1970s, watched it all happen. Ruff, who raised his family on another stretch of Hudson Avenue, several blocks to the west, remembered neighborhood meetings of that era: "Older families, from Hamilton, Hudson, Jay (streets), little old ladies, mostly widows—they'd come in to the neighborhood association meetings. They could just see their neighborhood slowly disintegrating," he said. People who had raised their families in the Pine Hills were dying out or moving on, and other families were not taking their place.

By the end of the 1960s, enrollment at Vincentian Institute entered a sharp decline. Its grade school, called the Child Culture Division (CCD), was operating at a loss: the glass school buildings (no longer predominantly glass, after efforts to weatherproof them) and other structures needed renovations, and the parish was short on funds. In his history of St. Vincent de Paul parish, author William Tyrrell notes that between 1966 and 1976, CCD went from more than 1,000 students to fewer than 450. Families were smaller, and the suburbs were calling.

When Sister Joan Byrne came to the parish in the early seventies to work as an administrator, the youngest members of the big Baby

Boom-era families were in the school's upper grades. "It was less of a family neighborhood" than it had been, she told me, "and the families that were there had way fewer children." Family life was changing in other ways, too, with further implications for the school. Take, for example, lunch. CCD had never had a lunchroom because children would go home to eat. But in the 1970s, there was a growing number of children who needed to stay at school over the lunch period. For some, it was because there was no one at home to feed them; their mothers were working outside the home. Others were the children of people who'd grown up in the neighborhood and moved out to the suburbs but brought their kids back to attend the school.

"It gives you an idea of how social change beyond your control impacts the parish and the neighborhood," Sister Joan said.

The high school was the first to succumb to the changes. Its building at Madison and Ontario was in pretty bad shape, and the small classes in the lower grades indicated that VI enrollment was just going to keep dropping. So Vincentian Institute closed in 1977, merging with Cardinal McCloskey High School to become Bishop Maginn.

Though the parish published a memory book project in 1982 titled *Vincentian: A Tribute/The First 65 Years,* there was not going to be a second sixty-five years. With grade school enrollment still falling off and per-pupil costs climbing, administrators reached the conclusion that if the school continued, educational quality was going to decline. They decided to close St. Vincent CCD after the 1984–1985 school year.

Ruff, a parent who had sent eleven children through the CCD, was the person who announced the closing to the school community. "We were down from 1,000 students to 125, and the sisters were retiring," Ruff said. "The biggest thing was not that we wanted to close it but it was that it was draining ninety thousand dollars a year from the parish funds."

"It was a sad time because it was a special place," he said. "Financially, we just couldn't struggle anymore."

"I'll tell you, that was a tough decision," Sister Joan said. She told me about one parent who simply could not believe that the neighborhood could no longer support the school. When his children had gone through CCD, "there had been 100 kids on his block of North Pine," she said. So he went door to door, counting children, to get a sense of how much the neighborhood had changed. What he found, Sister Joan said, was that on North Pine Avenue there was only one child under the age of five. The Pine Hills had become a different kind of place.

What the Pine Hills endured in the sixties and seventies was small potatoes compared to what happened to the neighborhood directly south of the state Capitol, where Governor Nelson Rockefeller swept the slate clean to make room for his own dream of Albany.

Built between 1959 and 1976, the South Mall was Rockefeller's plan to leave his mark, forever, on the capital of the Empire State. It was the era of urban renewal: to those who styled themselves as modern visionaries, cities seemed ugly, tired, past their prime. Why remodel when you could build—and not just build but *Build!*—build something bold and open and clean and white, ornamented with reflecting pools, public art, and soaring towers in timeless marble? And if there are people inconveniently living in the place you want to reinvent, well, there are workarounds for that, too. Constructing the South Mall complex required the demolition of more than ninety-eight acres of a "threadbare section" of Albany, or so reports called it, displacing thousands of residents and erasing their houses, schools, barbershops, delicatessens, and every other ordinary and irritating and cherished thing that makes a place home. "Mean structures breed small vision," Governor Rockefeller said once; and there may be something to that. But grand vision uproots more families. It was an ungentle way to remake a city.

Rockefeller's style of governance made its mark on the Pine Hills, too. America's move from the cities to the suburbs in the second half of the twentieth century happened alongside another cultural trend: the rapid expansion of university education. These two trends converged to change the Pine Hills neighborhood.

As the U.S. population surged in the years after World War II, state leaders and university officials realized something: in ten to fifteen years or so, those baby-boomers were going to be headed to college. Who was going to educate them? In New York, the state government took on that challenge.

Again, Governor Rockefeller had a sweeping vision—New York would build not just a state university, but a network of institutions. He pushed for a rapid expansion of state higher education, adding campuses, programs, and faculty at locations across New York. Under his plan, Albany would become one of four "university centers," by means of a comprehensive restructuring and expansion of its teachers college.

The institution that eventually became the University at Albany was founded in 1844 as the State Normal School. It trained young women and men to be teachers, drawing students from all over the state. By the 1950s it was known as the New York State College for Teachers and had a student body of a few thousand. Its campus, sandwiched between Western and Washington Avenues east of Lake, had little room for growth, not enough to accommodate Rockefeller's plans. He chose the site of the Albany Country Club, in the western reaches of the city off Washington Avenue, for the new university campus.

Students moved into the first finished dormitory quadrangle, Dutch Quad, in October 1964, commuting to the downtown campus for classes. By 1966, most classes were held on the uptown campus, and university buses provided transportation between the two locations.

The 1960s saw the university grow at a breathtaking rate, creating new degree programs and whole departments in its quest to become a full-fledged public research institution. Kendall Birr, author of an institutional history of the university, wrote that in the late sixties SUNY Albany added faculty at a rate of about 100 new members each fall. And student enrollment mushroomed: From 1962 to 1970, the student population swelled from about 4,000 to more than 13,200.

Its rapid growth, and its division over two campuses, made SUNY in some respects a school out of place. As Birr wrote of the late 1960s: "The downtown [campus] seemed remote from the centers of University activity while the Uptown Campus remained curiously isolated. Standard urban services (shopping, entertainment and general service facilities) never developed within easy walking distance of these uptowners." So it entered its modern era as a school that was not going to be contained to just one neighborhood—a circumstance that continued as, over the years, enrollment consistently outpaced dorm capacity. The university never had enough beds for all the students it admitted.

Rockefeller's uptown campus had been designed for ten thousand students. Within five years it was full, and enrollment kept growing.

A percentage of SUNY Albany's students commuted from local homes, of course. But over the years the university drew more students from other parts of the state, especially the metropolitan New York City area. The number of downstate students, Birr notes, grew through the 1960s. From the mid-1970s to mid-1980s the university tried to ameliorate its housing crunch by tripling students up in dormitory rooms and providing overflow housing at the downtown Wellington Hotel.

"Every room on each of the five quads was filled," began an article in the *Albany Student Press,* SUNY Albany's newspaper, in September of 1979. "Tripled residents of Pittman Hall complained of being 'smashed like sardines'; students slept in bunks in lounges in Brubacher and Sayles; the waiting list at the Wellington grew. And still they converged upon Perimeter Road, suitcases in hand—the Class of '83 and the new transfers who would soon call SUNYA home."

Another option for students was renting a local apartment. And behold: right between the two campuses, right on the SUNY bus lines, was a neighborhood full of flats—many becoming available as Pine Hills families moved out.

Living off campus was largely seen as a better deal, "less expensive and more attractive" than dorm life, as one newspaper article put it. Less restrictive, too, after New York state raised the drinking age in the early 1980s.

News stories throughout the eighties noted that splitting the rent on an Albany apartment was roughly the same cost as living in a dormitory—or cheaper. From a 1986 *Times Union* feature by Mark S. R. Suchecki, titled "Student renters squeeze an already tight housing market": "On-campus students at the state university will pay $1,666 for a double-occupancy dormitory room. . . . That works out to more than $330 per month for two students, an amount that would, according to a Fact Finders rental vacancy survey prepared for the city, be enough to lease one of more than half of Albany's 27,000 apartments."

Just how many off-campus students are we talking about here? A university spokesman told Suchecki that SUNY's projected full-time enrollment for the upcoming school year would be 15,830, with the university providing housing for 6,676. How many were local? Birr breaks down the 1986 freshman class: One quarter came from NYC; one-third came from Long Island; one-seventh came from the Capital Region.[1]

Decreased demand for dormitory space in the eighties meant that some SUNY dorm rooms were converted to faculty offices. The university's enrollment during that decade approached 16,000, and it wasn't just students who were cramped. Here's Birr again:

> How did 16,000 students, more than 700 teaching faculty, and several hundred support staff fit on a campus designed for about 10,000 students? To some degree they didn't. Space for every University activity—faculty offices, instruction, research, University Libraries, student activities, and physical education—was always at a premium, many felt cramped, and complaints abounded.

No arguing that the university was pressed for space. But it's worth noting that converting dorms to offices doesn't seem to reflect a commitment to increasing campus residency.

SUNY has added dormitories over the years, of course. Freedom Quad opened in 1988 with beds for 410; Empire Commons opened in 2002 to house a whopping 1,200 upperclassmen and graduate students. Liberty Terrace, in 2012, added 500 more beds. But enrollment has always far exceeded the university's housing capacity. It's reasonable to expect that a certain number of students will live off campus, either at their family homes or independently. How many? Did the university cross a line? I can't say. But I can say that the number of SUNY students renting off campus was great enough to mean change for the neighborhoods they settled in.

---

1. Later that year, the *Knickerbocker News* collected enrollment and housing data from SUNY, Saint Rose, Albany Junior College, Albany Law School, and the Albany College of Pharmacy. The total was 21,194 undergraduate and graduate students, 7,329 of whom would be housed on campuses.

SUNY, today known as the University at Albany, is not the only college that touches the Pine Hills. The College of Saint Rose, founded in 1920 as a Catholic college for women, is much smaller. But not only does it contribute to students' presence here, its growing campus is in the heart of the neighborhood.

In 1969, the year Saint Rose became fully coeducational, the college's full-time undergraduate enrollment was less than a thousand students. Over the next few decades, enrollment grew—and just as at the state university, these increases brought crowding, with parking seen as a particular headache. According to a 1994 history of the college, the space problem was such that, in the mid-1970s, Saint Rose administrators deliberated moving the campus out of Albany, to Glenmont—an idea that "was scuttled in favor of a renovation and construction agenda in the College's original urban setting," author RoseMarie Manory wrote. Saint Rose went on to add more classrooms, more dormitory space, and more students.

Saint Rose's expansion plans have sparked tensions among many of its neighbors for decades. In the late eighties, when the college took steps to make parking lots out of the old Vincentian athletic fields between Madison and Morris, it raised the ire of Morris Street residents who felt that Saint Rose officials didn't consider, or care, how the plans would affect the college's neighbors. Residents' anger is understandable: the fields were welcome greenspace on a thickly settled street. Goodbye community gardens; hello headlights through your front window blinds.

In recent decades, the college's expansion has led it to replace some Pine Hills houses with larger structures—dormitories, academic buildings—and more parking lots. The loss of some of those houses has come hard; they were beautiful old places that we'll never get back. I don't understand the relentless push to grow. Why must a college always admit more students? Why not just be small? I'm a lousy capitalist, I guess.

At the same time, considering how many old houses the college uses as offices and dorm space, the neighborhood could have lost more of its character, and more stability, if Saint Rose weren't here. It's a give and take. That's my opinion, anyway.

For the fall of 2012, the College of Saint Rose's undergraduate population was 2,881. Total enrollments, counting graduate students, was 4,504. Many Saint Rose students do not live on campus. A 2010 *Times Union* story quoted a college official as saying that "at best Saint Rose can only hope to house between 50 and 60 percent of its 2,800 full-time students on campus."

For the Pine Hills, the growth of the universities and the student renters that it brought didn't just mean new neighbors. It drove up rents and promoted real estate speculation. The demand for apartments prompted the conversion of houses into multiunit buildings.

It happened to our house, too.

In the late 1970s, Fred and Joan Spencer moved over near St. Peter's Hospital, where they worked. In the hands of their younger son, Keith, the West Lawrence Street house was transformed. He sheetrocked over the living room's wood-framed entryway. He enclosed part of the front porch; where the bay of three living room windows stood, he installed a door. He drilled pipe holes in the dining room floor and put a kitchen in there. The pantry became a tiny bathroom. And voila: the old house was now split into two apartments.

It was an ugly job.

"I cringed when I saw that," said Greg Spencer, Keith's brother. "I was only here a few times after that."

I cringe, too. Not only because of the indifference the renovations reveal for the beauty and balance of Craftsman workmanship, but because with those changes, the house I love morphed from a home into a money-maker. It was probably our house's most vulnerable moment; for many old places, getting chopped into apartments is a step from which they never recover.

Keith passed away in 2008; I never got a chance to talk with him. So I'll do my best to look at his actions from a 1970s perspective. There was no market for these big old houses, but there was a strong market for apartments. Splitting the house probably seemed like a good investment. And Keith was far from the only one taking that route: the houses on either side of this one had become multiunits, too.

Into the 1980s, tracts along Western and Washington Avenues had some of the lowest vacancy rates in Albany, along with some of the highest rents. "The students are willing and even eager to pay above-average rents by doubling and tripling up with roommates in apartments," noted Mark Suchecki in his 1986 story on the tight rental market. "By rooming together, a group can pay the higher rents an individual could not."

Rising rents made it harder for families to lease in the Pine Hills. "It's very difficult for a person with a family to be in competition with three or four students who can spend $450 for an apartment with no hardship," said the Eleventh Ward alderman, who in the 1980s was one of the strongest voices sounding alarms about the changes the neighborhood was enduring. He was a maverick Democrat named Jerry Jennings.

The biggest problem, Alderman Jennings argued, was not the students themselves but their absentee landlords. "They take advantage of a tight situation," he told Suchecki. "They don't reinvest the money they earn from the properties, don't keep them up. They're not doing the students a service by overcrowding them and charging each $150 a month."

When absentee landlords allow their properties to crumble, Jennings said in 1989, "It's like a cancer that's spreading through the neighborhood. . . . It's forcing a lot of residents who have lived here all their lives out."

Paint peeled, porches sagged. The students still lined up to rent.

Not every landlord is neglectful, of course. Many follow the law, keep up to code, treat their properties like the investments they are—and take the risk of renting to uncaring tenants.

After Mike Huber and his family moved to the suburbs in 1978, they rented their Hudson Avenue duplex to other families. When Mike returned home from college in 1987, he took over the management of the property from his mother. "Somewhere in that time," he said, "the neighborhood flipped a switch": nearly every home on his old street had become student housing.

Mike wanted to hold onto his childhood home, but being a landlord to students became increasingly hard for him to stomach. His house sustained a lot of damage. "They lose the keys, they break the glass to get in," he said. "The old beautiful glass doors." He visited the property once and smelled gas; the tenants were using the stove burners to heat the apartment because they didn't want to pay for oil.

"I went to college. I lived off campus," he said. "We did not abuse our landlord's property in the way these kids from SUNY did. It boggled my mind how much they were uncaring toward other people's property."

Elsewhere on the block, Mike saw other absentee owners shoe-horn more kids into their houses, even if it meant violating city code. "Another landlord told me I was a fool not to put another student up in the attic" to make more money off the apartment. "I said, 'There's only one staircase. There's no utilities up there!' He just looked at me: 'Doesn't matter. Doesn't matter.'"

Mike watched the neighborhood deteriorate to the point where he hated to imagine children growing up on such a run-down, chaotic street. When he would talk to prospective renters and learn they were parents, he would warn them away: "Uh-uh. You do not want to rent that apartment. You do not want to be in that block. You do not want your kids there."

"Once families go away, forget about it," he said. "That block was a goner."

The year that all the radiators froze and burst over winter break, Mike sat in his car outside the house and cried. "I told my mom, we're done. We can't do this anymore. That was the last straw." They sold the house in 2000.

"It breaks my heart," he said. "Not just what's happened to my house but what's happened to my entire neighborhood."

Compare the two passages below:

> Ruth Pfeiffer is sick and tired. She's sick of watching trash piles blossom on yards near her Hudson Avenue home. She's tired of being unable to find a parking spot on her own street. And don't even ask her about the noise. "I don't like to repeat what I hear," said Pfeiffer. . . . "It's screaming . . . continual carousing."

> Students drink and urinate in the streets. They scream deep into the night. They smash bottles and vandalize property. . . . In the morning, the sun rises on a neighborhood that's littered with red cups and broken glass.

Both passages are from *Times Union* articles on the student ghetto. The first was written in 1989; the second, 2014. The college students described in the first paragraph could be the parents of the college students in the second.

If you look through local newspapers from the 1980s, then the 1990s, and on to today, you'll find story after story decrying the state of the neighborhood and tenants' behavior there—and they're all the same: trash, noise, parties, vandalism.[2] Except for 2011—those stories are worse.

On the morning of March 12, 2011, after a night of pre–St. Patrick's Day drinking, hundreds of young people spilled out of house parties near Hudson Avenue and Quail Street and went wild: stomping on cars, throwing appliances off of second-floor balconies, fighting in the streets, and lobbing bottles at police who showed up to disperse them. Videos of the riot posted online show throngs of green-shirted revelers holding beer cans and red plastic cups, lining the residential blocks, hooting and hollering as groups of guys kicked out cars' windows and sun roofs. When the crowds were finally sent home, sixteen tons of debris were left behind.

The Kegs and Eggs Riot, as it became known, was a national embarrassment for Albany and for the university. The UAlbany president apologized, and the school moved the date of spring break for future years, in the hopes of reducing the number of students staying in Albany during the St. Patrick's revels. Students, intent on burnishing the university's image, went out on cleanup patrols. Police amped up their presence. There were town-gown engagement opportunities. But in the years since the riot, it's been tough to see if anything really has changed.

---

2. Pine Hills neighbors' concerns about off-campus students and the substandard properties being rented to them date back at least into the early '70s. According to a Pine Hills Neighborhood Association newsletter from October 1972, neighborhood groups had met recently with SUNY's student organization to urge some changes. The newsletter reported that the Student Association had tentatively agreed to contact student tenants "if neighbors forward complaints of noise, parking problems or other difficulties"; and the university's off-campus housing office was urged to "insist on a city certificate of occupancy in hopes properties which violate zoning laws will not be listed."

Is change possible? If so, what can be done?

Let's start here: people are responsible for their own behavior. Who the fuck *are* these guys?

Like Mike Huber, and probably you, and countless others, I once was twenty and utterly self-absorbed. I played my music too loud, drank too much, came and went at odd hours. But at the same time, I never littered. I somehow managed not to urinate on anyone's lawn. I never damaged property. You Just. Don't. Do. That.

As a Pine Hills homeowner, I'm willing to hear my neighbors throw one or two loud, late parties every year. They're entitled. Much more than that, yeah, I'd think it's inconsiderate. And yes, that's totally arbitrary. But isn't that what we do as communities—try to find a balance between my right to do what I want and your right not to be bothered by me? It's a negotiation, and different groups will reach different standards of what's acceptable to them. There's always a tension when neighbors have different ideas about how to use a neighborhood. That doesn't have to be a negative thing: it's good to be reminded we're not the only people here with rights.

But even so. Let's say my arbitrary guideline of two parties per household, per year, was the rule. There are thirty-six houses on the block where Mike Huber grew up, Hudson Avenue between Ontario and Quail, and nearly all of them are multiple-unit dwellings. If you lived on that block you could find yourself dealing with parties every week of the year. It's just too dense.

Laying a neighborhood's problems on the altar of personal responsibility is a move that's hard to argue with—and equally hard to turn into any real change.

Let's assume it's a minority of residents who are responsible for quality-of-life violations, because no doubt it is. Let's assume that it's the density of tenants itself that's the problem. If so, then perhaps it would be more effective to improve conditions through governmental controls. That approach—at least in theory, and back to that in a minute—sets aside the issue of who the tenants are. It's an important shift in focus, because there's no innate correlation between tenants' status as students and their worthiness as neighbors. Many students are quiet and tidy, and many assholes are nonstudents.

Over the decades, the city government has tried to address the neighborhood's problems on several fronts. One big push used the grouper law.

A law regulating how many unrelated people can live in a dwelling has been on Albany's books since the late 1960s. Called the grouper law, or the antigrouper law—interchangeable opposites, like "flammable" and "inflammable"—it prevents more than three unrelated adults from living together unless they are the "functional equivalent of a family." Till the mid-'80s the law had largely gathered dust. In 1985, the city stepped up enforcement against landlords; then, in 1986, officials took a new, bold step: they targeted SUNY student-renters.

In October 1986, twenty tenants and six landlords were summoned to appear in City Court on charges of breaking the antigrouper law. With fines of $250 per day, and with many charges back-dated three months, they faced fines of up to $25,000 and imprisonment of up to a year.

"The State University of Albany is irresponsible and creating this problem" by admitting far more students than it could house, said the attorney representing the city in court. "SUNYA expects us, the taxpayers, to put up with their students. . . . I think it's time we say to them, 'You want more students? Build more dormitories.'"

Lawyers for the SUNY Albany Student Association attacked the charges. One key argument was that Albany City Court did not have jurisdiction over code enforcement cases. That's a change that Mayor Tom Whalen had made not long before. Hoping to improve code enforcement, the city had moved those cases out of Police Court, where they were never a priority, and into Albany City Court. A ruling against that move could have thrown a wrench into Albany's whole approach to code violations.

There were also concerns that targeting student renters could hurt the city's relationship with the university. City insiders, speaking to the *Times Union* a few years afterwards, said Mayor Whalen believed the crackdown "had gone too far."

So the city blinked. Charges against students were adjourned in contemplation of dismissal. Charges against some of the landlords were adjourned as well; two others paid fines. Afterwards, Albany officials said they had made their point. They'd raised awareness, they said, so more people were now following the law.

Among those who disagreed was Alderman Jerry Jennings, who asserted in 1990 that there were just as many violations as ever, and he challenged city officials to walk the neighborhood streets and conclude otherwise.

These days, if you search "student apartment" on Craigslist or browse student-oriented property management websites (with names like albanystudentapartments.com and albanystudenthousing.com, it's obvious whom their target tenants are), you'll see plenty of units offered with four or even five bedrooms. Managers aren't hiding this information; ads mention how much each student will pay in rent split four ways. It seems pretty clear they're not in compliance.

Does it matter? Maybe, maybe not. You could argue that if the number of tenants per unit were kept at the limits required by law, it would ease the parking pressure on densely settled streets. It might even reduce trash and traffic. On the other hand, I'd take four considerate neighbors over one noisy jerk any day.

In 2013, I asked Jeffrey Jamison, then head of Albany's Department of Buildings and Regulatory Compliance, if the grouper law was still enforced. "Enforcement at this time," he told me, "is only on a complaint basis."

As an alderman, Jerry Jennings argued that the grouper law was not the way to fix the problems in the student ghetto; it was impractical and hard to enforce against a frequently changing contingent of renters. Winning cases required a lot of resources for just a handful of results. It would be better, Jennings believed, to go after negligent landlords and push them to take responsibility for their properties.

Jennings was elected mayor of Albany in 1993 and took office with a promise to crack down on building code violations. Under the system he inherited, code inspections were handled by the city Building Department, which had been criticized for having too few inspectors and for spotty record keeping that made it hard to track a history of complaints against a property. Inspections in Albany's machine era had long been seen as a patronage-riddled system. In 1995, Jennings gave the job of code enforcement to the Fire Department. Sixty fire officers were trained to do inspections ("That's 20 times what the Building Department had,"

Chief James Larson said in 1995), with the goal of eventually training the whole department.

Jennings sought to pay for the beefed-up inspection system by creating an apartment registry: Landlords would pay a $50 fee to register each apartment unit they owned, and the listing would be valid for thirty months, the period of time between mandatory code inspections. He also proposed a sharp hike in fines for code violations, with the maximum set at $5,000. Jennings's plan met strong resistance from city landlords and from some Common Council members, who saw the registry fee as a hidden tax. By the time the measures passed the council, they were a lot weaker, with the registry fee reduced to $30 per apartment and top fines capped at $1,000.

Giving code inspection work to the Fire Department was an interesting idea: Firefighters could look for potential hazards while becoming more familiar with buildings in their coverage area, something that could help them when responding to an emergency. But there are more than twenty thousand apartments in the city, and it's not like firefighters don't have other work to do. What's more, there are hundreds of vacant properties that require inspectors' attention, many owned by speculators who allow them to rot while waiting for their value to rise.

Complaints arose almost from the beginning that the Fire Department took too long to complete inspections, and the courts took too long to process violations. Hundreds of cases backed up in City Court. Funding was also an issue: The fire chief told council members in 1996 that apartment inspections cost his department sixty-five dollars a unit. The thirty-dollar registry fee covered less than half of that.

Lack of adequate funding was one of the problems cited in 2011, when Albany's code enforcement system became the first issue probed by the newly created city auditor's office. Inspections of rental apartments, chief city auditor Leif Engstrom found, were more than a year behind schedule, and a significant percentage of completed inspections were of dubious quality. Fees for registering rental apartments and vacant buildings were nowhere near enough to cover the related costs. Auditors could not determine whether complaints were handled promptly "because the date the Division receives the complaint is not recorded." Engstrom's team asked for a written copy of the city's code enforcement procedures, but the codes division never supplied one; auditors interpreted that to mean the procedures had never been written down. And an outdated computer system prevented officials from compiling a registry of rental properties. It took the city "months of trial and error" just to produce five years of inspection history for the audit.

"Information management is at the core of effective code enforcement," Engstrom's office wrote, and Albany's codes division fell far short. "This audit found severe data limitations and an absence of performance measures which limited our team's analysis." Among other recommendations, auditors concluded that the codes division needed better record keeping, a quality assurance plan, and "a clear mission and written policies and procedures designed to advance that mission."

After the audit, Jennings took steps to move code enforcement away from the Fire Department, first having the codes division report directly to the mayor's office, and then making Buildings and Regulatory Compliance its own city department in 2013. Firefighters, who received an annual stipend for their code inspection work, fought the changes. Their union filed a grievance when Jennings hired eight civilian code inspectors, and an arbitrator sided against the city, ruling that the move was in violation of the firefighters' contract.

After five terms as mayor, Jerry Jennings announced he would not run again. In 2013 voters chose Kathy Sheehan, city treasurer, to succeed him. Among the issues on her platform: increased penalties for code violations. Over the course of twenty years in office, Jennings had barely moved the needle on his signature issue.[3]

Not long before the 2011 Kegs and Eggs riot, a College of Saint Rose official spoke to the Common Council about two projects: a planned

---

3. Code enforcement wasn't the Jennings administration's only neighborhood revitalization strategy, of course. In 2004 and 2005, the city hired consultants to study the midtown area bounded by Central Avenue, Lark Street, New Scotland Avenue, and West Lawrence Street. The study culminated in a town-gown community investment plan to increase home ownership and owner occupancy. Employees of Albany's learning institutions—Saint Rose, UAlbany, the Sage Colleges, the Albany College of Pharmacy,

dormitory and a program to encourage home ownership among college employees. "We've lost Hudson and Hamilton," Mike D'Attilio, Saint Rose's executive director of government and community relations, said. "We don't want to lose Morris and Myrtle as well."

It was a sobering statement. Is that true—Are these blocks "lost"? What does it mean for a block to be "lost"? The absence of owner-occupiers? An irreversible slide into deeper and deeper decay? A date with the bulldozer?

"More changes are coming for the neighborhood," Jeffrey Jamison told me in 2013, "and not necessarily good ones."

Jamison was the person named to head Jennings' newly independent Department of Buildings and Regulatory Compliance. I spoke with him during Jennings' final year in office (though at the time no one knew that) to get a sense of what the city government saw in the neighborhood's future. It wasn't encouraging.

"Culturally there are differences between people who are renters and more transient, and homeowners," he told me. "You can look block by block and see the differences in quality of life."

Jamison presented me with a hypothetical: Let's say the colleges do add more student housing, he said. What will that mean for the Pine Hills? "The housing stock is still in existence. What are the owners going to do? Are families going to move in? Let's be honest," he said; "we have housing stock in the city of Albany for 140,000 people." With a population under 100,000, we have more houses than we need. Even if houses in these neighborhoods were renovated, Jamison said, owners wouldn't get a return on their investment because there's no guarantee people would want to live there.

It wasn't all gloom. He suggested the city could find other programs to encourage home ownership and investment in the neighborhood

---

and Albany Law School, as well as Albany Medical Center—could receive a $5,000 forgivable loan for downpayment and closing costs if they bought and lived in a home in the target area. For other potential residents, Citizens Bank would offer a similar loan. The plan faced economic hurdles—it was a time of rising real estate prices, followed by recession—but the program helped seventy-one homeowners in its first four years, according to the city.

and could maybe use city funds to beautify streetscapes, "a little bit of seed money to encourage others to take pride in their properties." But he didn't seem confident about the neighborhood's ability to attract investment.

"It's very difficult," Jamison said. "Once you've had students, it's probably still going to be rental property."

"We have not 'lost' Hamilton and Hudson. I don't believe that."

Leah Golby represents the Tenth Ward on the common council. It's the ward that contains much of the Pine Hills, including a good portion of the student neighborhood. She lived there herself—on Morris between Ontario and Quail—when she was at SUNY in the '80s ("Back then we were the only students on that block"). Today she owns a house on Myrtle, not far away.

"That was the attitude of the previous administration," she told me in 2015. "They were much more about demolishing and rebuilding. Sometimes you do have to demo, but most of these houses here are not lost. No, I wouldn't say they are lost at all. Not if there's life happening there."

Both as a neighbor and as a city official, she sees a plethora of reasons to feel optimistic about the Pine Hills. She loves the idea of a first-time home ownership program—"this neighborhood would be really great for that," she says—but sees that as only one way the city could encourage investment here.

Another way is a planned "road diet" for Madison Avenue. Madison between Partridge and Quail is the student neighborhood's main commercial strip, home to pizza places, bars, a tanning salon, a dry cleaner's. But remember that Madison is also US Route 20—four lanes of busy traffic navigating a street built for pedestrians and trolleys, not automobiles. The road diet has the potential to change that. Construction began in 2016 on 1.6 miles of Madison, cutting its traffic lanes from four to two and adding a middle turn lane. Studies suggest it will slow down traffic and reduce accidents. Golby believes it'll also change the way small-business owners look at the neighborhood. "It definitely has the potential to make those storefronts much more attractive to investors," she said. "That's what you see in city after city after these road diets are implemented: It becomes more of a walkable, livable neighborhood, instead of cars just zooming up Madison Avenue."

Better zoning should also help. Albany is updating its zoning map for the first time since 1968, part of a series of changes that should streamline the process of opening a business in the city. Golby hopes it will make it easier for people to reuse properties in creative ways.

There's reason to believe that code enforcement, too, is going to get better. In 2014, a city pilot program improved code compliance in the student neighborhood by focusing on education, not penalties. Inspectors checked whether apartments had residential occupancy permits, and if not, let landlords know what they needed to do to get one. What's more, the city is finally getting the software and equipment upgrades it has needed for so many years; that should make it easier to keep track of code violations and compliance. "I'm hopeful that when that rolls out we'll be able to manage all issues, not just critical issues," Golby said.

I don't live in the student part of the Pine Hills neighborhood, but it's not far away. My block of West Lawrence Street is a mix, and for the most part it's a working mix—owners and renters, professionals and students. Those of us who own our homes have used the tools available to us—code enforcement, p&z meetings—to oppose absentee landlords when we needed to. It doesn't always bring results. Do we think trying has given us better results than not trying? Absolutely. You get the neighborhood you fight for. At least, you *don't* get the neighborhood you *don't* fight for.

When trash vomits out of cans and collects on the sidewalks, when drunk shouting voices wake us at four in the morning, when I find footprints on the windshield of my car, I grit my teeth and recite: *Don't blame the many for the actions of a few. And judge not, for surely I, too, irk my neighbors from time to time.* In truth, I'm more inclined to think of absentee owners as the adversary. To me, overgrown yards, unshoveled walks, and broken steps reflect disregard for the neighborhood I love, and I resent it. I can't imagine they'd let their own houses—the ones they live in—get like that. Maybe they would, I don't know. But then

I remember that my beloved house is five years overdue for a paint job, and I'd better not cast that stone, either.

But man, it's hard sometimes.

Enter Carolyn Keefe to teach me a lesson. Something about "doing unto others."

"The neighborhood," she points out, "is not working all that well for the students, either."

Carolyn has had plenty of opportunity to observe what life is like for Pine Hills students: She and her husband have been surrounded by them for more than twenty years, raising their children in a house at the corner of Partridge and Hamilton. In the past two decades she's seen it all: Students move in, they move out, new ones move in. The rental houses around her get older. Noise, litter, and parking are problems year after year. Kegs and Eggs took place less than two blocks away.

"How many times I've heard students say, 'I can't *wait* to get out of here,' " Carolyn said. "This may be the first place people live in Albany. For many, this *is* Albany. Trash, noise, landlord problems—they send a message: This is not a city that values its neighborhoods."

I'd never thought about it exactly like that before, what the Pine Hills must look like to students. But then I remembered 1994: my own first glimpse of Albany was the student ghetto, and it was enough to drive me out of town. Out from under the umbrella of neighborhood nimbyism, I considered that poorly maintained properties reflect a disdain for tenants, too—disdain from the owners *and* the city. Everyone— students, families, the elderly, everyone—deserves to live with dignity in a dwelling that is orderly and safe. No wobbly handrails, no boarded-over windows, no shoehorning tenants into tiny bedrooms and renting flats to more people than the law allows.

If educated young people can't wait to leave Albany, that makes the student ghetto not just a student problem or a Pine Hills problem, but a city problem. As coordinator of the Pine Hills Improvement Group (PHIG), Carolyn Keefe is part of the solution.

Neighbors organized PHIG, an offshoot of the Pine Hills Neighborhood Association, in the fall of 2013 in hopes of moving beyond just voicing frustrations. They wanted to find ways to make the neighborhood better—cleaner, safer, friendlier. "Our goal is not to study the problem," she says, but to act: "What can we, with a small group of volunteers and just a little bit of money, actually do?"

Carolyn is a librarian by training, an information specialist with a focus on connecting small businesses with the resources they need to succeed. She takes the same approach to gathering ideas and organizing them into plans of action. After seeking input from neighborhood residents through surveys and meetings, PHIG settled on its first two goals: building community and beautifying the student neighborhood.

In Carolyn's view, students, full-time residents, university officials, city officials, and even absentee landlords are all partners, because they all have a stake in the neighborhood. "We didn't want it to be residents against students," she said. "We wanted it to be for the benefit of everyone."

And PHIG has succeeded in getting many of the various stakeholders to the table. It works with UAlbany, the Albany Police Department, neighbors, and other volunteers to host an annual "welcome back" picnic. The inaugural event, in 2014, invited students and full-time neighbors to a meet-and-greet with food and music at the Madison Avenue Playground, corner of Ontario. Displays introduced student renters to resources like United Tenants, Capital Carshare and the Albany Bike Coalition. There was information on recycling in Albany—what to put in, what to trash—demonstrations of how to use a fire extinguisher, a fire safety house to tour. The 2015 picnic added a fire demonstration room and a rock-climbing wall.

"For students, this is the first time, often, they're living on their own," Carolyn said. "So you have a bunch of 20-year-olds who might not know what is a good lease, or if an apartment is safe, or why we don't want them grilling on the porch. We wanted to make sure they're safe."

Another PHIG initiative coordinated a biweekly neighborhood cleanup with UAlbany student groups. ("They've been amazing," Carolyn said. "We couldn't have asked for more support.") PHIG volunteers beautified Madison Avenue's midtown commercial stretch by planting perennials under the sidewalk trees. They're trying to talk the city into putting in pedestrian-scale lighting and amenities like crosswalks. That's their mission statement: do as much as they can, and when something's too big for them to tackle on their own, urge other stakeholders to join in.

Sure, they're little steps. But they're taking them.

Carolyn believes in the power of small gestures. Doing away with the phrase "student ghetto," for example. It's not just an ugly name, she believes, but a self-fulfilling prophecy. The neighborhood's reputation steers investment away and teaches residents to undervalue their surroundings. "It's party central, so why bother?" she says. And it's not just the "ghetto" label that's the problem: Even the "student" part, Carolyn points out, is a misnomer. Pine Hills is hardly a monoculture. There are seniors, refugee families, and longtime residents like herself. "It's not just a student neighborhood," she says; "it just seems to *look* like a student neighborhood. That's been an excuse for not doing anything."

PHIG has a long list of goals, including reclaiming vacant lots as pocket parks or gardens and identifying places where blacktop could be replaced with grass. It is exploring ways to encourage a diversification of the business ecosystem—bringing in places other than bars and takeout joints. Members would especially like to see places that offer young people something to *do*, something that doesn't involve alcohol.

"It's important for the city to know that people see potential in this neighborhood," said Leah Golby. "The PHIG effort is bringing all the stakeholders together. It's the most promising thing happening in the neighborhood right now."

It's not just full-time residents taking strides to be good neighbors. The colleges, too, are looking for ways to contribute. Community engagement is nothing new, of course; for years representatives of UAlbany and Saint Rose have served on town-gown committees, attended neighborhood association meetings, tried to teach their students about how to be good off-campus neighbors. UAlbany has an "off-campus hotline" that anyone can call to report an issue on their block, be it a loud party, trash or vandalism, or a problem with a neighbor. In the years since Kegs and Eggs, the universities have initiated some interesting new programs.

In 2014, UAlbany created the Neighborhood Life division, a new entity under the auspices of the Office of Community Standards, which oversees student conduct. Luke Rumsey was picked to lead it. These days, if someone leaves a message on the hotline, he's the person they'll be hearing from. If a student renter is causing friction in the neighborhood, *they'll* be hearing from Luke, too. "For these types of complaints I will follow up with the students via a house visit," he told me. He wants students to be aware that "they can be held accountable for their actions through the school." And Luke may not come alone. He often brings an Albany police officer and a Saint Rose representative with him—in case it turns out the tenants aren't SUNY students. "APD, UAlbany & St. Rose all work very closely with one another," he explained.

A program that began in 2014 hired off-campus students to be "ambassadors," acting as a liaison between students and other neighbors on their block. Luke calls it "by far the most aggressive community engagement initiative to date." The ambassadors educate other student renters, address problems, and keep the lines of communication open between their neighborhood and the university. They are required to conduct door-to-door visits every two weeks, attend community meetings to understand the neighborhood better, and report any neighbor concerns back to the university. "The program received great feedback across the board," Luke said. "We are looking to expand."

What's so compelling about initiatives like PHIG and the ambassadors program is that they emphasize collaboration, not confrontation. They're not about pushing students out. They're about finding better ways to live together. Rolling up our sleeves and working together? It's so crazy it just might work.

Can the city do a better job of holding landlords accountable for substandard properties, and tenants for quality-of-life violations? Can the universities do more to encourage, or require, on-campus residency, and work to strengthen the neighborhoods their students call home? Can residents, both temporary and permanent, do a better job of communicating with one another and taking responsibility for their property, their block, their city?

Yes to all. In fact, I don't think any one piece of it will work without *all* pieces working. It's not a fight against landlords. It's not a fight against students. It's a fight against apathy.

17

Renewal

Being split into apartments in the 1970s might have been the beginning of the end for our house, making this just another old place with cracked walls, peeling paint, and an owner who lives elsewhere. Instead, it came into the hands of a man who saw it as something more than a rental. Michael Graham undid Keith Spencer's handiwork, restoring this house as a one-family home and investing his own muscle and sweat into its renovation. In our eyes, he's a hero.

When Michael bought the house in 1981, it was in pretty rough shape, he said. Why did he put his time, energy, and money into saving it?

"At the time I bought the house," he told me, "money was in short supply. The time and energy looked like a bargain—in fact, they were: The neighborhood is awesome, the people were down-to-earth and friendly. . . . By improving the house it was a good shot in the arm for the entire neighborhood."

"In the meantime," he added, "it was a roof over my head."

Michael, who worked in the software engineering field, had two qualities that helped him conquer projects that would've felled many a lesser DIY guy: an engineer's mind and a great affection for the house. I have that on authority of one of his old friends, Ric Chesser, himself a longtime Pine Hills resident. When I pointed out to Ric that one of Michael's projects, adding counter space in my kitchen, meant not only removing the back staircase but rerouting the first leg of the stairs that lead to the basement, he threw his head back and laughed. "That's exactly the kind of project Mike would do," he said. "I can picture him standing there with his dad, talking through calculations, figuring out how to do it."

Ric and Michael have known each other since they were kids, growing up across the river in their respective Greenbushes, East and North; they were acolytes together at the Lutheran Church. Before each bought a house in the Pine Hills, they shared an apartment on North Allen, across from School 16. Ric's a skilled carpenter himself; did he help with any of the projects in my house? "No, but I'd sit around and talk while Mike worked." Ric had his own share of home renovations to worry about; he'd bought his house, on Morris Street behind the Vincentian CCD school, in February 1980.

"Maybe eight to ten of the houses on that end [of Morris] changed hands in about a year or two," he told me. "A lot of them were in really bad shape," including his own. But as one Pine Hills generation passed on, and many younger householders looked to the suburbs, others like Ric and Michael saw something good in the neighborhood: opportunity. These shabby old houses were cheap enough to afford and interesting enough to make renovating them worth the effort.

Michael told me he took out the maid's staircase because "the traffic flow was painful" in the kitchen, and removing the stairs opened up space. A side benefit was that from the stairwell he was able to "harvest" the woodwork he needed to reconstruct the trio of front windows, where Keith had installed the apartment door. Michael hand-stripped and stained the interior woodwork and trim, which had all been painted white in some twentieth-century fit of modernization. He rebuilt the porches, dealt with drainage problems, had the roof replaced, remade the kitchen from the bare walls. ("Very sorry about not getting the kitchen windows at the same height," he told me; but you know what? I'd never noticed.) The house's hot water heater, plunked down for some reason in the kitchen, got banished to the basement where it belongs. Michael also cut the pass-through window between the kitchen and dining room. And the pipe holes in the dining room floor? He plugged them, I'm told, with sections of baseball bat.

When I tell him I'm going to call him a hero, he demurs and mentions the contractors he hired for some of the more daunting repairs. Okay, it's true that it wasn't his labor alone that redeemed our house.

But I'm sticking by "hero" even so. After all, he's the one who chose to sink money into this old place.

He declined my invitation to come and visit. Not everyone chooses to look back. But he did tell me one more thing about the house: "Glad you found the artifacts over the attic. I didn't have the heart to move them."

Thank you, Michael. Thank you.

Michael describes our block of West Lawrence, as he knew it in the 1980s, as "a friendly place." "It was a melting pot," he wrote me. "Students, professionals, tradespeople, and young people starting out." He recalls porch visits with an elderly neighbor and, during a World Cup soccer tournament, getting to know the Brazilian students next door. Despite their differences, he said, residents shared a respect for the neighborhood and for each other:

> Neighbors would stop on the street to talk to each other, which was interesting because none of us had that much in common. Considering the bland, siloed and self-similar neighborhoods of today, people in Pine Hills at that time had to identify their shared values through conversation. It wasn't a hardship, it was a sort of recreation. . . . We worked to know each other well enough to get along. That effort was the entry price that we all happily paid.

The picture Michael paints of life on West Lawrence Street is one that those of us here today might find warmly familiar: diverse, courteous, a little rough around the edges, maybe, but mostly positive, never homogenous and never boring. That stability is echoed in the reflections of another neighbor, Shamshad Ahmad, who's in a position to judge: with thirty years here and counting, he's the longest-tenured resident on our block.

A native of India, Ahmad and his family had come to Albany in 1979 when he joined the physics faculty at the state university. Before moving to this street in 1985, they were on North Lake Avenue. It was too crowded, he said, and they wanted to move somewhere with fewer rentals and more owner-occupancy. The Pine Hills stood out because of the neighborhood elementary: "School 16 was considered the best at that time," Ahmad said. But "that was a very difficult year to find a property," he added. They'd tried for several other places only to come up short, when finally they lit upon a house on West Lawrence. "Compared with [North Lake], it was a good place here," he said. "More peaceful, less traffic." It was something of a fixer-upper, nothing they couldn't handle, and another buyer's prior offer had just fallen apart. "Things fell in place," Ahmad said, "and I got it."

Huma, the second oldest of Ahmad's four children, was eleven years old when the family moved to the neighborhood. She wrote me from London, where she lives now, to share memories of her Pine Hills childhood.

It started with the thrill of getting her own room at last. The first time she set foot in the house, she recalls, she was carrying a tin box of her "most prized possessions" (sticker collection, Hello Kitty diary, oversized pencil) and claimed her bedroom—the red one—by leaving the box on its closet shelf. "There was no way my brothers were going to have this perfect room!" she wrote.

The neighborhood offered the freedom to explore and plenty of friends to explore with. They'd go out riding bikes—"going as far as Buckingham Pond on adventurous days"—or picking mulberries; Huma can still quote me the location of the best neighborhood bushes. She took her little sister to the library and spent summer days at 4-H camp in Ridgefield Park. "On holidays like Easter when everything was closed down," she remembered, "we could get our roller skates out and go around the Price Chopper parking lot or in the lot behind the bank on Madison."

Huma went to School 16, then Hackett Middle School, then Albany High. When she was a teenager, she and her friends liked to hang out sometimes up on Madison Avenue, where the sidewalk in front of Price Chopper had benches and a couple of stoic but amiable concrete tortoises. They'd buy a two-liter soda and meet "at the turtles" to talk. ("Yes, very exciting, I know," Huma said.)

"That we were Jewish, Christian, Muslim or Christian Pakistani didn't matter," she wrote. "We visited each other's houses, had birthday and pool parties and went through all the angst of growing up in the '80s and '90s together."

How has Shamshad Ahmad seen the neighborhood change over the past thirty years? Really, not much. "It was very much the same" when they first moved here, he said. The parking's gotten better. The student population has inched its way west. He recalled one period when there was a rash of car break-ins; he's glad that's behind us. "Renters come and go, the houses change hands," but by and large, he said, "it appears stable over 30 years." That's not to say Ahmad hasn't seen changes in the city during his time here. He observed that Albany's neighborhoods seem less racially segregated than in years past, and he's watched the local Muslim population grow "at an exponential rate." But this street's been steady.

The family has long been active in their religious community. In 2000, Ahmad was one of the founders of Albany's first mosque, Masjid As-Salam, and serves as president of its Board of Directors. His son Faisal gave up an engineering job at IBM to become an imam and is a founder of the Fiqh Institute, an Islamic educational center in Albany.

As the years went by, Ahmad said, he wouldn't have minded moving somewhere "a little quieter. To the countryside, or maybe to a suburb." He was born and raised in the country, he said, so that would have been his preference. "But none of my family members wanted to. The children were saying it would be too boring, too out of community." And after a while, the memories pile up, and nostalgia kicks in, and without a good reason to leave, they stayed.

"We didn't want to move because this is where our friends were, where our school was," Huma wrote me. "It's where we grew up. Simply put, it's home."

Three generations live now at the house on West Lawrence Street, and Ahmad's grandchildren go to School 16.

In 1994, the year I moved to Albany, Michael Graham sold our house to Carl and Anna Patka. Though he's a Philadelphia native, Carl had spent part of his childhood in the Pine Hills: his family moved to South Manning Boulevard when his father joined the philosophy department at the College of Saint Rose. "I had such wonderful memories of growing up there," he said. "It's a wonderful walking neighborhood, a walkable community." When he was in middle school his family moved to the suburbs. "I always kind of regretted it," he said. So years later, married and with kids of his own, he came back.

In the early '90s "there was a real movement to re-urbanize," Carl said. "FHA mortgages, low-cost home improvement loans: I knew a lot of people who wanted to do that, a lot of people with small kids. It was a really good atmosphere."

In those years Carl was an assistant counsel with the state Public Service Commission. Anna was working on a graduate degree at Saint Rose. They had two children when they moved in, plus another who came along a few years later.

This house "just had a wonderful feel," Anna said. "The three porches, such a nice feature. I loved the light and the sun and the space. We couldn't afford much," she added. "I was home with the kids; Carl was working but he had his student loans. It was the space that we needed and a good price." And it seemed like a good investment. A builder friend of Carl's looked the place over and told him, "This house is built like Fort Knox." Still, said Anna, "We were probably a little crazy to buy it. There were some huge problems." For instance, a crack in the foundation. Using a pickaxe, Carl dug down to the foundation along that entire side of the house, and then he sealed the crack. It took him a year.

"We had no money," Anna said, "but all the energy in the world."

Carl and Anna replaced many of the windows, rebuilt the upstairs bathroom and master bedroom from the studs, redid the ceilings in the dining room and the third-floor bedroom. They painted—in some rooms, several times, as old nicotine stains kept seeping through.

They had good friends in the neighborhood, and so did their kids. An empty corner lot on our block (no backstory there, no fire or demolition; it's just one of those lots that never got built on) was used for an informal community garden. "It was a gathering space," Anna said. "And there was so much food you had to share it."

"It was so much fun raising my kids at the house," Carl said, and letting them feel some of the independence he'd enjoyed in his own childhood. "The Price Chopper was right there," he said. "When I was a kid it was Central Market, and I remember my parents sending me with a dollar and some change to buy some milk and bread, some sugar—I'd walk up the hill in the corner—same hill, still there. I sent my kids on plenty of Ben and Jerry's runs." Then there were the little things that made him feel rooted to the past, like seeing the same crossing guard working on Madison Avenue. "Edna crossed me when I was a kid," said Carl, "and then she crossed my kids 30 years later."[1]

"You were able to have a sense of adventure a little bit, with everything so close," said Anna. "I could send Emily over to get a bagel when she was very young." The younger kids would "sneak" to Dunkin' Donuts on their walk home from the bus stop. "They just loved the idea of being able to go and do things independently."

Emily was their oldest, and she relished the Pine Hills' freedom as much as her father had in his day. "I would bike around with my friends, walk to a friend's house for dinner; it was all very close-knit," she told me. "That neighborhood made it really easy."

"The kids got to have relationships with other kids without our involvement," Anna said. "In the suburbs you have to be involved with your kids' activities because you have to drive them everywhere."

As much as the Patkas loved the house and community, in the early aughts West Lawrence Street had hit a rough patch. A next-door neighbor was dealing cocaine. ("Cars would pull up to the house at all hours and honk the horn," Anna said. A few times they went outside to chase customers away, which proves them braver than I'll ever be.) A guy in the corner house was raising pit bulls in his basement and shooting off air pistols in the back yard. The antisocial tenants didn't last—indeed, Gary and I never knew about them till years later—but there were other factors too. Emily was now middle-school age, and a chaotic first year at Hackett caused the Patkas to lose confidence in the

---

1. That was Edna Rinaldi, grandmotherly guardian to two generations of School 16 families. She worked the intersection of Madison and South Main from the mid-'70s until 2011, and in 2013 the city honored her on her one hundredth birthday by declaring it "Edna Rinaldi Day."

city schools. Other neighborhood friends and their kids were also moving away. Taking all this together, Carl and Anna felt it was the time for a change. They readied the house for sale and accepted a bid from the first people who looked at it. Us.

"Emily hated us for moving," Anna said, as the four of us sat on the deck of their home in Guilderland.

"I did," Emily agreed. "Well, I was really mad at you for a long time. I was just attached to that house. I can't explain it. I loved my room in particular, having the balcony. And it was my love for the neighborhood. There was just something special about knowing all the neighbors on our block."

The family relocated to a 1924 house off Western Avenue in Guilderland. It's a street that has more than a few echoes of the Pine Hills—lovely old houses, sidewalks, trees—but the traffic's a barrier to a free-roaming childhood. "It's close to many things," Anna observed, "but it's not walkable for kids." Speaking of Emily's younger sister, she said, "I couldn't let her walk to Stuyvesant Plaza."

"I do wonder sometimes what it would have been like had we stayed," Carl said. "Had we stuck it out I think the neighborhood would have gotten past it. Madison Ave. looks so much better now. And in many ways, that house was the real love of my life."

"We love this house just fine," Anna said. "But it just doesn't feel the same."

The Neighborhood You Fight For

Our house was one of the lucky ones, thanks to talented caretakers who looked at the old place and saw something worth saving. You could say the neighborhood was lucky, too—if you believe that people make their own luck. The Pine Hills' endurance, and its resurgence, has happened largely because of residents who were willing to devote their time and energy to protecting the neighborhood and making it better. I'll illustrate that point with the stories of four incidents from recent decades that could have been tipping points—moments where the Pine Hills kept a landmark, a resource, or part of its character, through the efforts of people who cared enough to work for it.

The Library

In 1985, the Pine Hills library got its eviction notice. The College of Saint Rose bought the Madison Avenue mansion that housed the creaky, leaky, but beloved neighborhood branch. The building never had been city property; St. Vincent de Paul parish had owned it and collected a nominal rent for its use as a library. The college put the city on notice that it was going to have to find another library location—eventually. It said it wouldn't force the library out till it was sure of its own plans for the mansion.

A library branch is the sort of place you can build a neighborhood around. Not just a place to get free books, or even a gathering space,

B.J. Costello, Fred Ruff and other members of the Pine Hills Neighborhood Association call attention to a trash container left for months in front of a Madison Avenue property, March 21, 1978. Photo by Jack Pinto. Courtesy of the *Times Union*.

it's a symbol of sharing. Libraries represent community. And losing one? It hurts.

The Pine Hills Neighborhood Association (PHNA) got a tip from a library insider that there was talk among trustees about not just closing the branch but moving it to another neighborhood.

"There was a real big possibility that we wouldn't have a library anymore," said Virginia Hammer. "It was a real concern."

Virginia is a South Allen Street resident and longtime Pine Hills firebrand. She's the sort of person every neighborhood needs: if there's a problem in the Pine Hills, Virginia is perfectly happy to be a pain in everybody's ass about it till something gets done. Back in the '80s, she was on the neighborhood association's library committee; the campaign to keep a library was her first foray into neighborhood activism.

Considering how much westward growth Albany had seen, it's not surprising the library board would at least explore the idea of putting a branch out that way, perhaps farther down Western Avenue. They wouldn't have been the only ones looking west: the firefighters at Engine 10 (updated from Steamer 10, the days of steam long gone) were making their own plans to move to a new firehouse on Brevator Street. But Pine Hills neighbors told the library trustees: We're still here. Establish another branch out there if you need to, but don't do it at our expense. And they set out to make sure city and library officials got the message.

"There is a very strong feeling that we want a Pine Hills library," PHNA vice president Henry Madej told the *Times Union* in 1986. "If you want to move it up the block, fine. Just don't close it down or move it to Central Avenue."

The neighborhood association "started making noise," as Virginia put it: circulating petitions, distributing fliers, holding meetings, going on TV. Members initiated a letter-writing campaign to the mayor, met with city and library officials, and kept the issue in front of the press. In October of 1986, Virginia told the *Times Union* that during multiple meetings with library officials earlier that year, "The possibility was raised of moving [the branch] out of the neighborhood." Library director William O'Connor downplayed that possibility in comments to a reporter but did acknowledge that they were considering one site outside the neighborhood.[1]

---

1. Despite assistance from the Albany Public Library, I was unable to locate APL Board of Trustees meeting minutes from the late 1980s to see how the branch relocation issue and the questions of public access were reflected in the official record. The minutes are not at the Albany County Hall of Records, nor could they be located within the library. In 2002, Albany voters approved making the library independent of city government.

"The big nut to crack," Virginia told me, "was the process of having your voice heard." The library board, whose trustees were all mayoral appointees, had faced criticism for its lack of responsiveness to the public. Meetings would be closed—or, if open, Virginia recalls, would not provide any time for public comments.

"It was very difficult," Virginia said. "People involved in the decision making were not interested in hearing from the people affected by the decisions." She had to school herself on open meetings law: "When we first started to show up at these meetings, we had to kind of force our way through. Apparently no one had ever tried to confront them before; they weren't used to having people there."

But she and others would go anyway. They would attend every meeting to watch, listen, and take notes. "I'm not sure we were ever really allowed to say anything to them," she told me, "but they knew we were there."

And they started doing their homework. They collected statistics on the Pine Hills branch use—"It was hugely popular. It contributed so much to the library's total circulation numbers"—and created a list of potential new branch locations. "They would say, 'There's no place in the neighborhood.' So the [PHNA] group went looking for real estate itself."

Frustrated that library trustees weren't acting fast enough, the PHNA kept on their heels. What the neighbors feared was that if the board waited till the last minute, it would declare itself out of options. "What's going to happen when the college is ready to move in?" Virginia asked in 1986. "The library's going to be out on the sidewalk."

A few possible locations were floated, including the Engine 10 firehouse, which was a serious contender to become the new library till engineers concluded the building couldn't handle the weight of the books. The question wasn't settled until 1988, when the city purchased the New York Telephone Co. building on Western Ave., right across from the Madison-Western Point. Weight wouldn't be a problem there: the place was built in the 1930s to hold heavy telephone switchboards. Its first floor provided double the space of the old library branch, allowing the library to expand its collection and add community meeting space. In 1990, staff and volunteers moved thirty-five thousand volumes into their new home.

Did the neighborhood pressure help influence the outcome? Virginia thinks so. I do, too.

"From what we had to go through just to get in there and talk, I think there wasn't the biggest consideration there for the feelings of neighborhoods," she said. "We felt like they basically didn't give a darn. If somebody had presented them with something, they'd look at it, but they wouldn't go out of their way. *'Close it? Oh well.'*"

When the ribbon was cut to open the new Pine Hills Library, Virginia saved a piece of it. "Everyone was happy. We had this happy library. But we almost lost it."

The Firehouse

As the old telephone exchange was transformed into the new Pine Hills branch, another building at the Point was standing empty, too. Steamer 10 couldn't cut it as a library, but someone else approached the city with an idea for the firehouse.

Ric Chesser had been doing theater around Albany—in parks, school auditoriums, any place he and the rest of the Washington Park Theatre Company could set up a stage—since the 1970s. In the early '80s, thanks to his daughter, Ric found his niche: children's theater. "Emily was two," he told me. "I was looking for things to take her to, and most of it was just awful. I realized at some point, '*I* know how to do this!' And that was how Kids' Fare got started." When the performers saw the energy and excitement that live theater inspired in young audiences, they were inspired too, and they started looking for a permanent home.

The city agreed to let them rent the firehouse for use as a children's theater for a dollar a year, plus utilities, but that hardly made it a cinch. Ric's theater group had to pull together the money and labor to turn the station into a performance space. They built more restrooms, updated the plumbing and electrical systems, fixed ceilings, and of course added a stage, not to mention seats for the audience. The work cost hundreds of thousands of dollars.

Steamer 10 Theatre opened in 1991, and it's still chugging along. As executive director, Ric offers between 120 and 150 performances a year to some 11,000 patrons, directing actors, building props, even writing many of the scripts himself. Fliers needed to tell subscribers about upcoming shows? He designs them. Grant applications due? He writes them. Concession stand out of cookies? He buys them. Toilets overflowing? He plunges them.

Ric and his cohorts provide not just entertainment but education, offering theater classes for children and productions in which kids are the actors. In recent years, our daughters have been among them. It's just the sort of place a young person needs when she's entering adolescence: safe, silly, nonjudgmental, and full of positive energy.

Steamer 10 brings thousands of families into the Pine Hills every year—most of his mailing list, Ric says, is in the suburbs—and at least some of them must grab dinner or coffee on Madison Avenue before a show. And who knows? Perhaps some of them will like the neighborhood so much they'll want to stay. Ric hopes so. "It's the only way the city's going to survive and thrive," he said. "You have to get families with children committing to the city." That neighborhood focus is part of Steamer 10's mission statement. "We all grow together," a part of it reads. "There is no doubt that we can only exist through the goodwill and efforts of our community, so we seek to not only further the interests of our community, but the solidarity of that community." To that end, the theater offers meeting space for neighborhood groups and plays a pivotal role in the Upper Madison Improvement Group, a nonprofit that has staged events like the Pine Hills street fair and free summer concerts.

Steamer 10's a Pine Hills treasure. How many neighborhoods can say they have a children's theater within walking distance? But even people without young children can appreciate that it's keeping the lights on in an uptown landmark, making it a vital part of the neighborhood.

The Cinema

By the early 1990s the curtain was falling on the Madison Theatre's single-screen era. "It's a dinosaur," complained a lawyer for its owner, Barry Rosenblatt, whose family was trying to sell the place. It was by then one of only two neighborhood theaters remaining in Albany, and one of only a handful around the country. In 1994 the cinema got a new owner, who tried to keep it alive in the era of the mall multiplex by carving the draperied hall into five smaller screening rooms. It was given a new name befitting a place with one foot in the past: the Norma Jean Madison.

Norma Jean wasn't the only dinosaur on upper Madison; independent bookstores were breathing in the meteor dust, too. Clapp's, which had been open in one of the theater's retail spaces since the early days, threw in the towel in 1996, one of the many small bookstores nationwide that couldn't cut it against giants like Borders and Barnes & Noble. "The students are all mobile now and they've been raised in malls," Clapp's owner Susan Milner told the *Times Union* as news of the closing went public. "Mine is a neighborhood store, and it just doesn't attract the young people anymore."

When Clapp's closed, the cinema claimed its space and added two more screens. But financial troubles dogged its owner. Historic Albany put the theater on its endangered building list in 2000, and, at last, in 2003, the Norma Jean closed its doors, perhaps for good.

People still held out hope that someone would work out a plan for the theater. And indeed, in 2004, a plan did come forward—though it was hardly what the neighbors had in mind. CVS, which runs the pharmacy on the corner of Madison and South Main, proposed tearing down the old cinema and its attached retail spaces to build a much larger drugstore—thirteen thousand square feet—with a drive-through window.

Faced with the specter of losing not just the theater but part of the neighborhood's pedestrian character, residents came forward to protest. Letters to the editor hit the *Times Union* within a week, lamenting the loss of another Albany landmark and questioning the kind of "progress" this plan represented. One asked: "Do we think much-anticipated newcomers to our city will be impressed with another drive-through box rather than a theater that they could walk to?"

Lorraine Weiss was one of the people troubled by news of the CVS proposal. She didn't live in the Pine Hills, but as a historical preservation planner, she had years of experience with Albany preservation efforts. And she saw that if people were going to organize in support of the

Madison, there was no clear flag-bearer: The theater sits near a ward boundary, and the area isn't part of a historic district or a merchant's association. "Nobody 'owned' the issue," Lorraine told me. But "we knew that we needed to get the conversation going. We needed to get ahead of the game before it went too far." Someone suggested to her: "You should talk to Anne Savage and see about organizing something." Anne hadn't lived in Albany for very long, but through work she'd done for Citizen Action of New York and People Advocating Small Schools, which pushed for a school renovations bond act in 2001, she had gained a reputation as a skilled organizer interested in community planning. "So I landed on Anne's doorstep one night," Lorraine said, "and I said, 'Hi, we need to do something about the Madison Theatre.'" Lorenz Worden, active with the PHNA, joined them. In all, a coalition of about a dozen came together. They called themselves Friends of the Madison.

"Why I thought we could accomplish anything, I don't know," Anne told me, "but the CVS plan seemed like such an obvious disaster for the neighborhood."

Friends of the Madison's goals were to gather information on the theater—its architectural significance, its history, its role in the neighborhood—and share that information with influencers: city planners, lawmakers, the media. They took common council members out to breakfast one by one. They also started compiling examples of old theaters that had been successfully converted to other uses. "It was like stone soup," Lorenz told me. "Everyone came and offered what they had to offer." An engineer did a pro bono structural analysis of the theater. An attorney and an architect offered their skills. Computer-savvy people set up a listserv, which hundreds joined.

A survey of Pine Hills residents found near-universal support for saving the theater and near-universal rejection of the CVS plan. Though there wasn't a groundswell of drive-through pharmacy backers—"It's just not an interesting thing to be in support of," Lorenz said; "It's like being interested in blacktop"—the campaign to save the Madison was hardly unanimous. Some said Albany needed to stop living in the past and embrace projects that would improve the tax base. "We just kept presenting the information that taking away business space—reducing business space—was not a viable option," Lorraine said. To replace something as uncommon as a neighborhood cinema with a chain store, a parking lot, and the increased car traffic they would bring, they argued, was to squander the Pine Hills' economic potential. "This was a pedestrian-focused neighborhood," Lorraine said, "and it was a unique place in this part of Albany."

"If we try to be Guilderland," Anne said, "we will fail. They will always be better at being Guilderland than we are. People choose Pine Hills because they can walk to things. We need to be who we are; we need to compete in a way we can win. And we *are* competing—because people are choosing where they will live. If we try to be someone else, we will lose every time."

Lorraine remembers one PHNA meeting where a developer's representative was trying to sell the CVS idea. Several neighbors had stood up to talk about why they love the Pine Hills, how they'd moved here for its walkable character. The rep's response, Lorraine recalled, was to emphasize how mothers with children and senior citizens would be able to drive through the pharmacy. And then he added: "This isn't really a pedestrian neighborhood. Downtown is your pedestrian neighborhood. This is a *suburban* neighborhood." His script was written, and there was no deviating from it.

In October 2004, the city rejected the CVS plan, determining the size of the proposed drugstore exceeded zoning limits and lacked adequate parking. "We were one happy group of people," Lorenz said. "We were partying in the street that night."

But what next? Friends of the Madison had plenty of love but no money, and since love don't pay the bills, they turned their efforts to assisting the hunt for a buyer and encouraging the city to keep its aim on that target.

On a winter's night in early March 2005, Friends of the Madison held a community meeting at the College of Saint Rose. A blizzard hit the city that evening, but more than 150 people showed up anyway. ("Because they *walked* there!" Lorenz laughed.) Mayor Jennings stopped by to pledge his support. Neighbors were hopeful that the Madison could be reopened, or, if no operator could be found, that the building could be reused as some other type of arts venue. Participants made heartfelt speeches about neighborhood and community, about the past and the future, and about the theater's role in both. They listened to Friends of the Madison's ideas for the building and shared some of their own. "People idealized their childhood memories of the theater," Lorenz said. "They said they wanted to bring their grandchildren here. That helped, that people really cared about the place in a personal way."

At that meeting Lorenz noticed a man sitting at the back of the room, not saying anything. As he found out later, the man was an Amsterdam theater owner named Joe Tesiero.

A couple of weeks afterwards, Tesiero bought the Madison. It was the neighborhood's passion for the theater, he said, that helped convince him to invest. He told the *Times Union*: "After listening to the Friends of the Madison, we are quite confident that the Pine Hills area wants their theater back and we will try our hardest to give them a theater that their community deserves."

Lorraine, Anne, and Lorenz, needless to say, were thrilled—but they emphasized that credit for the victory spread far beyond them. "We had a lot of good luck," Lorraine said. "But the luck wouldn't have come without the nucleus of energy that rose from the citizenry." Having strong neighborhood associations and politically active residents had allowed them to mobilize quickly. As Anne put it: "We stood on the shoulders of who came before."

After the sale, Tesiero sat down with Friends of the Madison and talked about the property's future, a gesture they appreciated. "We had no standing," Lorraine said. "We weren't official. He wasn't necessarily seeking input, but he allowed us to give him input." In particular, they urged him to seek a coffee shop for one of the theater's retail spaces—an idea mentioned repeatedly by neighbors in brainstorm sessions—in favor of the Quizno's he was considering. The Quizno's never materialized, but a coffee house did.

Over the next several years, the theater didn't change much. It was still pretty shoddy, and it didn't appear that Tesiero invested much money or time into making it anything more than it already was. But its doors stayed open till another buyer came along—and for that he has the Friends of the Madison's respect, and mine.

"He deserves a lot of credit," Lorraine told me. "Even though we weren't happy with his management afterward, he stepped in. He was the caretaker, the guard at the gate, for how many years. In hindsight, his main gift was to be a transition to a more successful management with more commitment to the neighborhood."

With the theater reopened, Friends of the Madison started meeting with other merchants, looking for ways to strengthen and support the business district. The theater group's efforts spurred the creation of the Beautify Upper Madison Project (later, it was renamed the Upper Madison Improvement Group), which works to promote the business district with beautification projects and community events.

The years that followed were good ones for the commercial corridor: The city engaged consultants to survey residents and prepare a report to guide neighborhood commercial development. An underused block of Yates Street was repaved to add parking. A 2009 renovation doubled the size of the Pine Hills library. A lively restaurant scene developed on Madison, with all the storefronts filled once again. At one merchant meeting, according to Lorraine, "the CVS people were there. They said things had improved for them, that shoplifting was down, because there was more life on the street."

"This project was really the catalyst for the neighborhood taking other steps, to work toward other planning projects in the neighborhood," Lorraine said. "It's a great planning story: where a neighborhood resource can serve as a catalyst for stabilization and further development."

Tesiero kept the theater till 2013. Then it passed to Gunther Fishgold and Darren Grout, who a few years earlier had assumed the role of Pine Hills caffeinators when they opened Tierra Coffee Roasters next door to the Madison. "I believe in that neighborhood more than any I've ever been in," Fishgold told the *Times Union*. Their renovations reduced the number of screens at the Madison from seven to three, restored a retail storefront, spiffed up the marquee, finally got rid of that musty smell, and added a live performance venue in the back of the house. Now they host films, concerts, and comedy acts, and they make the best movie-house popcorn ever popped.

A healthy business district, Lorenz believes, is part of what makes the Pine Hills so well suited to be a model for twenty-first-century urban living. "The whole tenet of the time is the refocusing on neighborhoods as the heart of the cities," said Lorenz, who these days is championing the construction of protected bike lanes as president of the Albany Bicycle Coalition. "The more this traffic is calmed, the more it will come to people: 'Let's go to the theater; let's walk, take a bike, take the bus.' If we're going to solve this global warming, this has to be part of the solution."

"We always wanted the Madison Theatre to be part of the neighborhood picture," Anne said. "That was part of the short arc. The long arc was to increase home ownership in Pine Hills—to make this the kind of place where families want to be. Supporting the merchants supports the vital, urban, walkable community."

"You need good neighborhoods," Anne added. "That's what you need to make cities succeed."

The Landlord

Tensions between neighbors are nothing new. Neither are tensions between homeowners and absentee landlords. But when a property on your block goes out of control, and no one answers for it, what can you do?

On the corner of North Allen and Lancaster was a building that held twenty-six apartments. Online records list the property as 5,921 square feet; by my math that averages out to about 227 square feet per unit. The area was zoned for one- and two-family houses, but the big old place had been grandfathered in because, like practically every other house in the neighborhood, it predated the 1968 zoning code. It was owned by Roger Ploof, one of Albany's largest landlords.

In the early aughts, the property had a reputation among neighbors for troublesome tenants and ongoing problems with noise, trash, and rowdyism: fights that spilled out into the street; used condoms and syringes tossed into a neighbor's yard; and nearly a hundred police calls to the building in eleven months in 2003. Nearby residents said they felt afraid to walk past the building.

After years of complaining to Ploof, neighbors said, with no results, in 2004 they took a new approach. City building code allows for challenges to nuisance properties that don't conform with zoning law. But an Albany property's neighbors had never before pursued such a challenge; the tactic had been used only by city officials. The New Albany Neighborhood Association, which represented the area, led a push to have the building declared a nuisance property, submitting petitions that prompted a zoning board hearing.

Ploof said that was the first he heard of any problem with the apartment house. "The neighborhood association never called me; the police never called me," he told the *Times Union*. He pointed out that his properties almost always pass code inspections, and he said he believed police calls on the building were "lower than average" for Albany apartments.

The board sided with the residents, ordering Ploof to cut the building's twenty-six apartments down to two. It was an order he defied until the city took him to court. Then, with potentially $200,000 in charges hanging over his head, he emptied the building of tenants.

A few years later, another group of Pine Hills residents used the same approach to mount a challenge against a second Ploof property. Since the landlord had purchased the seven-unit house at 32 South Allen in 2007, neighbors said, living conditions there had plummeted. In 2010 they collected enough petition signatures to force a Board of Zoning Appeals hearing, and they went before the board to describe trash dumped out of upstairs windows and blowing into nearby yards, blaring stereos, and parties that lasted days. When they complained, they said, tenants had threatened them. Police provided data that showed a sharp increase in the number of calls to the property since Ploof had bought it.

Again, the landlord downplayed problems at the house: "There's not drug dealing or shootings or things of that nature," he told the paper. (Oh, well, that makes it all right then.) Ploof claimed his properties were being targeted because of his largely minority clientele. Unmoved, the zoning board slashed the number of units allowed in the building from seven to two.

Virginia Hammer, who lives on South Allen, was one of the foot soldiers in that fight. "That took a lot of work," she told me. "It took a really, really, really long time because we had to learn how to do it," how to prepare petitions that would stand up in court. In the end, she said, it was a bittersweet victory: during the years when Ploof fought through the appeals process, some neighbors moved away. "We won the battle but we sort of lost the war," Virginia said. "People hung on as long as they could."

And yet—it's a precedent. "I think that it says, 'Look, the neighborhoods aren't just going to allow landowners to come in and do what they want with the properties without any consequences,'" said Jeff Jamison, who argued the case for the city during Ploof's appeals.

Neighborhood activism's not always successful, of course. Pine Hills residents fought to keep a post office and lost it anyway. They couldn't stop the College of Saint Rose from expanding across Madison Avenue. But even when they fail, these efforts have value. They help people identify their shared commitments. They give us an opportunity to articulate what's important to us and see others stand up for it too. Even a campaign that falls short can strengthen the bonds that make a neighborhood something more than a collection of houses.

Before coming to Albany, I'd never lived anywhere long enough to see how things got the way they are. I thought they just . . . were. I read the papers, of course; I noticed when the city approved this project or rejected that one. What I didn't see were the months of effort behind those decisions. So to the people who interrupt their family time and their comfortable evenings to sit through meetings, brainstorm ideas, go door to door, be the squeaky wheel, file petitions, write grants, change minds: thank you.

19

Building / Community

On a summer weekend in 2012, a group of volunteers gathered at the corner of South Main and Madison. Their goal: to bring a bit of the Pine Hills back to life.

On the side of the CVS drugstore was a mural, flaked and faded after thirty-five Albany winters. Neighbors had organized to restore it. Donations paid for sealing and repointing the brick; businesses offered supplies. And people—longtime residents, former residents, newcomers—showed up to paint. Gary and I were there; we brought our kids, our backyard umbrella, some lawn chairs, and our talents, so-called, which were best suited to fetching paint for others, trying not to fall off ladders, and maybe filling in large rectangles devoid of any detail. But we wouldn't have missed it for anything.

Guiding the efforts was Constance Dwyer Heiden, the woman who had designed the original mural in 1977. Touched by neighbors' enduring affection for the work, she had come to Albany from her home in Lancaster, Pennsylvania, to oversee its renewal.

Connie had grown up on North Main Avenue in the 1950s and '60s, between Madison and Western, in a charming row of houses with little porches across from St. Andrew's Church. She left Albany after graduation. Getting that distance helped her see the value of her Pine Hills childhood—a value that sprang not just from its people or from the place, but from an interweaving of both. The friends she'd giggle with at the Madison. Sitting in a booth at Stittig's with a high school date. Her elderly neighbors, some of them Pine Hills pioneers, the first owners of their lovely old houses.

"It made me appreciate how nice it is to know people and have people know you," Connie told me. "Having connections."

She came back to Albany and began working with the City Arts Office, which used federal funds to create public art and arts programming in the city in the 1970s and '80s. One outreach project arranged crews to paint murals around the city, and when Connie learned they were considering the side of Mack's Drugs at Madison and South Main for one of them, she knew she had to get involved. After all, she'd grown up just across the street.

"There was no doubt about it," she said. "This was my baby."

She wanted to make the mural a "homage to the neighborhood" she grew up in. But how could she paint the sense of community she'd come to value? The answer came to her "in a flash": a tribute to the small businesses at the heart of the Pine Hills.

"How many hours I'd spent in Mack's Drugstore and Stittig's and the Petit Paris, and Ann Petersen's—we'd go there to get our hair cut," she said. "Mom would run out of something and we'd have to run over to Cal Heller's, a narrow store where the groceries were stacked up to the ceiling."

So she made the center section of her design a collage of signboards for neighborhood stores. A panel on the left pays tribute to the city with a rendering of City Hall; on the right is the Steamer 10 firehouse. Flanking the panels are trees, because, as Connie says, "We have to have roots so we can grow and branch out."

Over the years, Connie's tribute to the landmarks of her childhood became a neighborhood landmark itself. And when it faded, Pine Hills residents saw its restoration as a symbol of the neighborhood's vitality.

You know, "restoration" isn't quite the right word, because after the loose flakes were removed and the wall prepared for painting, the mural was barely a shadow. More than "restored," it was reborn—drawn and painted anew, based on Connie's guidance and photographs of the original. So if the mural project was a symbol for a wider sense of community, then let's linger on that symbolism for a moment: the past may be our starting point, but *we* are the ones who make a neighborhood.

Several years ago, a dear friend from Myrtle Avenue moved to Saratoga County. She now has a big, modern house on a quiet street lined with immaculately maintained properties. She has a lovely swimming pool in her backyard. She misses the Pine Hills.

"I never see my neighbors," she says. "When they come home they pull their cars right into their garages and go inside for the night."

Blame television, blame cars, blame developers: for decades house design and neighborhood planning turned inward, emphasizing back decks instead of front porches, three-car garages instead of sidewalks, cul-de-sacs instead of mixed-use districts. In her 1961 landmark planning book, *The Death and Life of Great American Cities*, writer and activist Jane Jacobs castigates twentieth-century urban planners for their misunderstanding of how cities work. In housing projects, superblocks, and other urban renewal projects, she saw assumptions worth challenging: that each function of a city should be separated into its own tidy district; that the presence of other people is "at best a necessary evil"; that the street is inherently an unwholesome public space. Others looked at a jumbled city and saw disorder, but Jacobs saw an order of a different kind: something organic, and maybe chaotic, but useful, vital, and human.

When Connie talks about small businesses being the heart of Pine Hills life, she's seeing the threads of what Jacobs calls "a web of public respect and trust"—hundreds of casual interactions that add up to something greater than the sum of their parts. Maybe it's enjoying a good gripe about city snow plowing with the Price Chopper cashier, nodding hello at the coffee shop to someone you recognize as a friend of a friend, or stopping under a streetlamp to let your dog take a good sniff of a stranger's pup, and exchanging a "Have a good night" with the woman on the other end of the leash. Moments like these may seem trivial, Jacobs writes, but they add up to something with real value: a shared sense of trust. Not just "I trust you," but something more, as in, we hold our community "in trust"; we all are responsible in some way for its success or its failure, and we perceive that others are invested in it, too. "Lowly, unpurposeful and random as they may appear," she writes, "sidewalk contacts are the small change from which a city's wealth of public life may grow."

It's not about knowing everybody you pass on the sidewalk—indeed, quite the opposite. In cities, Jacobs writes, privacy means more than just shutting the window blinds; there's a public kind of privacy that allows us to reap the benefits of economic and social contact with the people around us without having to invite them all into our personal lives. Casual public connections don't imply that we have to visit them on their birthdays or invest in their financial schemes, but these interactions *do* reinforce that we share a basic level of public responsibility for this place we have in common, and for one another.

This web strengthens not only a neighborhood's identity but also its political agency. Because a neighborhood is part of the larger city, people in it ideally will have ties to their street and also ties to people and organizations outside the neighborhood. These overlapping networks—which take years for people to form, Jacobs emphasizes—help the neighborhood draw on resources when it faces a problem too big to solve on its own. And this is the value of neighborhood: much more than a sentimental flourish, it is the base fabric of the urban tapestry.

The connections a city makes possible have material benefits, too. Studies of urban scaling quantify the worth of the human social network: living close by other people increases per-capita productivity and creativity, a pattern that appears to hold true independent of a city's size, geography, or history. Of course, social negatives like crime and disease increase, too—but then, so do innovations for dealing with them.

To develop this web of connections, we need to have places where we can connect with each other. That's why it matters how our neighborhoods are built. Jacobs emphasizes the importance of mixed-use districts; a neighborhood that contains residences and offices, plus shops and other services, she argues, will be healthier economically and socially: socially because people will have more opportunities to run into each other out on the street; economically because having both workers and residents means more patrons for local businesses at different times of day and a larger customer base that can support a greater diversity of businesses. What's more, she argues, giving people a plenitude of reasons to get out on the streets can make the neighborhood safer: "A well-used city street is apt to be a safe street," she writes, because the watchful eyes of people who feel proprietorship of the neighborhood will do more to enforce the norms than a patrol car ever could.

These days, the idea of mixed use is an important part of conversations about urban neighborhoods, often tagged with the buzzword "walkability": Do we have to jump in the car every time we need a loaf of bread? Do we have sidewalks to bring us to a neighborhood playground?

These are questions more and more people are asking. A 2013 poll by the National Association of Realtors found that 60 percent of respondents favor a neighborhood where homes are within easy walking distance of shops and other businesses. Other assessments have shown that neighborhoods with high "walkscores"—a measurement of how many shops and services are within walking distance—have seen a recent increase in real estate values. A 2010 University of New Hampshire study reinforced Jacobs's observations: residents of walkable neighborhoods trusted their neighbors more and had greater community involvement. And the study's authors pointed out that having higher levels of social capital, as sociologists call it, has been linked to better health and increased economic opportunities.

Public spaces near our homes—a small commercial district, a playground, a library—offer opportunities to connect with the people around us. Walkability helps turn a jumble of houses into a community.

And that's what makes this Albany's moment.

Albany has assets other cities would love to have: Neighborhoods. Housing stock with character. Walkability. Small shopping districts. Good trees! And the thread that weaves it all together is residents who care enough to get involved. As more people embrace a new urbanism, cities like Albany—and neighborhoods like the Pine Hills—should roll out the welcome mat. How can we promote our assets and work to strengthen them? One way, perhaps, is to think of urban revitalization as something that starts in the neighborhoods, not in a megacorp office block garnished with tax breaks.

Seen from that perspective, the goals of development would shift. Small-business investment would loom large. So would small-scale infrastructure improvements and beautification projects. In neighborhoods where a high turnover of tenants has weakened the social fabric, we'd establish programs to encourage home ownership and address blighted or vacant properties. We might see more plans like the Madison Avenue road diet that emphasize *living* in our neighborhoods instead of just rushing through them. Residents might push for walkable, mixed-use districts and urge that zoning laws be adjusted where necessary.

And, finally, perhaps we'd see our old houses and narrow streets not as headaches but as part of what makes Albany unique and stately and, yes, beautiful. Not everything from the past can be preserved, nor should it be. I'm not *that* sentimental. But our built environment is inseparable from Albany's identity, inseparable from that interweaving of geography, character, history, and spirit that people sometimes call authenticity, or a sense of place. It is the warp on which the weft of all our stories lies.

Albany has the ingredients to remake itself into a twenty-first-century city. That's what I see here in the Pine Hills: potential. It radiates from rich history and fresh ideas, from lifelong residents and passionate newcomers. If our vision is colored by love, what of it? It doesn't obscure the challenges. It might even help us work through them.

It's a late-summer evening here on West Lawrence Street, at the fading end of twilight, and Gary and I have uncapped a couple of beers and settled into our front porch chairs to catch up on the day. Seen from up here on the hill, the neighbor's porch bulb underlights the tree; it frames our view in a way that reminds me of a stage set. The sidewalk *is* a stage, in a way, and we're here watching the show.

From the yard across the street, Charlie and Wrigley, our dogs' best dog-friends, hear our voices and bark once to say hello. A car blasting music idles at our corner and revs its engine; we roll our eyes and wait for a green light to send this annoyance away. Two young women walk by, lugging home groceries; seeing them makes Gary remember he'd better run to Tierra to buy a bag of coffee or we'll regret it in the morning. He crosses Morris Street, and in just a few more steps he's out of sight up Price Chopper's mulched bank: the same shortcut Carl Patka and his kids used to use. Teens on skateboards whiz down the street. From somewhere a car alarm starts beeping and is silenced, then starts beeping again and is silenced again. The breeze carries the laughter of children and the opening notes of someone's dinner preparations: garlic and olive oil.

The street's never empty for more than a minute or so: a car, a jogger, a dog-walker, a man with a bag of empties. I wave to a neighbor kid who's walking past. Then it's Gary's turn to recross the stage; on his way up our sixteen steps he stoops to snag a candy wrapper in the grass.

It's nothing special, our street. It's just people being people, flawed and careless and noble and human. And yet there's something hopeful in hearing the music of the other lives being lived around us. It's comforting. And it's humbling to know that I, too, have a voice in this song.

My phone buzzes; it's our girls, who've been up at the Madison with friends. They're texting to say the movie's over and they're coming home.

Sources, Notes, and Notes on Sources

When quoting sources I have tried to preserve the capitalization, punctuation, and spelling of the original. Similarly, I've tried to use whatever name an institution called itself at the time under discussion; that's why, for example, I refer to the State University of New York at Albany as "SUNY Albany" in passages about the 1990s, but call it "UAlbany" when writing about recent years. And when a story came from the decades when the *Times-Union* used a hyphen in its name, I hyphenated too; when the newspaper dropped the hyphen, so did I.

Chapter Two

My main sources for information about the Marx family are federal and state census data, city directories, and local newspapers. The first time I saw Ludwig Marx's name (in this instance, it was "Lewis Marx"), it was written across my property on plate O of the *City Atlas of Albany, New York, from official Records, Private plans and Actual Surveys; Based upon Plans Deposited in the Department of Surveys* (Philadelphia: G. M. Hopkins, 1876).

Judge Gillis's account of the first rail journey was included in *The History of the First Locomotives in America, from Original Documents, and the Testimony of Living Witnesses* by William H. Brown (New York: D. Appleton, 1871). Brown's book also reprints 1831 newspaper accounts of the journey that ran in the *Albany Argus*. Brown, a silhouette artist, happened to be in Albany on the day of the train journey. He made a sketch and then a silhouette cutout of the locomotive, tender, and first two passenger carriages, and according to several accounts they were accurate depictions. The silhouette is now in the collection of the Connecticut Historical Society.

For more on the rail journey, see Cuyler Reynolds' *Albany Chronicles* (Albany: J. B. Lyon, 1906), Arthur James Weise's *The History of the City of Albany, New York* (Albany: E. H. Bender, 1884), and a pamphlet by Joel Munsell, "The Origin, Progress and Vicissitudes of the Mohawk and Hudson Rail Road and The First Excursion on It," read before the Albany Institute on April 20, 1875 (digitized and available online at books.google.com/books?id=SR4tAAAAYAAJ). Also see Thurlow Weed's memories, published in *The New York Times* on May 25, 1882 ("The First American Railroad: Thurlow Weed's story of the first trip from Albany to Schenectady").

Jack McEneny's Albany history book, the source of the turnpike quote, is *Albany: Capital City on the Hudson* (Woodland Hills, Calif.: Windsor, 1981).

I found reports on Robert Harper's disappearance in the *Albany Evening Journal, Albany Evening Times, Albany Argus, Troy Daily Whig, Troy Daily Times,* and *New York Times.* Biographical information about Harper came from a rather breathlessly laudatory entry in George Howell and Johnathan Tenney's *Bicentennial History of Albany: History of the County of Albany, N.Y., From 1609 to 1886* (New York: Munsell, 1886).

I mention a Charley Mooney column in which an "old-timer" wrote to him about Pine Hills hotels. It ran in the *Knickerbocker News* March 2, 1973.

The quip about the "diseased dog" on Albany's sand plains is usually attributed to Joel Munsell, whose *Annals* and *Collections on the History of Albany* chronicle many snippets of life in the city's earlier days. But I haven't been able to find the passage in his writings. I did see it, however, in the *Albany Argus* of May 24, 1867, and reprinted the next day (and attributed to the *Argus*) in the *Albany Morning Express* in a front-page article titled "A Stupendous Land Swindle."

Reports of little Ludwig Marx's death ran in the *Albany Times* and the *Albany Evening Journal,* April 17, 1882.

For accounts of the development of Washington Park, I'm indebted to *Albany Architecture,* ed. Diana Waite (Albany: Mt. Ida, 1993) and to the *Proceedings of the Board of Commissioners of the Washington Park of the city of Albany* (Albany: Argus Co., 1879, 1881, and 1884). Also see Howell and Tenney's *Bi-centennial History* and Cuyler Reynolds' *Albany Chronicles.* For more on Norway maples as Albany street trees, see the article "The Norway Maple," in *The Country Gentleman* 69 (June 9, 1904).

The New York Times account of Governor Hill's Ridgefield toboggan ride was published January 19, 1886. It was also the *Times* that put the height of the toboggan run at fifty-five feet, and if you can't trust the *Times,* who can you trust? In the November 16, 1886, *Albany Evening Times,* a report noted that season's run, on which construction was nearly completed, would be sixty feet high, with two-hundred-foot chutes that dropped one foot over three. An item in the December 29, 1885, *Albany Express* gave a few more details about its construction:

> The toboggan shute (sic) on the Ridgefield grounds was being paved, yesterday, with blocks of ice six inches thick, with a surface of 16x32 inches. The shute is filled to its entire depth with layers of block ice which are held in place by cleats nailed to the side of the structure. When the work of paving the slide is completed, probably by tomorrow, the incline will be flooded in order to permit it to freeze over into a smooth surface. The slide cannot be used, however, until snow comes.

A good summary of the Ridgefield club and its athletic exploits is "Ridgefield Grounds Memories Recalled by their Transfer," *Times-Union,* June 29, 1899, written as the organization turned over its property to the YMCA. Howell and Tenney also provide a brief club history. Traces of the Albany Cricket Club appear here and there in periodicals and municipal documents, such as their 1878 request to the Washington Park commissioners to play on the croquet grounds (noted in the park *Proceedings*), and a writeup in the May 1882 *Outing* magazine that notes the club had leased space in another city park for the season. *The Albany Hand-Book: A Stranger's Guide and Residents' Manual* by H. P. Phelps (Albany: Brandow & Barton, 1884) lists the club's trustees in its inaugural year as the Ridgefield Association; and in *Hudson Mohawk Genealogical and Family Memoirs* (New York: Lewis Historical Publishing, 1911), Cuyler Reynolds calls Charles Lansing Pruyn the "leading spirit" of the club's founding.

My main sources of information about School 18 are the *Proceedings of the Board of Public Instruction of the City of Albany* and various annual reports made by the Board of Public Instruction to the common council. The Committee on Hygiene's report was made at a board meeting on November 19, 1888, and was included in *Proceedings of the Board of Public Instruction of the City of Albany*, vol. 11 (Albany: Van Benthuysen Printing House, 1887).

The approval of the transfer of the Junction property to the Board of Fire Commissioners took place in 1890, per the school board's *Proceedings,* vol. 12. The board held a special meeting on May 7, 1891, to address the proposal to put the Steamer 10 firehouse behind School 4, and the issue was noted in the *Albany Evening Journal* on May 8.

The date in its gable reads 1891, but according to newspaper accounts the Steamer No. 10 firehouse was still under construction in May 1892, and officers were not appointed to the new house until the Board of Fire Commissioners meeting of September 20, 1892. That's also when the fire chief was directed "to prepare a new running card to include assignments for steamer No. 10." The Public Building Commission did not turn over the building to the fire commissioners until September 30 (*Times-Union*, May 3, 1892; *Times-Union*, September 21, 1892; *Albany Morning Express*, October 1, 1892).

Notation of Albany Railway's first electric car journey comes from Cuyler Reynolds's *Albany Chronicles* and is corroborated by an article written by John W. McNamara, president of Albany Railway, in the September 24, 1890, edition of the *Electrical Engineer* magazine. Reynolds also notes Albany Railway's horse sale was in May 1890.

The Albany Land Improvement and Building Company incorporated in January 1888 and started advertising in local newspapers just a few months later. One of the earliest newspaper accounts of their plans I have found is "Albany's Westward Growth," which ran in the *Albany Sunday Express* of January 29, 1888. This article also notes that one of the new company's trustees was architect Franklin H. Janes, who had prepared a variety of home plans for selection by Pine Hills buyers. It also notes that Pratt had a family connection to the original Pine Hills development parcel: the land had belonged to a man named Horace D. Hawkins, and Pratt's sister had married Hawkins's son.

Some years later, on November 23, 1893, as the business was falling apart, the *Albany Morning Express* printed a story headlined "Local Concerns in Trouble," which gives another account of the company and its history. See also a profile of the company (in the "Pine Hills" column of the *Times-Union*, September 30, 1892) that calls Logan, Pratt, and Peabody the "moving spirits in this enterprise" and rhapsodizes about what they've done for the city.

The advertisement that proclaimed, "There are no Indians or wild beasts at PINE HILLS!" can be found in the *Albany Evening Journal* of July 28, 1891. Ads promoting the Pine Hills as "the most healthful and desirable residence section of the city" ran in the 1891 city directory. The ad in which they sing the praises of the Albany Railway ran July 8, 1891, in the *Albany Evening Journal*. And the ad that lists Pine Hills buyers by name ran in a magazine called *The New Albany* 1.2 (July 1891).

The Pine Hills Association's complaints about sand wagons were reported in the *Albany Evening Journal* on August 28 and 29, 1901.

The early growth of School 16 is chronicled in the school board's annual reports; see in particular the years 1906 and 1907. The superintendent's quote comes from his 1913 report.

Chapter Four

Lorenz Willig and William Madigan's flight over Albany was the subject of a story in the July 28, 1941, *Knickerbocker News*. The reporter identifies the new buildings Willig noticed alongside of Buckingham Lake as an apartment development on Home Avenue, but Home isn't near the lake, and the Stonehenge apartments are; plus, they were built in 1941.

The real estate agent quoted in the March 27, 1903, *Albany Evening Journal* article is unnamed (the story calls him just "a prominent real estate man"). The 1907 quote (*Albany Evening Journal*, March 1, 1907) is from a Mr. Chism of Chism Brothers, which was an Albany real estate firm.

The description of Willig's building methods comes from the *Hudson Valley Times* of Mechanicville, New York, March 21, 1922.

There are a limited number of house blueprints and building plans archived at the Albany County Hall of Records; my house's plans happen to be among them. A testimonial from architect Harry Wichmann, whose name is on the 1910 blueprints, was included in *Examples of Success by Correspondence Training* by Thomas J. Foster, president of International Correspondence Schools of Scranton, Pennsylvania (International Textbook Co., 1912). https://books.google.com/books?id=aAw-AAAAYAAJ. Accessed January 8, 2011.

I learned about the Woodlawn Improvement Association Transportation Corporation from the following sources: *Proceedings of the Common Council of the City of Albany*; *Twelfth Annual Report of the Public Service Commission, Second District*, for the year ended December 31, 1918, vols. 1 and 2 (Albany: J. B. Lyon, 1919 and 1920); several articles in a trade magazine called *Bus Transportation*; and accounts in the *Albany Evening Journal*, *Albany Evening News*, and the *Knickerbocker News*. Two must-see sources: an *Albany Evening News* feature on WIAT's history, September 11, 1936; and an article, "Bus Line Follows Real Estate Development," *Bus Transportation* 1.4 (April 1922).

The article I quote about the Central New York Mortgage and Homebuilding Company ran in the *Saratogian* on April 19, 1922.

For examples of Sears kit house advertising in Albany, see the *Albany Evening News* of September 16 or September 22, 1927 ("Skyscrapers are ready-cut") and March 8, 1928 ("Build your home the Skyscraper way"). I quote Rosemary Thornton from an article on her website, *Sears Modern Homes*: "All My Friends Who Have Seen This House Are in Love With It." www.searshomes.org/index.php/2013/03/08/all-my-friends-who-have-seen-this-house-are-in-love-with-it/. And it was another one of her articles that sent me looking for evidence of a "Modern Home Sales Center" in Albany, which I confirmed in the city directories: "Is Your City on This List? If So, You Should Be Look-

ing for Sears Homes!" www.searshomes.org/index.php/2011/06/06/
is-your-city-on-this-list-if-so-you-should-be-looking-for-sears-homes/.

Information about the Winchester Gables development comes from
Albany Architecture. If you happen to own one of these houses, or if
you just like to go full-court geek into building details, you may want
to check out the *Albany Evening News* of November 13, 1929: on pages
21 and 22 contractors and suppliers for the development ran ads that
detail original construction features and list many of the model home's
fittings and supplies by brand name.

Lorenz Willig's passport application is one of countless historic
records that have been scanned and made available on *Ancestry.com*.
Willig's YMCA work in Europe is corroborated by a listing in *Albany's
Part in the World War* (Albany: General Publishing, 1919); also, his
interview and examination for YMCA service was noted in the *Albany
Evening Journal*, August 16, 1918.

See Lorenz Willig's songs in Library of Congress, *Catalogue of Copyright Entries Part 3: Musical Compositions for the year 1931* (Washington,
DC: Government Printing Office, 1932). Digitized at https://archive.
org/details/catalogofcopyrig263libr.

Lorenz Willig died on May 15, 1962, and his death notice ran in
the *Knickerbocker News* that week. A "Community Notes" item in the
Altamont Enterprise and Albany County Post, May 25, 1962, counted his
surviving descendants.

Chapter Five

Here's some information on the 1813 city map: Van Alen, Evert, surveyor. "Map of the City of Albany by Evert Van Alen 1813." *Eighty-
Three Maps of the City of Albany C. 1820 Labeled as "New Topographical
Atlas of Albany and Schenectady Counties."* Albany County Hall of
Records, microfilm inventory No. 8904308000. Van Alen's map was
copied in 1897, and a large photocopy of the copied map is available
in the ACHOR research room. You can read about the history of the
1813 map in an appendix to the *Annual Report of the City Engineer*

of Albany, N.Y., for the Year Ending January 1, 1898 (Albany: Journal Co., 1898), which excerpts 1813–1814 common council proceedings on the commissioning and adoption of the map. https://books.google.com/books?id=yoI1AQAAMAAJ&pg=PA157.

I'm grateful to an article on *HistoryNet.com* for teaching me enough about Captain James Lawrence and the *USS Chesapeake* that I could write a paragraph about them (Adkins, Roy, and Leslie Adkins, "Don't Give Up the Ship," *HistoryNet.com*. August 1, 2008. http://www.history net.com/dont-give-up-the-ship.htm/1.

Other maps I reference in this chapter:

De Witt, Simeon. *Plan of the City of Albany* [map]. 1794.
Schuyler, H. P., surveyor. *Map of Parts of the 5th Ward, City of Albany, survey by HP Schuyler, Officer in the Clerk's Office, 1799*. Albany County Hall of Records.
Jacob, E., surveyor. *Map of the City of Albany, with Villages of Greenbush, East Albany & Bath*. Albany: Sprague & Co., 1857.

The Albany common council appointed the Special Committee on Changes of Names of Streets on January 5, 1891, and the *Albany Evening Times* reported on the issue on January 6 ("What the Common Council Did at Last Night's Meeting"). The committee made its report to the council on March 16 of that year. See *Proceedings of the Common Council of the City of Albany, A.D. 1891* (Albany: Argus, 1892). The petition to change West Lawrence Street's name to Euclid is noted in the minutes of the common council meeting of May 16, 1910.

Chapter Six

My main sources of information for John A. Scott's early life were census data and city directories, with a smattering of church records thrown in. More on those in a moment.

How did I trace a man with a name as common as John Scott over many years and through multiple career changes and new addresses? One way I assured I had the right person was to cross-check for his unmarried sister. Mary E. Scott lived with John and his wife for many years. She was a bookkeeper and stenographer, which earned her her own line in the directory, and since she shared John A. Scott's address, she assured me that I was following the right Mr. Scott around town. I also cross-referenced the directory information with the state and federal censuses.

During the time he worked for Albany Perforated Wrapping Paper, John Scott's occupation is listed as "shipper" in city directories but as "bookkeeper" in his wedding announcement (*Times-Union*, October 25, 1893), so take your pick. The wedding notice called him a "popular and rising young Albanian." Mary and John were married that day at 9:00 in the morning, had breakfast with their families, and caught the 10:05 train to Boston to begin their honeymoon.

The Scott Paper Mills of Albany is noted under "New Corporations" in *The Bookseller, Newsdealer and Stationer* trade magazine 22.10 (May 15, 1905), retrieved July 22, 2016, from books.google.com/books?id=Z9RTAAAAYAAJ&pg=PA444&lpg=PA444. And John A. Scott of Albany is listed under "toilet paper, roll and package" in *Lockwood's Directory of the Paper, Stationery and Allied Trades, 31st Annual Edition* (New York: The Lockwood Trade Journal Co., 1906). But he appears to have moved into manufacturing earlier than that: In the 1901 city directory he is named in his residential listing as a "toilet paper manuf.," he's in the business directory under "Paper Manufacturers," and the name of the wholesale dealership has been changed to simply G. T. Thompson and advertises itself as the "successor to Scott & Thompson."

The Scott Paper warehouse was at 87 Lawrence Street. The building's unusual history—first it was Broadway Methodist Episcopal Church, then, by 1870, a pork packing plant, then for thirty-five years a warehouse—is outlined in a story in the *Knick News* on May 29, 1942. Its headline is "Old Lawrence St. Building May Become Church Again": The dissolution of the paper business—by then it was Henry Streibert's business—prompted Streibert's grandson to sell the building to Mount Calvary Baptist Church. That church held services there until 1957, when it moved to its current location at 58 Alexander Street in the South End.

About Albany's Lumber District: the labor union publication I quote from is the *Illustrated History of the Central Federation of Labor, Representing the Various Trades Unions of Albany and Vicinity* (Syracuse:

Boyd Press, 1898). Read more about Albany's lumber trade in Howell and Tenney's *Bi-Centennial History*; James Elliott Defebaugh's *History of the Lumber Industry of America*, vol. 2 (Chicago: The American Lumberman, 1907); and *The Albany Lumber Trade: Its History and Extent* (Albany: Argus, 1872). Also see Plate I (the letter I) of the 1876 Hopkins maps, and a *Map of the Albany Lumber District* (Albany: Hoffman, Pease, and Tetley, 1857) in the collection of the Albany Institute of History and Art (Map 50b, Digital ID DI 505), www.albanyinstitute.org/details/items/map-of-the-albany-lumber-district.html. Accessed March 23, 2016.

The trade journal in which Henry Streibert announced his intention of building a "large factory" for Scott Paper Company is *The Paper Box Maker and American Bookbinder* 25.1 (November 1906).

Cuyler Reynolds' *Albany Chronicles* notes the 1895 opening of the Speedway on Washington Avenue from Quail to Manning. The common council approved an "ordinance authorizing the mayor to sign a petition for the improvement of Washington avenue from Quail street to the Manning boulevard" on January 6, 1913; and the city paved it as far west as Manning in 1914. See also "Willig to open Pine Hills tract," *Albany Evening Journal*, May 15, 1915, and a note in the last paragraph of "Beaverwyck Park (sic) may be enlarged," *Albany Evening Journal*, March 26, 1914.

Advertisements for and stories about the "Pine Hills Park" auction ran in Albany papers from mid-May to early June 1915. The sale was held on May 29 and 31. Auctioneer Fitz-James E. Browne ("He put the 'Real' in 'Real Estate' ") ran the sale under the management of M. Morgenthau Jr. Company of New York City, which featured its success in Albany in an advertisement in the *New York Times*, September 26, 1915, p. 92. The ad noted that the land's original cost was $15,000 and total sales were $38,700, and "perhaps you have a similar proposition of merit for us to handle. Consult *now!*" A June 2 *Times-Union* story said the sale total was $35,000; and a piece in the "Real Estate News" column of the *New York Herald*, June 3, 1915, reported that Scott and Willig bought the property for $15,000 about three years previous, and that "the owners realized about one hundred per cent on the original purchase price."

I accessed the records for Ash Grove Methodist Episcopal Church and Calvary Methodist Episcopal Church at The Reverend Charles D. and Ouida Schwartz Archives of the Upper New York Conference of the United Methodist Church, located in Saratoga Springs. However, this facility consolidated with other upstate Methodist archives, and its records were moved to Liverpool, New York, in 2017. The Albany records I reviewed include baptism and membership records, pamphlets, photographs, newspaper clippings, and accounts of church history written by members.

Scott's selection as a member of the Albany Real Estate Board's original Board of Governors was reported in "Real Estate Men Organize Board," a story in the *Albany Evening Journal*, December 23, 1914.

The Central New York Mortgage advertisement that asserted, "The greatest need of America is homes" ran in the *Albany Evening Journal*, Nov. 1, 1921. And I quote from "Chamber members hear home building plan from business men of Albany," a front-page story in the *Hudson Valley Times* of Mechanicville, April 6, 1922. The *Times-Union* editorial praising Hackett's efforts with Central New York Mortgage ran on November 1, 1921.

Legal actions against Central New York Mortgage and Home Building Co. by Florence Holmes and by the state attorney general were filed in state Supreme Court, Third Judicial District. Hackett's dismissal of the Holmes suit as a "scheme to attract votes" was quoted in the *Albany Evening News and Albany Evening Journal* on October 19, 1925. News of the lawsuit and other developments were reported, usually as briefs, in many of the communities where Central New York Mortgage had operated. One of the more informative articles on Holmes's suit is the piece that references the "so-called exposure" story: "Local Man Involved in $665,000 Suit to Discredit Hackett" (October 19, 1925). (The "local man" in the headline was Ellsworth Cohen, head of the city's Board of Trade and Schenectady representative of Central New York Mortgage and Home Building.) The granting of the preliminary injunction against the company was noted in many newspapers, including the *New York Times*, which ran an Associated Press brief ("Stock Concerns Enjoined," December 5, 1925).

Ottinger's 1927 speech was reported by the newswire International News Service; I saw the story in *The Daily Argus* of Mount Vernon, NY, February 25, 1927.

These are the books written by John A. Scott's granddaughters: *The Empty Chair: The Journey of Grief After Suicide* by Beryl Scott Glover (Oklahoma City, OK: In-Sight Books, 2000) and *Booze at Breakfast* by Catherine Scott (XLibris, 2013).

Robert Hamilton Scott, the younger of the Scotts' two sons, was interviewed about his professional life in 1985 as part of a master's thesis project (Wilbur Lewis Rykert, "History of the School of Criminal Justice at Michigan State University, 1935–1963," master's thesis, Michigan State University, 1985. http://cj.msu.edu/assets/Rykert.pdf).

The profile of Mary Ainsworth Scott ran in *The Evangelist*, the newspaper of the Albany Catholic Diocese. The clipping in the file is undated, but the story notes that Mrs. Scott turned 103 years old "this week," which would place it in early March 1974, as Mary Scott's birthday was March 4.

Chapter Seven

Henry A. Slack's *Pine Hills Bird Notes* was privately printed ca. 1915 (essays in the book range in date from April 1907 to April 1915); my copy of the book, which I bought on eBay, contains no copyright or publishing information. The book has been digitized, however, by the Smithsonian Libraries, and may be read online at https://archive.org/details/pinehillsbirdnot00slac.

Chapter Eight

Newspapers, directories, and census data are primary sources of information on the Elwood family. The Elwood-White wedding announcement ran in the *Amsterdam Evening Recorder* on July 3, 1908.

Profiles of Everett's father, apiarist Philip H. Elwood, can be found in *The Bee-Keeper's Magazine* 17.1 (January 1889), *American Bee Journal*

62.8 (August 1922), and the *Evening Times* of Little Falls, NY (May 18, 1922).

Conditions for the insane at the Albany poorhouse were described by Dorothea Dix in a report dated January 12, 1844, and included in the *Documents of the Assembly of the State of New York, 67th Session*, vol. 1 (1844). Nellie Bly's reports on the Blackwell's Island asylum were published in the *New York World* newspaper, then subsequently in a book titled *Ten Days In a Mad-House* (New York: Ian L. Munro, 1887), http://digital.library.upenn.edu/women/bly/madhouse/madhouse.html.

Records from the State Charities Aid Association are kept in the New York State Library. Its finding aid gives a historical sketch of the organization's work (www.nysl.nysed.gov/msscfa/sc19816.htm). The State Charities Aid Association changed its name in the 1960s to the State Communities Aid Association and then, in 2000, to the Schuyler Center for Analysis and Advocacy, under which name it is still active today.

About the Folks-Elwood pamphlet "Why Should Anyone Go Insane?": 585,000 copies had been printed "to date," according to the *Report of the Commissioner of Education for the Year Ended June 30, 1912*, vol. 1 (Washington: Government Printing Office, 1913). A copy of the pamphlet is held in the Manuscripts and Special Collections of the New York State Archives.

Elwood's quote on the "so-called personal right of indulgence in the use of alcohol" comes from "Mental Defect in Relation to Alcohol with some Notes on Colonies for Alcoholic Offenders," a paper he gave at the National Conference of Charities and Correction held in Memphis, Tenn., in 1914. Its proceedings (Fort Wayne, Ind.: Fort Wayne Printing Co., 1914) were digitized by Google Books. His assertion that "at least 20 per cent of all insanity" is linked to alcohol use comes from this source, too.

The phrase "privation, mental anguish, and physical diseases" is found in the State Hospital Commission's 29th Annual Report, July 1, 1916 to June 30, 1917 (Albany: J. B. Lyon, 1918; online at https://books.google.com/books?id=xc1NAAAAMAAJ); but Elwood makes the connection between poverty and mental illness earlier in his career, when he was still in New York City. See, for example, his article "Social Aspects of the State Hospitals for the Insane," in *Proceedings of the Fourth New*

York City Conference of Charities and Correction, vol. 4 (Albany, J. B. Lyon, 1913; https://books.google.com/books?id=7zQrAAAAYAAJ).

Other key sources: Elwood's "The State's Opportunity in the Prevention of Insanity," *State Hospital Bulletin* 8.1 (May 15, 1915); and Elwood's "The State Hospital and the Parole System," in *Proceedings of the National Conference of Social Work* (Chicago: University of Chicago Press, 1920).

The records and ephemera of the Pine Hills Fortnightly Club are kept by the Department of Special Collections and Archives in the University at Albany library.

Two sources that taught me about Peter Kinnear, John Wesley Hyatt, and the Albany Billiard Ball Company: Carl Johnson's "So where was celluloid invented?" on the *My Non-Urban Life* website, http://mynonurbanlife.com/so_where_was_celluloid_invented/, February 26, 2010; and Paul Grondahl's *These Exalted Acres: Unlocking the Secrets of Albany Rural Cemetery* (Albany: Times Union, 2013).

The *New York Times'* brief about Elwood's departure from state service was headlined "Dinner for E. S. Elwood: Work of Former Secretary of Hospital Board is Praised." It ran July 21, 1921.

Chapter Nine

Marguerite's memoir is the backbone of this chapter, with details corroborated by census, newspaper, directory data, church records, and the extensive collection of family records kept by Greg Spencer and Lynn Devane. Information about the Pine Hills business district in the 1920s is gleaned from city directories.

In old directories and documents, George Stickles's profession is listed variously as "health gymnastics," "massage doctor," and "hygienic," another term for the regimen. I found his first wife, Catherine, in the 1900 federal census, where she is listed as a widow. She is also identified as "Cathrine wid George" in the Milwaukee city directory.

The quote about Kinderhook's Electric Park comes from a brochure preserved in the local history scrapbooks at the Nassau Free Library. The privately printed Nassau village history booklet can also be found in the library: *A Brief History of the Village of Nassau*, Kurt Vincent, ed., Village of Nassau Historic Preservation Commission, 1994. The description of Stickleville came from an oral history recorded in the book.

The marriage record for George Stickles and Marguerite Claffee is in the Albany County Hall of Records (No. 937, September 11, 1912). On it, George notes that this is his third marriage but does not acknowledge his divorce. Naughty, naughty.

Calvary Church records note the Stickles girls' baptisms and their eventual withdrawal from the congregation. After George's death Marguerite brought the family into her Catholic faith.

George Stickles' death certificate notes that he died at 9 a.m. October 14, 1926. Cause of death: carcinoma of face. His death notice ran in the *Times Union* on October 18, 1926, page 25.

Chapter Ten

My main sources on the Madison Theatre's opening are the inaugural program, in private collection, and a feature in *Motion Picture News*: "Simplicity of Decorative Scheme Feature of Madison Theatre, Albany, N.Y.," *Motion Picture News* 39.27 (July 6, 1929): 75–76. Digitized and available online at http://archive.org/stream/motionnew40moti#page/n0/mode/2up. See also page 100 of the same issue for a photograph of Albany mayor John Boyd Thacher and some Stanley-Mark Strand bigwigs at the opening.

A few relevant newspaper articles: "New addition to Albany's theatrical world," *Albany Evening News,* May 29, 1929, p. 8; and "New Madison Theatre in Pine Hills Opens Tonight," *Times-Union* May 29, 1929, p. 16; also see ads on pages 17 and 18.

To read more about Vincentian and its "glass school," two indispensable sources are books published by the Church of St. Vincent de Paul: *Vincentian, a Tribute: The First 65 Years* (1982); and *A Century of Spiritual Service: Church of Saint Vincent de Paul* by William Tyrrell (1985). Both books are available in the Albany Public Library's main branch.

The passage I quote on therapeutic sunbathing is from "The Science of Health and Natural Healing: Lesson No. 8: Rest and Sleep," by Herbert M.

Shelton, who in 1928 founded Dr. Shelton's Health School in San Antonio, Texas. books.google.com/books?id=-h6wvrnO2TwC&pg=PA24-IA22.

Father Charles's quote comes from a *Knick News* feature, "Character Building Plan Stressed at Vincentian Institute," October 20, 1938. The *Knick News-Times Union* photo archives are where I found pictures of the students at their desks in sunglasses and sunsuits. Also see a November 20, 1948, *Knick News* story, "Vincentian's Growth Rapid Since Start of School in 1917."

For more on George Hawley and his Madison Avenue mansion, see *Albany Architecture*. Also see an editorial page testimonial that ran in the *Times Union*, October 16, 1928, after Hawley's death.

Personal interviews (with Greg Spencer, Ed Girzone, Joseph Girzone, Gerry Conway, and Thomas Ravida) and local newspapers were my main sources for information about life in the Pine Hills during World War II. A *Knick News* feature on postman Bill Gannon, "Pine Hills 'Remembers' Bill Gannon, THE Postman," ran on February 15, 1947. I'm also indebted to Paul Grondahl's *Mayor Corning: Albany Icon, Albany Enigma* (Albany: SUNY Press, 1997), for providing context on early 1944, when Mayor Corning and Pete Girzone both received their draft notices.

See the *Knick News* editorial on Girzone and the draft policy in the February 4, 1944, edition. The *Times-Union* ran a photograph of Pete, his wife, and all of their children on February 3, 1944. The Associated Press picked up Girzone's story and sent it out as a newswire item. His failure of his physical examination is corroborated by an item in the *Knickerbocker News* of March 7, 1944; the story as I tell it here came from Girzone's son Ed.

News coverage of the Thirteenth Ward monument drive and dedication: "Ground Broken for Ward Memorial," *Knickerbocker News*, July 10, 1944 (photo); "13th Ward Memorial Committee to meet," *Knickerbocker News*, September 13, 1943; "13th Ward Ceremony Date Set," *Knickerbocker News*, October 25, 1944; and "Mother with 7 Sons in U.S. Service Unveils Monument in 13th Ward," *Times-Union*, November 12, 1944. The seven Ravida brothers came home and joined the local post of the Italian American World War Veterans, as reported by the *Knickerbocker News*, August 3, 1946. By the way, the granite obelisk wasn't the first war monument up at the Junction: the Pine Hills Association had planted a memorial tree there in June of 1942.

The *Knickerbocker News* of Aug. 15, 1945, describes the scene downtown as Albany learned the war had ended.

Chapter Eleven

Personal interviews shape this chapter, with Greg Spencer as the primary source. Georgea Stickles Perrin's personal account of her alcoholism and recovery came to me via Greg Spencer, her nephew, who provided me with an unpublished cassette recording of two speeches she had made at AA state conventions in 1995 and 1997.

Young Sylvia Stickles's affinity for entering contests (a hobby she shared, actually, with Marguerite) is revealed by the prizes she won here and there, such as an honorable mention in a 1930 *Times-Union* essay contest for her piece on Abraham Lincoln. She also won the *Times-Union*'s Easter coloring contest in 1931. The Harry Neigher features I mention can be found in the *Times-Union* of November 15, 1930, and December 18, 1930.

Sylvia's death was front-page news in the Capital Region during the first week of November 1952. Here's a sampling of the local coverage: "Former Albany Woman Drowns During Miami Midnight Swim," *Knickerbocker News*, November 1, 1952; "Miami Police Hold Albanian in Drowning," *Times-Union*, November 2, 1952; "Albany Man Faces Miami Quiz in Woman's Death," *Times-Union*, November 3, 1952; "Miami Police Probe Albany Woman's Case," *Troy Times Record*, November 3, 1952; and "Albanian Faces New Quiz in Death of Sylvia Stickles," *Times-Union*, November 4, 1952. The story also went out on newswires and was printed as far away as Phoenix (*Arizona Republic*, November 2, 1952) and Nashville (*Tennessean*, November 3, 1952), as well as in papers around Florida and across New York state.

Chapter Twelve

My information on Pine Hills life in the 1950s draws on personal interviews and email exchanges with Chris Cohan, Tom Whitney, and Gerry Conway, as well as Greg Spencer and Lynn Devane.

The shooting of Theodore Wendell at the Madison Theatre was reported in the *Knick News* on February 23, 1952 ("Albany Boy, 14, Shot in Theater, Given Fighting Chance to Survive") and February 28, 1952 ("Waitkus Sends 'Best' to Boy Shot in Theater"). In 1962, the *Knick News* reported that a young man with the same name and home address received an art degree from Albany Junior College.

A few key news articles on the National Little League's first season: "Little League Delays Debut," *Times-Union*, June 2, 1952; "Little League Teams Ready For Openers," *Knickerbocker News*, June 6, 1952; "1,000 Watch Little Bow," *Times-Union*, June 8, 1952; and "1,000 Watch Little League Make Debut," *Knick News*, June 9, 1952. I'm grateful to Greg Spencer for the loan of his scrapbook of news clippings, programs, and other items from that first season.

In a 2012 interview with an NBC affiliate news station, Fred Neulander asserted his innocence in the 1994 murder of his wife. The interview can be seen at www.nbcphiladelphia.com/news/local/Rabbi-Fred-Neulander-Expects-to-be-Exonerated-138801454.html.

Chapter Thirteen

First, a few articles about the meat business in Albany in 1947: "Upsurge in Meat Price Felt in Albany Markets," *Knick News*, June 11; "Meat Sales Off 25 Pct., Albany Dealers Report," *Knick News*, September 16; "Meatless Tuesdays Begin in Albany," *Knick News*, October 7; and "Albany Meat Sales Not Affected by New Setup," *Times-Union*, October 9, 1947, which contains the quote I included about "meatless Tuesdays."

I interviewed and exchanged correspondence with two of Peter Girzone's children, Joseph and Edward. They shared photographs and other family mementos, including news clippings and pictures of the West Lawrence Street market.

Father Joseph Girzone passed away in late 2015. Since then, I've encountered errors when attempting to connect to his blog at joshua-mountain.org; it may not be available in the future. The undated blog post that I quote is titled "Who Said there's no God?"; I first accessed it in 2012 at http://joshuamountain.org/postings/?p=2707. It was still findable as a cached Google web page in June 2016.

The *Washington Post* article I quote from is "Priest writes his own rags-to-riches story" by Laura Sessions Stepp, April 6, 1991. I first encountered the piece reprinted in the *Daily Gazette* of Schenectady ("Capital Region's Girzone writes own rags-to-riches story," June 22, 1991).

Chapter Fourteen

Georgea's memories made their way to me via some speeches she gave in 1997, recorded onto cassette tapes by her nephew, Greg Spencer.

Central to this chapter are my interviews and correspondence with Father Peter Young and Greg Spencer, corroborated by newspaper accounts and other documents. A great account of this era of addiction treatment, especially of the relationships between AA and professional treatment, can be found in *Slaying the Dragon: The History of Addiction Treatment and Recovery in America,* by William L. White (Bloomington, Ill.: Chestnut Health Systems, 1998).

On May 8, 1967, the Albany County Board of Supervisors adopted Resolution No. 75, "Authorizing a public program for alcoholics in the county of Albany through the Community Mental Health Board and appropriating the sum of $10,000 therefor." The board minutes are preserved at the Albany County Hall of Records. The *Knickerbocker News* editorial I mentioned ran on May 11; the paper also had a story on the alcoholism program on May 9.

The *Times-Union* article on Fred Spencer and the Albany Citizens Council on Alcoholism can be found in the May 5, 1968, edition. Georgea's statement on the opening of Perrin House is quoted in "Facility for woman alcoholics finished," a *Knickerbocker News* story by Marv Cermak, February 3, 1987.

The ACCA presented Joan with the honor I mention at its Community Recognition Dinner on September 30, 1993. I have a photocopy of the certificate she was given, which is in Greg Spencer's possession.

Greg lent me other documents on the careers of Georgea, Joan, and Fred, including copies of various honors they received over the years, letters of recognition, an early brochure from Perrin House, and the press release on the opening of Perrin House, which notes that Georgea "was one of the first women to receive membership in the New York Federation of Alcoholism Counselors (NYFAC), and to receive her license as a Credentialed Alcoholism Counselor (CAC)."

Chapter Fifteen

Information about Marguerite Stickles's death and the transfer of the house ownership came from her obituary, deed records for the West Lawrence Street house, and the Nassau-Schodack cemetery.

To learn more about the Madison Theatre's 1967 modernization, see "A $200,000 Complete 'Do-Over' For Stanley Warner's Madison, in Albany," a feature in the trade magazine *Boxoffice*, February 19, 1968. See also the *Knickerbocker News* of October 5, 1967, pp. 21A, 22A, 23A, for congratulatory ads and laudatory copy on what they called its "grand opening."

I don't know as much as I'd like to, yet, about the Aurania Club's 1964 fire. Here are a few key news articles: "Fire Wrecks Aurania Club; Police Investigate Arson," the lead story of the *Knickerbocker News*, June 26, 1964 (also see the jump page, 2A, for a sidebar on the club's history); "History makes way" (standalone photo with cutline), *Knick News*, January 6, 1965; and "Club Opens Season in New Quarters," *Knick News*, September 18, 1965. Also, see *The History of the Paid Albany Fire Department: A Story of Fires and Firemen From 1867–1967*, Warren Abriel, editor, and Joseph Winchell, photographer (Albany: Argus Greenwood, 1967) for photographs of firefighters battling the 1964 blaze.

School 4 sustained its partial cave-in on June 22, 1968. Questions about the condition of the school, and about the city's and school board's actions before and after the roof collapse, lingered for the rest of that year and into the next. A particularly biting *Knick News* editorial (September 16, 1968) grimly notes Albany's long-deteriorating public infrastructure, and contrasts the finding that School 4 was structurally unsound with the Board of Education's previous reports that the building was in "good shape." Decrying a "lack of openness on the part of school officials," the editorial board observes: "One is led to wonder how expert were the previous 'experts' who had inspected the damage."

The *Knick News* editorial on the city's park plans is "A Restrained Bravo," April 19, 1967. The article I quote about building a new Ridgefield Park fieldhouse ran on June 21, 1968. And a must-read on the state of the city's showcase park is "Washington Park Today: A Victim of Shabbiness and Neglect," by Carol Schlageter, *Knick News*, August 24, 1968.

Kennedy's *O Albany!* is an essential source for stories about 1960s community organizing, especially the groups the Brothers and Better Homes. The trash collection issue saw widespread local news coverage; some key stories are "Albany Groups Declare War on Trash," by Mike Wales, *Times-Union*, June 12, 1967; "Trash Pickup Hurts Poor, Survey Shows," *Knick News*, July 17, 1967; "Permanent Trash Pickup Systems Proposed to City," by Chris Weber, *Knick News*, July 27, 1967, with sidebar, "Rally Slated For New Trash Plan"; "Corning Gets Some Questions on Trash," *Knick News*, August 17, 1967; "Mayor Accused of 'Bad Faith' in Trash Pickup Hassle," *Times-Union*, September 3, 1967; "Mayor Aims To Push Trash Plan," by Richard Gaikowski, *Knick News*, October 17, 1967; and "Trash Pickup Cost in Albany Assailed," by David Eno, *Knick News*, November 21, 1967.

B. J. Costello talked with me in 2015 about his early days in Albany and the Pine Hills Neighborhood Association.

Gregory Maguire and I exchanged a number of emails about the neighborhood we both love. His 2012 piece about growing up in the Pine Hills can be found at blog.timesunion.com/norder/gregory-maguire-writes-about-albanys-pine-hills-neighborhood/1611/.

Chapter Sixteen

This chapter is built on the extensive local newspaper coverage of town-gown relations, particularly from the 1980s forward; on a number of interviews; and on a few key books. The University at Albany's institutional history was invaluable to me in crafting this chapter: *A Tradition of Excellence: The Sesquicentennial History of the University at Albany, State University of New York, 1844 to 1994,* by Kendall Birr (Virginia Beach, Va: Donning, 1994). I also relied on *Albany Architecture* and on Tyrrell's 1985 history of Saint Vincent de Paul parish.

For this chapter I conducted personal interviews with Michael Huber, Fred Ruff, Sister Joan Byrne, Ric Chesser, Jeffrey Jamison, Leah Golby, and Carolyn Keefe; and an email interview with Luke Rumsey.

Tyrrell's book touches on a couple of other interesting elements. In November 1979, volunteers conducted a parish census, visiting six thousand households within its boundaries; they found that twenty- to twenty-four-year-olds were the largest age group in the parish. In another measure of the parish, he notes a review of neighborhood real estate records between 1979 and 1983 and writes: "The lowest price at which these were sold remained relatively stable, ranging from $10,000 to $12,000. However, the top price had increased from $120,000 to $217,000. A prospective buyer was left with choosing between low-priced, inferior housing or having to compete with real estate specula-tors to buy expensive property beyond the means of most individuals."

Notes on some specifics from this chapter follow:

The term "A neighborhood under siege" came from a *Times Union* editorial on March 27, 2011.

The "our town" quote from John MacDonald, manager of Clifton Country Mall, is found in "'Meet me at the mall': Shopping centers substitute for town squares," by Maureen McTague Dana, *Knick News*, April 4, 1977.

The reference to the South Mall neighborhood as Albany's "thread-bare section" came from a cutline, "Aerial view of mall cleared for con-struction of state buildings," *Knick News*, December 30, 1964.

The SUNY Albany student newspaper also wrote regularly about housing and overcrowding. The paragraph I quote is from "Off-Campus Housing Is Scarce," by Aron Smith, *Albany Student Press*, September 11, 1979. The article was the second in a two-part series; also see the first story, "High Acceptance Rate Puts Pressure On Housing," September 7, 1979.

Mark S. R. Suchecki's story "Student renters squeeze an already tight housing market" can be found in the *Times Union*, August 25, 1986. Suchecki is also the one who observed that off-campus life in Albany is "generally less expensive and more attractive than renting dormitory rooms, according to students and university housing administrators."

The history of the College of Saint Rose is *Of Glory, Of Praise: A 75-Year History of The College of Saint Rose* by RoseMarie Manory (Albany: College of Saint Rose, 1994). The book is available online via the Saint Rose archives at strosearchives.contentdm.oclc.org/cdm/compoundobject/collection/p16074coll7/id/258/rec/1.

The tensions between Pine Hills residents and Saint Rose over the college's expansion plans were outlined for me in personal interviews with Ric Chesser and Fred Ruff, as well as in local news coverage from spring 1987 and stretching on into 1988. Issues of contention included not only the parking lot plan but also the expansion of office and classroom space to the south side of Madison Avenue and unauthorized paving behind a dormitory. A few articles to get you started: "Parking-lot plan faces fight," by Bruce Scruton, *Knick News*, May 15, 1987; "Albany college, neighbors at odds," by Brad Kelly, *Knick News*, June 12, 1987; "Neighbors fight CSR expansion," by Deborah Gesensway, *Times Union*, June 15, 1987; and "New Saint Rose Parking Lot Still Riles Neighbors," also by Gesensway, *Times Union*, August 31, 1988.

Those tensions didn't end with the '80s. See, for example, the 2010 *Times Union* story I quoted about Saint Rose on-campus residency: "College expansion concerns neighbors," by Jordan Carleo-Evangelist, November 5, 2010.

Jerry Jennings's quote on absentee landlords and blight spreading "like a cancer" is from "Student ghetto housing conflict arises on Hudson Avenue," by Catherine Clabby, *Times Union*, December 17, 1989. The 1989 "sick and tired" passage is from the same story.

On the grouper law: Albany city code defines a "family" as follows: "Four or more persons occupying a dwelling unit and living together as a traditional family or the functional equivalent of a traditional family"; it notes, "It shall be presumptive evidence that four or more unrelated persons living in a single dwelling unit do not constitute the functional equivalent of a traditional 'family.' " Retrieved on June 28, 2016, from http://ecode360.com/7686557#7686557 and http://ecode360.com/7686560#7686560. The "functional equivalent" wording was added in May 1986.

According to *Knick News* reporter Greg Smith ("Students defy Albany's anti-grouper law," September 19, 1986), the city of Albany prosecuted eleven landlords for grouper law violations between January 1985 and March 1986, mostly concerning apartments in the student-heavy midtown neighborhoods. SUNYA's Student Association, with sixteen students and one landlord as plaintiffs, pushed back in 1985, challenging the city on the law's constitutionality. For more on that case, see the *Albany Student Press*'s "SA granted stay in Grouper Law suit against city," by Ilene Weinstein, October 29, 1985; "Albany wins round in anti-grouper suit; class action rejected," another *Knick News* story by Smith, November 21, 1986; and the *Times Union*'s "City's 'grouper' law ruled constitutional; definition of 'family' at issue," by Shirley Armstrong, November 21, 1986. See also Richard Wexler's "City, opponents miss legal change: New grouper law affects suit," *Times Union*, November 26, 1986; this story also concerns the 1986 grouper law case in which tenants were charged.

Representing the city in that case was Attorney James Linnan, whose criticism of SUNYA for "creating this problem" was quoted in "University hit for lack of housing" by Greg Smith, *Knick News*, October 29, 1986.

Other key articles on the 1986 case:

Smith, Greg B. "26 arrested in Albany grouper-law crackdown." *Knick News*, October 20, 1986.

Smith, Greg B. "Anti-grouper law crackdown gets mixed reaction." *Knick News*, October 21, 1986.

Wexler, Richard. "SUNYA students' lawyer rips city tenant prosecutions." *Times Union*, October 21, 1986.

Wexler, Richard. "Tenants arraigned in court." *Times Union*, October 30, 1986.

Smith, Greg B. "Law change scrambles anti-grouper cases." *Knick News*, December 4, 1986.

Kelly, Brad. "Albany grouper case finishes in standoff." *Knick News,* April 9, 1987.

Wexler, Richard. "After enforcement war, all quiet on grouper front." *Times Union,* May 21, 1990.

A smattering of other coverage touching on student residents of the Pine Hills, including the 2011 riot:

Kelly, Brad. "SUNYA students work to alter image; community participation is key." *Times Union,* August 26, 1988.

Clabby, Catherine. "Student housing targeted: Code violations, rowdiness eyed." *Times Union,* March 8, 1990.

Clabby, Catherine. "Pine Hills neighbors address rowdy student problem." *Times Union,* October 19, 1990.

Jochnowitz, Jay. "City attorney gutted proposal, Jennings says." *Times Union,* November 6, 1990.

DeMare, Carol. "Albany's grouper law faces federal challenge." *Times Union,* January 1, 1993.

Campagna, Darryl. "UAlbany plans to build new dorms." *Times Union,* February 28, 2001. (Story notes that about 6,000 out of 17,000 UALB students live in dorms.)

Carleo-Evangelist, Jordan. "St. Rose dorm project gets key ok." *Times Union,* March 8, 2011.

Yusko, Dennis. " 'Kegs, Eggs' and arrests." *Times Union,* March 12, 2011.

Carleo-Evangelist, Jordan, and Bryan Fitzgerald. "Riot a rift in town and gown." *Times Union,* March 15, 2011.

Matteo, Kayla. "Blight aside, it's still a student community," Letter to the editor. *Times Union,* April 6, 2011.

Grondahl, Paul. "Students act to clean up image." *Times Union,* September 30, 2012.

Churchill, Chris. "Broken tree at root of couple's frustrations." *Times Union,* September 7, 2013.

Churchill, Chris. "A mother stays as her neighborhood decays." *Times Union,* November 20, 2014.

Any review of town-gown relations should include this *Times Union* series published in the wake of Kegs and Eggs:

Churchill, Chris. "Albany's 'student ghetto': From energy into decline." March 24, 2011.

Churchill, Chris. "Neighborhood on the edge." March 24, 2011.

Carleo-Evangelist, Jordan. "Holdouts coping amid hostility." March 25, 2011.

Lee, Stephanie. "Students get what they pay for." March 26, 2011.

Waldman, Scott. "The struggle for a solution: Everyone agrees the culture of Albany's student ghetto needs to change, but how?" March 27, 2011.

And a public apology by UAlbany president George M. Philip was made in a letter to the editor printed in the *Times Union*, March 15, 2011.

The common council, per its proceedings, voted unanimously on December 19, 1994, to authorize firefighters to conduct building inspections, and Jennings signed it into law the next day. On September 18, 1995, the common council voted to raise fines for code violations. A few important news stories about Jennings's codes work and the creation of the building registry:

Metzgar, Sarah. "Albany fire officials rev up to crack down on code violators." *Times Union,* November 16, 1994.

Gurnett, Kate. "Fire chief outlines code-inspection work." *Daily Gazette*, February 2, 1995. Chief James Larson's quote comes from this story.

Benjamin, Liz. "Audit faults apartment inspections." *Times Union,* May 12, 1999.

And the following reporting by Jay Jochnowitz for the *Times Union*:

"Landlords fight city hall over code violations." May 8, 1995.

"Softened housing code headed for council vote." August 17, 1995.

"More tinkering likely for Albany housing code plan." September 5, 1995.

"Landlords get council panel to revise code violation penalties." September 12, 1995.

"Albany considers increasing fines for scofflaw landlords." October 12, 1995.

"Aldermen balk at apartment-registry fee." January 4, 1996.

"Albany panel backs rental unit registry." July 12, 1996.

"Jennings presses common council on registry." August 15, 1996.

"Albany Common Council ok's rental registry." August 20, 1996.

The audit by the City of Albany Office of Audit and Control ("Performance Audit of the Division of Building and Codes, Part 1: Code Enforcement Operations," by Leif Engstrom, chief city auditor; Debra Perks, and Abigail Fox. September 2011) is available online at www.albanyny.gov/_files/2011CodeEnforcementAuditPart1.pdf.

And "Albany's building commissioner steps down" by Jay Jochnowitz (*Times Union*, June 17, 1995) gives a picture of what code enforcement was like in the Corning era.

Kathy Sheehan's platform from her 2013 mayoral campaign is outlined on her campaign website at http://www.sheehanforalbany.com/issues.htm. Accessed August 8, 2016.

Jordan Carleo-Evangelist and Bryan Fitzgerald reported on March 15, 2011, after the Kegs and Eggs riot, that Mike D'Attilio had "recently" said, "We've lost Hudson and Hamilton" to the common council ("Riot a rift in town and gown"). According to common council minutes (http://ecode360.com/documents/AL0934/public/9828084.pdf), D'Attilio spoke before the council on February 24, 2011.

Information on the Madison Avenue road diet can be found at www.albany2030.org/road-diet; and information on zoning updates can be found at http://rezonealbany.com/. The Pine Hills Improvement Group's documents, plans, meeting notes, and other materials are at sites.google.com/site/phiggroupinfo/home. And more information on UAlbany's Neighborhood Life initiatives, including the Off-Campus Ambassadors program, can be found at www.albany.edu/neighborhoodlife/.

Chapter Seventeen

This chapter relies on interviews. I spoke with Ric Chesser and Shamshad Ahmad, as well as Carl, Anna, and Emily Patka. I corresponded with Michael Graham and Huma Ahmad by email. Though I don't quote him,

I also exchanged emails with Imam Faisal Ahmad. In 2007 the *Times Union* ran a good profile of the imam and his Albany roots, "Imam: Made in America" by Marc Parry, September 16, 2007.

Chapter Eighteen

Interviews shape this chapter, too. I spoke with Virginia Hammer, Ric Chesser, Lorraine Weiss, Lorenz Worden, and Anne Savage.

The *Times Union* article about possible plans to move the library out of the neighborhood was "Pine Hills site sought: Group to lobby for library branch" by Daniel Gold, October 15, 1986. Other news coverage of the Pine Hills library branch relocation follows:

Kelly, Brad. "Pine Hills trying to keep its library," *Knickerbocker News,* April 9, 1986.

"Residents trying to save library." *Times Union,* July 15, 1986.

Connell, Nancy. "Possible move of Pine Hills library branch concerns neighbors." *Times Union,* July 15, 1986.

Gold, Daniel. "Neighborhood council to flex watchdog muscle." *Times Union,* September 4, 1986.

Wexler, Richard. "Pine Hills' Engine 10 to close; fire station to become a library." *Times Union,* October 22, 1986.

Kelly, Brad. "Albany makes offer on NYTEL building." *Knick News,* July 9, 1988.

Clabby, Catherine. "Pine Hills library 'worth the wait.'" *Times Union,* October 25, 1990.

Steamer 10 Theatre's mission statement can be found at www.steamer10theatre.org/about-us/steamer-no-10-theater-inc, and you can read more about its history at www.steamer10theatre.org/about-us/history. For a good profile of the organization, see "Steamer 10 finds its success in loyalty," by Amy Biancolli, *Times Union,* February 25, 1996. These two articles report on plans to convert the firehouse into a theater: "Albany firehouse being revived as children's theater to move in," by Martin P. Kelly, *Times Union,* January 15, 1989; and "Pine Hills fire station to become Albany theater," by Catherine Clabby *Times Union,* June 7, 1990.

The Madison Theatre "dinosaur" quote was included in "Future's bleak for single-screen theaters," by Michael Hill of the Associated Press. I saw the syndicated story in the *Ocala Star-Banner* of December 10, 1994, via the digital archive at news.google.com/newspapers. The Clapp's quote comes from "The End: Clapp's, a neighborhood bookstore in Albany, will soon close, another victim of the trend toward suburban superstores," by Paul Grondahl, *Times Union*, January. 4, 1996.

Historic Albany Foundation has released its Endangered Historic Resources List every five years beginning in 2000. The lists are online at www.historic-albany.org/ehr/, or available upon request at the HAF office.

The letter to the editor I quote was by Duane Barker, published in the *Times Union* on August 30, 2004.

Key articles on the Madison Theater include "Will the show go on?" by Rick Marshall, *Metroland* 28.10, March 10, 2005, and the following stories by the TU's Brian Nearing:

"Drugstore plan may doom theatre." August 18, 2004.

"Theater drama awaits ending." January 2, 2005.

"Flicker of life for old Madison movie house." March 25, 2005. Tesiero's quote is from this article.

"Silver screen's glitter spreads." March 26, 2005.

Gunther Fishgold was quoted in "New brew on Madison," by Chris Churchill, *Times Union*, September 6, 2013.

Read more about the upper Madison consultant's report, prepared by Troy Architectural Program, on the city Department of Development and Planning website at http://www.albanyny.gov/Government/Departments/DevelopmentandPlanning/Neighborhoods/Midtown/Upper-Madison.aspx. Accessed August 1, 2016. Also see "Repaving to provide more commercial parking," by Brian Nearing, *Times Union*, May 9, 2006.

Regarding 80–82 North Allen, see these stories by Brian Nearing for the *Times Union*:

"Apartments spawn nuisance hearing." September 9, 2004.

"Landlord told to close units." September 23, 2004.

"Landlord complies with city order." January 27, 2006.

On 32 South Allen, see the following stories by the *Times Union*'s Jordan Carleo-Evangelist:

"Landlord trouble again?" March 17, 2010.

"Neighbors: Stop the noise, trash." April 15, 2010.

"City to landlord: Buildings are a nuisance." June 25, 2010.

"Judge decides against landlord." October 26, 2011. Jeff Jamison's quote appears in this story.

"Court upholds ruling against Ploof." December 14, 2012.

Also see *Roger Ploof vs. G. Michael Apostol, as Chairperson of the Zoning Board of Appeals of the City of Albany, et al.* State of New York Supreme Court, Appellate Division, Third Judicial Department. No. 514809, decided and entered December 13, 2012. http://decisions. courts.state.ny.us/ad3/Decisions/2012/514809.pdf.

Chapter Nineteen

I wrote about plans to restore the Pine Hills mural in a 2012 *Times Union* article ("Mural's restoration will capture the spirit of community in Albany," March 22, 2012). See also "A new coat of spirit," by Chris Churchill, *Times Union*, July 14, 2012.

Here's the full bibliographic info on Jane Jacobs's book: *The Death and Life of Great American Cities* (New York: Random House, 1961; Random House Vintage Books edition, 1992).

How to quantify the value of cities? Physicist Geoffrey West is one theorist who's trying: his data-driven approach considers the city as a system, something akin to an organism, and looks for the laws that govern its behavior. One pattern he says he's identified is that every time a city doubles in size, its per capita productivity and creativity—measured by data such as wages and number of patents—go up by 15 percent. Crime and disease go up, too, and at the same rate. For a good overview of his theories see the *New York Times Magazine* piece "A Physicist Solves the City," by Jonah Lehrer, December 17, 2010; or West's TED talk, "The surprising math of cities and corporations," filmed July 2011 and available online at www.ted.com/talks/geoffrey_west_the_surprising_math_of_cities_and_corporations?language=en#.

More about the "walkscore"—a measure that ranks an area according to factors such as intersection density and how many services and amenities are within walking distance—can be found at www.walkscore.com. Some studies that examine the relationship between walkscores and real estate values:

Cortright, Joe. "Walking the Walk: How Walkability Raises Home Values in U.S. Cities," *CEOs for Cities*, August 2009. http://blog.walkscore.com/wp-content/uploads/2009/08/WalkingTheWalk_CEOs-forCities.pdf.

Sohn, Dong Wook, Anne Vernez Moudon and Jeasun Lee. "The economic value of walkable neighborhoods." *Urban Design International* 17.2 (May 2012).

Leinberger, Christopher B., and Mariela Alfonzo. "Walk this Way: The Economic Promise of Walkable Places in Metropolitan Washington, D.C." Brookings Institution study, May 25, 2012. http://www.brookings.edu/research/papers/2012/05/25-walkable- places-leinberger.

Another good read: "Now Coveted: A Walkable, Convenient Place," by Christopher B. Leinberger, for *The New York Times,* May 25, 2012. Leinberger was one of the researchers on the Brookings Institution study.

The 2010 University of New Hampshire study I mention is Shannon Rogers, Kevin Gardner, Cynthia Carlson, and John Halstead, "Examining Walkability and Social Capital as Indicators of Quality of Life at the Municipal and Neighborhood Scales," *Applied Research in Quality of Life* 6.2 (June 2011). A summary from the UNH media relations office can be found at www.unh.edu/news/cj_nr/2010/dec/bp13capital.cfm.

About the National Association of Realtors' 2013 poll: The researchers said the 2013 Community Preference Survey, conducted online, polled "1,500 adults chosen to be representative of the U.S. population," according to a synopsis on PlannersWeb.com: Joseph Molinaro's "National Realtors' Survey Indicates Strong Interest in Walkable Mixed-Use Neighborhoods." Posted March 27, 2014, at http://plannersweb.com/2014/03/national-realtors-survey-indicates-strong-interest-walkable-mixed-use-neighborhoods/. Molinaro was involved with the survey. Results can be viewed at http://www.realtor.org/reports/nar-2015-community-preference-survey.

Index

Photographs, illustrations, and maps are noted in the index by the abbreviation "fig." followed by the text page number preceding that set of illustrations.